The Complete Idiot's Reference Card

Cyberetiquette

➤ Make sure you include a name, date, and place in the subject line of your messages.

➤ Quote only the pertinent portion of someone else's message.

➤ Make sure you use both upper- and lowercase letters in your messages. Using all uppercase letters is considered SHOUTING.

➤ Don't include your surnames at the bottom of your messages, because this messes up search engine operations once the messages are archived.

➤ Check with the recipient before sending large files as attachments to e-mail. Large files can mess up e-mail programs.

➤ Remember how difficult it is to convey emotions through e-mail. Using emoticons can help.

➤ Try to keep your message on topic when you are replying on a bulletin board, newsgroup, or mailing list.

➤ Keep personal information out of newsgroup discussions and in private e-mail.

Tips for Using the Internet

➤ Plan the work and work the plan. Concentrate on a single family line when you first begin.

➤ Always keep track of what you have done, and what sites you have visited online.

➤ Learn all the ins and outs of any particular search engine, so that your searches will be most effective.

➤ Organize your bookmarks or favorites, so that you can easily find saved URLs (Web site addresses).

➤ Don't assume the information you want will be on the first page of a given Web site. Take the time to search throughout the site.

➤ When you use search engines, remember to search the more uncommon words first to better narrow your results.

alpha
books

Types of Sites Found on the Internet

➤ Directories—organized lists of sites

➤ Search engines—sites designed to search other sites

➤ Databases—names, dates, and places found in searchable files

➤ Family Web sites—pages created by fellow researchers and devoted to given families

➤ General Web sites—pages created by libraries, societies, and companies

Sites to Get Started

Search Engines

➤ AltaVista (www.altavista.com/)

➤ Excite (www.excite.com/)

➤ HotBot (www.hotbot.com/)

➤ Infoseek (www.infoseek.go.com/)

Directories

➤ Cyndi's List (www.cyndislist.com/)

➤ Genealogy Most Wanted (www.citynet.net/mostwanted/links.html)

➤ The Genealogy Home Page (www.genhomepage.com/full.html)

Software Sites

➤ Family Origins (www.parsonstech.com/genealogy/index.html)

➤ Family Tree Maker (www.familytreemaker.com/)

➤ Generations (www.sierra.com/)

➤ Ultimate Family Tree (www.uftree.com/)

Online Databases

➤ Ancestry.com (www.ancestry.com/)

➤ GenealogyLibrary.com (www.genealogylibrary.com/)

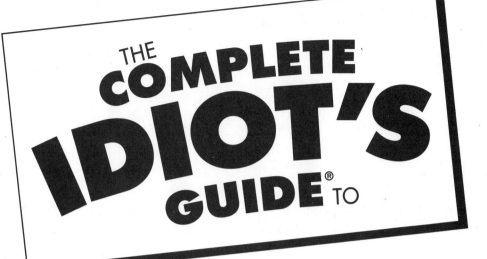

THE COMPLETE IDIOT'S GUIDE® TO

Online Genealogy

by Rhonda McClure

alpha books

201 West 103rd Street
Indianapolis, IN 46290

A Pearson Education Company

Alpha Development Team

Publisher
Marie Butler-Knight

Editorial Director
Gary M. Krebs

Product Manager
Phil Kitchel

Associate Managing Editor
Cari Shaw Fischer

Acquisitions Editor
Randy Ladenheim-Gil

Production Team

Development Editor
Terrie Lynn Solomon

Production Editor
Michael Thomas

Copy Editor
Faren Bachelis

Cover Designer
Mike Freeland

Illustrator
Jody P. Schaeffer

Book Designers
Scott Cook and Amy Adams of DesignLab

Indexer
Angie Bess

Layout/Proofreading
Angela Calvert
Cheryl Lynch
Donna Martin
Jeannette McKay

Contents at a Glance

Contents

Foreword

Computers are changing the face of genealogy. It's still the same fascinating hobby, but now we have a new tool to assist in the process. However, learning how to use this new tool is a big, and for some, a scary step. Rhonda McClure guides the reader through the process.

Remember, we were all beginners when we first started doing research. Some of you reading this book will be seasoned genealogists who have been enjoying the challenges of this hobby or avocation for years, yet know little about what's available through the Internet. Others will be new to the field, don't really know much about family research, and perhaps know even less about how to tap into the vast resources now available on the World Wide Web. Now is the time to learn.

Understanding the jargon is half the battle. Sometimes there is no one around to ask questions of, or sometimes it's just embarrassing to let others know how uneducated you feel. No matter what the reason, it is comforting to have a book that explains the meaning of those "techie" terms and tells you how to find helpful information on the Internet. Believe it or not, soon those terms and your newly developed surfing skills will become part of your everyday life.

When you go to your public library, you find some books that are strictly about genealogy and others that have a wider audience. Both can be put to good use when solving your genealogical riddles. The Internet is very similar. Some sites will be devoted exclusively to genealogy. Other sites will be non-genealogical yet contain information useful to family researchers. You will find Web sites hosted by individuals, societies, government agencies, and commercial enterprises. All can be valuable in your search for those elusive ancestors.

Genealogists were quick to understand the advantages of the Internet. The ability to contact thousands, perhaps millions of people, and to send out queries to others was eagerly endorsed by genealogists. Learning how to post messages and what should be included are new experiences for some. The need for documentation of facts is also something beginners often overlook. In addition, in their eagerness to share, some have ignored privacy and copyright issues. Most of the guilty are probably just naive. Ms. McClure provides some helpful guidance on these issues that are of great concern to longtime genealogists.

Using the Web should not be intimidating. Yes, there is lots to explore, and it takes a while to discover just what is out there. But, between the covers of this book you will find a road map to guide your way. From genealogical basics to surfing the Web, you will discover tips that will bring success to your research projects. And that's what it's all about—discovering new information about your ancestors.

—Shirley Langdon Wilcox, CG

Shirley Langdon Wilcox has been certified by the Board for Certification of Genealogists since 1973 as a Certified Genealogist. She has been active for over thirty years in the genealogical community, serving in many leadership positions. This includes the presidency of two national organizations—the National Genealogical Society (NGS) from 1996–2000 and the Association of Professional Genealogists (APG) from 1991–1993.

Shirley is a 1995 recipient of APG's highest award, the Smallwood Award of Merit, and a 1985 recipient of Prince George's County (MD) Genealogical Society's highest award, the McCafferty Award of Excellence. She edited four publications for the latter society between 1975 and 1985 and served twice as its president, in 1973, and also from 1975–1976. She also served as Fairfax County (VA) Genealogical Society's president from 1986–1989. Since 1995 she has been a genealogical teacher with the Fairfax County Public Schools Office of Adult and Community Education.

Introduction

Genealogy is a fascinating look into the history of those who have come before. It's fun to discover an ancestor who had long dark hair, like you, or who was good at fishing, your favorite pastime. But for many who enjoy genealogy, tracing family history is a grounding influence.

To most who take up genealogy, tracing family history quickly becomes an addiction or an obsession. Other family members and friends will begin to joke about you, putting a bumper sticker on your car that reads "Will brake for cemeteries." That's okay, because while they are laughing at their clever jokes, you will be having the time of your life solving the biggest mystery of them all: your roots.

When I first became interested in family history, I remember going to a library that had a genealogy department. And, because I was quite young at the time, I could feel the librarians' eyes watching me. For them to see someone so young as I was then actually working on tracing her family's history was unusual at that time. Of course, today genealogy is one of the most popular hobbies, and it now transcends age, race, and gender. Everyone is interested in his or her family history. What has made this difference? The advent of PCs has made it easier to keep track of all those limbs on the family tree. Genealogy software has helped us to more easily record the data we find, and has made it easier to share potential family information with possible cousins. The Internet has made communicating with other family historians even easier. And in many cases, the Internet's ever-growing popularity has peaked the interest of those who previously thought genealogy was just for "little old ladies wanting to join snobby societies." People now realize that researching your family's history is much more than an elitist obsession.

This book will show you how to learn about genealogy. If you are completely new to genealogy, then this book will get you started with the fundamentals, and get you ready to take your research to the Internet. If you are new to the Internet, this book will provide you with an easy-to-follow overview of what is available on the Internet and how to find what you need. Some chapters offer you help in communicating with other genealogists—help that can minimize your frustration and disappointment. Although the Internet doesn't have all the information we seek, it does offer access to many other genealogists who will be eager to help you. And with this book, too, you will be able to find other people who share the same interests as you.

How This Book Is Organized

The Complete Idiot's Guide to Online Genealogy shows you step-by-step how to get started with your genealogical research, and then how to begin to use the Internet to further your research. In the final parts of this book, I show you how to create your very own family history Web pages, so that you can share the information you find with other researchers.

Part 1, Computers and Genealogy, introduces you to what you'll need in the way of PC hardware to truly get involved in online genealogy. In this section, you'll learn about the terms and etiquette you encounter in the online world. In addition to this PC primer, I've explained different technical aspects of the Internet and the World Wide Web. I close this section with an overview of the currently available genealogy software programs.

Part 2, Genealogy 101, is designed to give you an overall introduction to genealogy. In this section, you'll get a look at the common genealogy forms you are likely to use, and where to find the information you need to get started to launch your family history research in the right direction. If you are more experienced with genealogy, this section offers a good refresher of items to keep in mind when you are researching genealogical information online.

Part 3, Surf's Up, introduces you to conducting genealogical research on the Internet. In this section, you'll see ways in which you can communicate with fellow online researchers, via such electronic methods as mailing lists, newsgroups, and chat rooms. In this part, I show you how to write effective queries, so each query you write will have the best possible chance that someone will answer it.

Part 4, Diggin' Up Bones—Online Style, presents an overview of various record types that genealogists have been using since the dawn of genealogy. Now, in the Internet age, these records are available electronically and many of them are online. With the addition of genealogical records to the online research world, searching census and land records, or reading obituaries from countless newspapers has never been easier or more convenient. This section also introduces you to the currently available online searchable databases, an additional benefit of the PC age.

Part 5, Mining for Family Gold, places your family's history within the overall context of history. Learning about the very historical events your ancestors lived through will give you a deeper insight into the personal family history you discover. In this section, I also present information on available resources for those who are re-searching their ethnic ancestry. In addition, Part 5 gives you a brief tour of some of the records available online from other countries.

Part 6, PJs and Slippers Time, is the section to remind us of how the Internet has simplified our lives. In this section, you'll learn ways you can search library catalogs before you ever physically reach the library. This section also surveys the best genealogy library ever, the Family History Library. You'll also learn the basics about online genea-logical education—classes that you can take almost anytime. In Part 6, I'll also show you how to create your own family history Web page to share your genealogical re-search with the rest of the online world. You never know when a cousin will be surfing the Internet in the middle of the night and link to your family Web site.

Extras

Throughout this book, you'll also find little helpful hints and tidbits to further educate you about the ins and outs of beginning your online genealogical research, call attention to problem areas of research and PC use, or offer caution about any potential difficulty. These extra insights come in the form of sidebar information: Lineage Lingo, Heritage Hints, Cousin Counsel, and Genie Goodies. Here's a quick summary of what to expect from each:

Genie Goodies

These notes offer more details on a given subject, offering you added details to enhance your understanding.

Lineage Lingo

This set of sidebar information offers you definitions to genealogical and computer terms with which you may not be familiar.

Heritage Hints

These boxes offer clues to making your genealogy research or your online session more productive.

Cousin Counsel

With these little boxes, you can learn little warnings to help you avoid mistakes and pitfalls that others, who have more experience with online communications and genealogy, have experienced.

Each of the chapters concludes with some highlighted tips in "The Least You Need to Know."

Acknowledgments

My appreciation to all those at Alpha Books (they are listed in the front of the book) who have worked on this project to see it come to fruition. Special thanks go to Jessica Faust who gave me this chance, and Randy Ladenheim-Gil who took up the steering, listened to my concerns, and offered her own insight. Thanks to Terrie Lynn Solomon for her efforts to keep it all together. Appreciation also to Beau Sharbrough for keeping me on the straight and narrow technically.

A special thank you to Rhody. Without her, I would not be writing today. She saw a writer in a "wet-behind-the-ears" kid many years ago. Under her tutelage, I have grown and progressed in the writing craft. She is my mentor and my friend, and I love her dearly.

Finally, thanks to my family. First, my grandfather, who believed in me all those years ago. And to my husband and children, Michael, Marie, Ben, Elizabeth, and Jessica, who have put up with an almost absentee mother and wife. They have tolerated my late nights and fuzzy thinking from lack of sleep, as I strove to complete this project. Without them, I couldn't have done this book.

Trademarks

All terms mentioned in this book that are known to be or are suspected of being trademarks or service marks have been appropriately capitalized. Alpha Books and Pearson Education cannot attest to the accuracy of this information. Use of a term in this book should not be regarded as affecting the validity of any trademark or service mark.

PAF, FamilySearch, Ancestral File, International Genealogical Index, and Family History Library Catalog are trademarks of the Church of Jesus Christ of Latter-day Saints.

Family Origins is a trademark of FormalSoft, Inc. (Parson's Technology).

Family Tree Maker and Ultimate Family Tree are trademarks of Broderbund Software.

Generations is a trademark of Sierra On-line.

RootsWeb is a trademark of RootsWeb, Inc.

The forms found in Appendix D are used with permission from Genealogy Research Service and Tracey Converse.

The pedigree chart and family group sheet are used with permission from Evertons, Inc.

Part 1
Computers and Genealogy

The past meets the future through computerized genealogy—this seems like the ultimate in irony. Genealogists are discovering all sorts of newfangled methods and resources from this futuristic, computer-based technology.

Unfortunately, for many would-be genealogists, the idea of buying a PC (personal computer), trying to use it, and attempting to go online are synonymous with jumping out of a plane without a parachute. Some people would rather take the jump than sit down in front of a PC.

With this prevalent attitude in mind, I wrote this section, which gently introduces you to PCs and the "geek speak" that permeates PC use. Part 1 introduces you to what PC hardware requirements you'll need to access the Internet and go online. Additionally, you will also learn about online etiquette on the World Wide Web.

Chapter 1

What Is Online Genealogy?

In This Chapter

➤ Genealogy is genealogy, maybe

➤ Everyone's family is online now

➤ What can you find in cyberland?

➤ Getting to that cyberinformation

Genealogy is one of the world's favorite hobbies. In fact, a recent issue of *Time* magazine devoted its cover story to searching for family history. This isn't surprising, because researching family history has long been one of the top three hobbies worldwide. Some proponents even say that genealogy is the most popular hobby, having finally surpassed stamp collecting.

Combining the power and fascination of new online technology—namely the Internet—with this intriguing hobby has really given a boost to genealogy. In the 1970s, genealogy got its first boost when Alex Haley's *Roots* was made into a miniseries for television; genealogy was no longer considered just for the rich and famous as a way to validate their riches or their fame. As Haley showed that it was possible to trace his African American lineage back through slavery in the United States to Africa, those who read the book or watched the miniseries came to realize that they could also trace their family history, and that their interest wasn't in finding rich or famous people on the tree, but just to see where the family came from.

Genie Goodies

Genealogy is many things to different people. To some it is an attempt to prove a lineage for membership in a society of some sort. To others it is the definition of who they are, especially true among adoptees who are researching their biological lines. Genealogy is a personal journey through history to discover those who have come before you that have played a part in making you the person you are. After all, without your ancestors as they were, you would likely be a different individual in looks, heritage, or beliefs.

And now through the Internet, genealogy is no longer considered available to just those who have the freedom to hang out in libraries all day long. The Internet offers even individuals with demanding jobs and families a way to begin searching for their family history. Now, anyone with a computer and a modem can get online after the kids are in bed and begin to follow his or her ancestors' trails back in time.

Heritage Hints

Novice genealogists are those who have just begun to search. They have questions about all aspects of this hobby. The hobbyists have surpassed the novice in knowledge and perhaps in time they devote to their hobby. And the professional researcher has taken it to a higher level. Each level brings a different view to a discussion, giving you a wealth of information.

Online genealogy also brings you into contact with individuals that you wouldn't have had a chance to meet in any other way. Genealogists long to meet cousins and others researching the same surnames and looking in the same counties, states, or countries as they do. The Internet helps to bring together distant and not-so-distant relatives from across the world.

Throughout this book, we will look at the information and individuals that you will discover by visiting the Internet's genealogy sites. And there are plenty of sites available. Recently, those who track the Internet's growth determined that genealogy features the third largest number of Internet sites. Considering that we concentrate on the past when we focus on genealogy, we have certainly seen that we can take full advantage of modern technology to help us reach even further into the past.

What's the Difference Between Online and Regular Genealogy?

You may be thinking that there's no difference between online and traditional genealogy. To a degree, this notion is true. After all, the end result is the same. Your goal may be to find out who your great- or great-great-grandparents were and where they came from. However, when you compare traditional genealogical research to the online version, you'll discover that the information you may find and the way in which you find that information may be different.

Most genealogists are quite familiar with looking through books and microfilm. In fact, they are quite comfortable listening to the whir of the microfilm reader as it cranks up a film. Many seasoned genealogists have developed a system for effectively using the various records available at libraries and other information repositories. Some genealogists would even be insulted if you questioned their organizational abilities when it comes to tracking their research.

Somehow, when these same genealogists work with personal computers (PCs), they forget that they are masters of such machines. These skilled humans throw out the window all their tried and trusted methods for searching information. I sometimes wonder if the PCs "enjoy" the little "power trips" that result when machines get the best of humans. Not infrequently, I find myself talking to my PC, especially when it stubbornly refuses to do what I've asked.

Yes, I'm one of those guilty of assigning a personality to my PC. Generally, my PC and I have a very close bond. But every once in a while that relationship gets tested as my PC fails to pick up my e-mail or visit the Internet site that I anxiously wanted to check out. Everyone knows, however, that we control the PCs—they don't "think" for themselves—so learning how to make your PC do what you need is an additional important part of mastering online genealogy.

Lineage Lingo

E-mail is a PC-based, usually Internet-delivered electronic form of writing a letter or message to someone. Your PC sends the letter or message directly to the recipient by way of the Internet using the e-mail account you must set up with the company that provides you Internet service. E-mail arrives more quickly than via regular postal mail, and without a postage-due warning on it. Because it's fast and free, you'll find yourself using it more and more as you become familiar with the Internet.

The biggest difference between regular genealogical research and tracing your family online has to do with the accuracy of the data. When you compare the types of genealogical records on which you are relying, the possible number of levels between the original source and what you see online creates the potential for errors. With

Internet records, someone has entered the information that you find on most of the Web sites currently available. When someone enters the genealogical information into a form suitable for presentation on the Internet, transcribing the information into electronic form opens up the possibility of the typist entering errors should he misread the original information. With traditional, non–PC-based genealogy, when you visit a library or archive, you are more likely to be viewing and studying original documents. Granted these originals may be on microfilm, but you are seeing a representation of the original written document, not a transcribed version.

Another of the differences that online genealogy has brought about is the rapid change of information. Because the Internet is not a static entity, Web site content is in a state of constant change. Part of this continual change is directly related to the ease in which people can replace what they currently have on their Web sites with new content. This ability to change content is, however, a benefit to genealogy. Because the information can be changed, researchers are more willing to share what they currently know. They understand they can post their additional findings as they come upon them.

In the past, genealogists would sit on their research for years before publishing. Authors wanted to make sure their research was as complete and accurate as possible because publishing it was a major expense. And once it was published, you couldn't change it. You had to publish another edition. Now, as researchers discover new information for the family tree, they can update the Web page on which they are displaying the information.

The ease of families relocating is another cause of the constant change. People may move for business or other personal reasons. This causes them to search for a new Internet service provider (ISP). This may mean that a family's home page moves to a new ISP and now has a new Internet address. The Internet address of the old home page—the address that you have bookmarked or saved—is no longer valid six months later.

The Internet's constant state of change can really throw a monkey wrench into your research, especially if you need to revisit a particular Web site. We have ways, however, to overcome such obstacles brought on by today's constant change, and I will discuss specific techniques to help you with such problems later in the book.

Cousin Counsel

Because it is so easy to post your family history information on the Internet, there is the chance for more error. In their zeal to share what they know, some researchers are not verifying the accuracy of their data. Keep this in mind as you discover Web sites about your family surnames and verify everything.

Cousin Counsel

Internet Web pages have nasty habits of moving from their original locations. Although some pages move because the individual who owns them has to physically move, sometimes the Web page relocation issue is much simpler. The person who owns the Web page may rename it, not keeping in mind that changing the name may cause previous visitors to be unable to relocate the page.

Is My Family on the Internet?

It may surprise you, but it is possible that some of your family information is already on the Internet. Remember that there are thousands of people busily typing family information into their computers, and, in turn, they then post that information to the Internet. Of course, if you are researching the ZUCKNICK family, you may not find nearly as many Web sites or family Web pages as someone researching the SMITH family.

If you are researching a name like ZUCKNICK, though, you do enjoy a positive benefit. Usually with a unique name such as that, when you find something online, you can pretty much be assured that you can connect to that person. When it comes to the more common surnames, there are plenty of sites out there, but you may have a tougher time connecting to one of them. In fact, I currently have three different SMITH lines on my family tree. They are all in the New England area, and at present they don't connect to each other in my regular research.

What Can You Expect from the Internet?

So, just what can you find on the Internet about your family? The wealth of Web sites and information will surprise you. And the astounding fact is that new sites are popping up each day.

Genealogy thrives on people. The more people you can contact, the better your chance of cracking through that "brick wall" that is stopping your research path. The Internet offers you the chance to reach millions of people. These are people who share the same interest, or obsession, as my family would say, that you do. They will read your comments and commiserate with your inability to gain new information on your genealogical research. Even better, they may be the ones who offer you the suggestion that helps you to push through that brick wall and gain the information you need to trace your lineage back another generation.

Sometimes, we find it difficult to grasp the magnitude of the Internet. As we sit in armchairs or little offices surrounded by our genealogy files, happily skipping from one Web site to the next, to a large

Heritage Hints

When you click on a link in the World Wide Web, you are sending out a data packet requesting a specific Web page, and the Web page you then see on your screen is a data packet that is sent back to your PC. These packets hop from one system to another, and can sometimes get stalled along that route. So some slowdowns can be caused by a system other than yours or your Internet service provider.

Lineage Lingo

A **hop** represents the jumps from one computer system to another computer system that occur behind the scenes to get you from one Web page to another.

degree, we still don't understand what is going on throughout cyberspace. I suspect if we had to "ride" the Web to go from site to site, we might need to invest in some Dramamine to handle the circuitous route of necessary hops through the greatness of the World Wide Web (WWW).

When you click on a link on a Web page, you are not going from your computer directly to the computer that has that Web page. You are hopping from one computer to another until you get to the one that actually houses the page you are interested in. Of course all this hopping takes place behind the scenes. Usually, too, the hopping is so quick that you forget the hundreds or thousands of miles the information is traveling.

Genealogy's Far Reach on the Internet

I recently went to one of the many Web search engines that allow you to search on subjects for possible Web sites. I typed in the word *genealogy* on AltaVista (www.altavista.com) and discovered that at present there are some 2,054,844 hits on that word. The search engine said that it found some 1,306,903 Web pages that fit my search. That's a lot of genealogy out there.

Since not everyone thinks of his or her research in terms of the more technical term of genealogy, I did another search on the term *family history*. This time I received 376,627 hits on that term. AltaVista then informed me that it found 202,488 Web sites on family history.

Lineage Lingo

A **hit** in search engines is a result that fits your search criteria. If the term is *genealogy*, any Web page that has the word genealogy somewhere in the code searched by the search engine will be displayed as a hit in the results list.

Goodness, that's a lot of Web sites devoted to genealogy. What a great feeling I have knowing there are many others as involved in genealogy as I am. Of all those millions of hits on the WWW, I can presently claim only about 10 of those pages, assuming that each of my subpages was considered a separate page.

There may have been some Web sites that were included in both of the searches made above. That is because many genealogists use the terms of *genealogy* and *family history* interchangeably. Regardless, we can safely estimate that the Web features at least 1 million sites currently with some genealogy interest to them.

Genie Goodies

While the terms **genealogy** and **family history** are often used interchangeably, they actually denote different approaches to the tracing of a family tree. Genealogy concentrates more on the names, dates, and places of a biological lineage or descent. Family history incorporates family stories, occupations, and other history to flesh out the family and is more apt to include non-bloodline relationships, such as adoption.

As you begin to visit the vast array of genealogical Web sites, you will find that they vary as to content and emphasis. The Web page's publisher—the person who took the time to create the page—had the Web page's goal in mind. Each Web page's goal greatly affects what information the designer uses and how it is displayed. Content of genealogical sites can include the following:

➤ Pages devoted to specific surnames

➤ Pages that include transcribed records

➤ Pages that deal primarily with history of a place or person

➤ Pages meant to teach

➤ Pages designed to encourage discussion among researchers with a common interest

➤ Pages maintained for commercial purposes

➤ Pages that contain a person's family history as he currently knows it

These examples just scratch the surface. With 1.5 million content pages bursting out the edges of cyberland, it's easy to see that you could easily spend hours flitting from site to site. That's why you should try to have a goal for each time you log on. We need to avoid new traps that come with online technology that are merely online versions of the old traps we still suffer from in the offline world—such as trying to keep ourselves from avoiding the paper trap of continuously returning to the same books in a library only to be disappointed again.

Who Can Access Online Information?

The Internet is effective because millions of people can reach the information it displays. With such an audience, the Internet has become a major marketing force. The ability to reach so many people with a relatively inexpensive medium is amazing.

Look at almost any Web page these days and you will see banners. Just like commercials interspersed in a television show, Web sites have their own commercials, which have come to be known as *banners*.

Genie Goodies

There are two main types of advertisements found on Web sites that genealogists are apt to visit. A banner is usually displayed at the top of the Web page. It is a rectangular box with an ad in it that you can click on to be taken to the site being advertised. The other type actually opens a separate, smaller browser window. The advertising text appears in that smaller window. These windows will open automatically when you visit a Web site that uses them. The first time you experience this type of Web-based advertising, it can take you by surprise. Don't worry. Internet advertising can take you off track, but you won't stay lost forever.

Genealogy is a hobby that thrives on this worldwide access. The more people we can reach, the more successful genealogists we are. After all, it doesn't help me to work hard writing up a detailed description of my family history only to tuck it away in my hope chest. While it may stay nice and clean and preserved in the dust-free confines, I won't get contacted by anyone who has read my genealogical work and might be able to help me add some new bit of information to it.

As long as you have the necessary computer and phone equipment, you have the potential to access the Internet. You don't even necessarily have to own this equipment. In Chapter 2, I show you how you can access the Internet even if you are "computerless."

The upside to the Internet is that everyone can access it. The downside is that everyone can access it. Unfortunately there are some less than ethical folks out there who might be able to use information you share online. Chapter 3 talks about this subject, showing what to watch out for and things to keep in mind.

The Least You Need to Know

➤ Researching your genealogy online is different than researching at a library.

➤ Using the Internet, you will likely find some significant information on the family you're researching.

➤ Using the Internet, you will be able to find Web pages that emphasize all aspects of genealogy and family history.

➤ With more than a million sites featuring genealogy on the Web, learning to be selective about what Web sites you visit can save you a great deal of time.

➤ Because anyone can access the Internet and its information, the potential to access tons of information is a reality, but so is accessing misleading or inaccurate information.

Chapter 2

Getting to Genealogy Cyberland

In This Chapter

➤ What are your computer's capabilities for accessing genealogy information online?

➤ What should you do when your computer ties up your phone line?

➤ What is an Internet service provider (ISP), or Internet provider (IP)?

➤ What other ways can you get genealogical information from the Internet—even if you don't own a computer?

If you take time to think about it, the technology we use today is wonderful. From our living room or family room, we can access genealogical information from around the world. Through online genealogy, we can meet and talk online with people that we may never see face to face. Yet these people may have a direct impact on the outcome of our genealogical research.

However, to get connected with these people out in cyberland, you must have certain PC components and software. I'm sure you knew we'd get to the PC technical part of it before we hit the hardcore online genealogy stuff.

Are You Up to the Computer Challenge?

If you are a PC owner, you already know that if you are thinking about purchasing a new software program, you need to make sure that the software's system requirements are exceeded by those of your PC. The system requirements software manufacturers list on their packaging is the minimum any PC has to have to be able to run the software. (Notice, I did not say *effectively* run the software; that's another issue.)

The Internet itself also has certain system requirements. There is a reason that the Internet has become known as the Web. While each Web site that you are likely to visit is stored on a computer independent of other computers that store other Web sites, all of these computers are interconnected to become what we know as the Internet or World Wide Web. You could think of this as a large spider web. Each ring is interconnected with other threads in the web. The spider can move from ring to ring by following the various connecting threads.

To effectively use the Internet, you need certain things:

➤ a computer, sometimes called a PC (for personal computer)

➤ a modem

➤ a phone line with a modular connector

➤ an Internet service provider (otherwise known as an ISP)

➤ a web browser

Computer

Of course, you already know you need a PC to get hooked up to the Internet. However, the speed and RAM of your computer can greatly affect your ability to get online and do any effective searching.

The speed on your computer is displayed by MegaHertz units (usually seen as MHz in computer descriptions). The theory goes that the higher the number, the faster your computer should go. This is affected by other aspects of your computer, including the RAM. *RAM* (no, it is not of the goat variety) stands for Random Access Memory. You can think of it as the working area for your computer. While we are working on a particular family from our family tree, it is not unusual to take the files and copies we have on that family and lay them out on our desk. This makes it easier and quicker for us to refer back to a given resource. RAM is the desk where your computer puts the files it feels it will need to refer back to. Again, the higher the number the better, because the higher the number, the more space the computer has to put the files. Sort of like going from a 13-inch round table to a 6-foot conference table to lay out your files. When you are sitting in front of your PC waiting for graphics files to load, you'll find the Internet to be an extremely tedious place. Even a few seconds pass like minutes, and even the smallest of images downloading to your PC seem huge and never-ending when you are using an older, slower system—especially if you have ever worked on a faster, newer PC at work, a friend's house, or elsewhere.

So what is the ideal PC for the online genealogist today? The ideal system would be the fastest and spiffiest system you could possibly buy *tomorrow*. Yes, I said tomorrow, because the moment you leave the store with your computer and load it in the car, your "new" computer is most likely already the older model, as computers are a fast-moving and ever-changing industry. But don't let the predictable and imminent demise of your new costly PC purchase worry you. When considering a PC purchase for any reason, you should always base your purchase decision on the task you need to accomplish. For online genealogy, you need a PC that can run your genealogy database software and, in this day and age, hook you up to the Internet.

So, if you are selecting a PC strictly for the purpose of online genealogy, you can afford to spend less than you would for "tomorrow's" best PC. But, if you want to be able to access the Internet and not get frustrated with long delays, you'll probably want at minimum these system specifications:

➤ 150 Mhz 486 motherboard

➤ 14.4 bps modem

➤ 16 MB of RAM

With these listed minimum system requirements, you'll be able to access the Internet, but your connection will not be fast. However, if you are just now heading out the door to purchase a computer for the first time, you will find that the currently available systems are much faster and more powerful than the one listed above. And best of all, the cost of the newer, faster computers is lower than the prices some of us old-time computer users paid a couple of years ago.

When you are looking at the new crop of computers, remember that in general the higher the number, the faster that particular component will be. The modem, for example, usually doubles. We went from 14.4 to 28.8 to 56 bps. This number is actually in thousands and has to do with the amount of data that can travel through the modem and out over the phone lines at any given moment. The motherboard, which is the main component of your computer, also will help keep the computer running faster if it has a higher number. The motherboard is to the computer what a mother is to a household. The motherboard is responsible for making sure that all the other components attached to the computer and inside the computer work together. It is sort of like how a mother keeps things working smoothly in the home.

If you already own a PC, making some minor changes to it to improve its performance is a great alternative. What results may not be the speediest, or most high-tech, setup but you can judge for yourself what an acceptable Internet delay is.

Of course, my minimum list of requirements work together. The higher the numbers are for a PC's motherboard speed and the amount of RAM the PC has, the better the PC's performance. And if your PC performs well by itself, then it will usually perform better on the Internet.

If your computer doesn't meet my list of minimum requirements, you may want to see what deals for upgrading you can find at your local computer stores. Sometimes, all you need is one minor item to upgrade some aspect of your computer's performance without great expense, and you can have your local computer store install it or set it up for you. Adding more memory or getting a faster modem—both for under $200—are good examples of small purchases than can mean improved performance in many instances.

Later in this chapter, I'll show you other creative ways that you can use to get on the Internet. One of these might work better for you if upgrading your personal home computer is not an option at this time.

Lineage Lingo

RAM stands for random access memory. Your computer puts information into RAM for easier and quicker access. As a rule, this area can be written and rewritten to many times during a single session on the computer. This type of memory can be easily expanded by having a qualified technician add chips to the motherboard. You could think of this as your computer's work space.

Modems

The modem is the device that allows your computer to convert its digital information to sound, which can then be sent over a normal phone line to another modem. The other modem converts it back to digital information, which is then interpreted by the receiving computer. Through modems and related devices, personal computer users are able to send information back and forth, via the Internet or other online commercial service.

If you cringe because you know what I'm going to discuss next, just relax. What you need to know about modems is fairly easy. Yes, there are different types of modems—some go inside your PC and some sit outside your PC. The primary difference between modems, though, is their speed, which currently runs from 28.8 bps to about 56.6 bps. (Regardless of your modem's speed, you will see some variation in send and receive speeds.) If these numbers confuse you, just remember the greater the number, the faster the Internet transmission speed is generally. However, just because you have the fastest modem on the market, does not mean you will always be speeding along the Internet. Other aspects of online communication will affect your speed, including the capabilities of the modem on the other end. Some outside considerations can affect modem transmission speeds, though, including "noise" (static) on your phone line, which can slow down communications transfer rates.

Internet Service Provider (ISP) or Internet Provider (IP)

Your Internet service provider (ISP) or Internet provider (IP) is your "virtual" on ramp to the Internet. Your modem connects to the ISP's or IP's modem, and through this connection you actually gain access to the Internet.

Later in this chapter, we will look in more detail at ISPs and IPs. Selecting a service provider is not so simple, and I have several suggestions that can help you.

Browser

Once you have all the hardware necessary for your PC, you have your modem, and you have at least decided on an ISP, then you need to see whether you have all the software needed to make your Internet connection and track all those great genealogical tidbits you'll be discovering as you surf your way from Web site to Web site. The software that transforms you and your PC into a genealogical cybersurfer is called Web browser software.

If you pay attention to any national news, you probably already know there are two Web browsers dominating that area of the software world—Microsoft Internet Explorer and Netscape Navigator—and both companies are in a bitter battle that now involves some fairly significant antitrust lawsuits. Which Web browser you select is entirely up to you, because both are solid programs. Microsoft has just released its Internet Explorer V5.0 browser, which comes as a part of Microsoft Office 2000. If you prefer Netscape Navigator, this Web browser's latest version is V4.51.

Getting Web browser software is usually quite simple and oftentimes costs nothing. Many software programs, including word processing programs, genealogy programs, and software office suites (such as Office 2000), now offer to install at least one version of either the Explorer or Navigator browsers as you are installing other software. For example, when I recently installed a financial program, the installation program asked me if I wanted to install Internet Explorer also. The financial software developers have made Explorer available to its customers at no extra charge so this company can entice you to visit its Web site, too, when you're online. Software companies count on your visiting their product-specific sites. The Internet is now a major publicity tool, in addition to the benefits that genealogists get out of it.

Heritage Hints

Web browser software reads files created in a certain way and converts them to the pretty pictures and fonts that you see on your screen. If you are curious to see what is "behind the scenes" with any particular Web page creation, click the cursor somewhere in the browser window, then click the right mouse button, and select View Source. I think you will be surprised at what you discover.

Another way to get your needed browser software is when you sign up with an ISP. Often, if you are new to the Internet, the ISP will provide you with a packet including the ISP's preferred browser. Sometimes ISPs may prefer that you use either Explorer or Navigator, primarily due to the software and hardware the ISP uses at its location. Most times, though, your ISP won't care. Determining which browser you should use is simply a matter of personal preference. The browser's "look and feel" should be comfortable to you.

Once you're online, you may want to visit the sites where you can download the one browser that you do not currently have and try it out to see which one you feel more comfortable with. You can then uninstall the one you no longer wish to use. When visiting the Web site to download the program, keep in mind that the program will be a large file. It may take upwards of two to three hours to download.

Heritage Hints

A great way to compare Explorer and Navigator is to install them both and then run them at the same time. Select a particular site and have each browser visit it at the same time. Compare the sites in both browser windows to see which browser you prefer.

Internet Explorer is available by visiting the Microsoft site at www.microsoft.com and selecting its download section.

Netscape Communicator is available by visiting the Netscape site at www.netscape.com. You can download Netscape's latest version of its browser at this location.

Both of these programs are free if you download them from the software vendors' sites. Netscape Communicator also offers a downloadable commercial version that offers you technical support help.

Finally, if you wish, you can purchase both of these browsers at your local computer store. You will generally find them located with the Internet software. And there is quite a lot of it currently available on the shelves.

It's Not My Teenager, It's My Computer Tying Up the Phone

When I first got involved in online genealogy, our house had only a single phone line. Sometimes, people would complain that they couldn't get through because my phone line was always busy. Sadly, I couldn't even blame my busy phone line on my teenager. At the time, I only had a four-year-old, a three-year-old, and our dog. Somehow I didn't think anyone would believe me if I said the dog was tying up the phone.

When you work online, people who used to be able to call you at all hours of the day and night may find it a little harder to get through. When you use your modem to connect to the Internet, you are using the phone line, too. Your modem converts the computer data into an audible tone that is then carried over the phone line. Because of this, when you tell your modem to connect to your ISP, you are basically telling your computer to make a telephone call.

In order to still be able to hear from the living family members, *and* be able to surf the Net, many people opt to get a second phone line—but this addition is not an absolute necessity. I suggest it so that you can still maintain contact with the non-Internet world. Just be aware that your phone is "busy" to anyone calling you when you are connected to the Internet.

Also, if you have any spiffy phone features like call waiting, these options may interfere with your online performance. You will want to find out whether your local phone company offers a way to temporarily turn off such features.

For example, if you have call waiting, your telephone signals an incoming call to you with a click you hear in your earpiece while you continue to talk on the phone. Unfortunately, your modem hears this same sound and it disconnects from your ISP. If you were on the last three minutes of a very long file download when this click occurred, you might want to bash the computer or strangle the phone. Taking your frustrations out on the PC or phone may make you feel better for a few minutes, but you'll still have to get back online and start your file download over again. So avoid this little headache by disabling the call waiting before you go online the first time.

You will also want to spread the word to any teenagers or others who are in the house who might dare to try to use the phone even though they know that you are online. If anyone picks up an extension elsewhere in the house, he or she will knock you off your Internet connection.

In my house, we have certain unwritten rules. Everyone knows not to move anything in my office, because I use a very intricate piling method and would be lost if anyone moved something. Likewise, they know not to pick up the phone when I am on the Internet. My oldest, now 14, has made comments about my tying up the phone more than she ever has. Because my daughter is now the teenager, I finally have someone that I can blame for our excessive phone use.

Genie Goodies

Many telephone companies are now offering phone lines specifically for online usage. ISDN lines offer a digital alternative that is much faster than regular modems. Of course, along with the speed comes the cost. These special phone lines are more expensive than your regular monthly phone charges for your home phone. You usually end up paying a higher rate to the phone company and the ISP. At present this technology is not available in all areas.

I See an ISP

Earlier I mentioned that you need an Internet service provider in order to be able to get connected to the Internet. If you open your phone book and look in the yellow pages, you may be surprised at how many local ISPs have popped up in your own community.

I live in a very small town. We were excited when a small movie theater opened up about a year ago, so we now have one movie theater showing a single movie in week-long runs, but we have *three* local ISPs. Larger cities have many more to offer than this.

Is a Local ISP for You?

Internet service providers come in many shapes and sizes. Some offer you unlimited time each month for a set fee. Some may have a set number of hours that you can use for your fee. Usually these types of ISPs have set that limit high enough that the average surfer doesn't reach that limit. Other ISPs will throw in Web space for you to create your own home page.

Perhaps the only downside to a local ISP is that sometimes they don't anticipate the large volume of people who may be trying to dial in to the Internet at a given time. When this happens you are sometimes left with frustration because you get a busy signal instead of a chance to surf the Web.

With that said, though, many times you will find that the local, smaller ISPs are friendlier. They are sometimes more willing to help you with any technical problems you may have. This can be important when you are new to the Internet and not sure what is going wrong.

One thing I have discovered is that when you are frustrated, you want the answer *now*. You want the person on the other end of the phone to appreciate your problem for what it is. We've all been there. So it is a major plus in my book if the technicians in the support department are helpful and understanding when I call.

An ISP That Travels with You

If you find yourself traveling a lot and want to be able to connect while on the road, then you will want to more thoroughly investigate the national ISPs. These larger providers offer local phone numbers in many major cities around the country.

The downside to this is that if you live in a small town, such as I do, then you may discover that while they cater to the larger cities, they do not have a local number for you.

Cousin Counsel

When you are shopping around for an ISP, compare before you settle on a provider. Call each one you're interested in and ask them about monthly fees, hourly limitations, available Web site or home page space, and local access numbers.

While my solution may not be suitable for everyone, what I have done is to actually have two Internet service providers. I use one of the local ones when I am happily surfing at home. However, when I head off to Salt Lake City to the Family History Library, or set out to attend a conference, I then rely on my national service provider.

Other On Ramps

In addition to signing up with an ISP, you have some other ways to access the Internet. Truly, the Internet has permeated many areas of our everyday life, resulting in several alternative areas where you can access cyberspace and its wealth of information:

➤ Commercial services

➤ Libraries

➤ Educational institutions

Commercial Services

You've all seen the ads for Prodigy Internet or America Online (AOL) on television. I suspect you even have your very own collection of AOL CDs that have come to you through the mail. If you subscribe to any PC magazines, you have probably received at least one such CD this past year. Because I subscribe to a number of PC magazines, you can bet that my collection of free-but-unused CDs is impressive. But you never know when you might have to reinstall either AOL or Prodigy, so I always have a new CD on hand. In addition to Prodigy Internet and AOL, CompuServe and Microsoft Network (MSN) are also other commercial online services.

All commercial services have one thing in common: content. In fact, each commercial service has an area devoted entirely to genealogical research.

Each of these commercial services also offers an on-ramp to the Internet. Because the Internet has so permeated the commercial services, most of them have adopted a browser-styled approach to the services' content areas to make each of them more user-friendly.

Cousin Counsel

Because commercial services have gone to a more browser-oriented feel, you sometimes cannot tell whether you are on the commercial service or the Internet. If you need to leave your e-mail address online for anyone, always assume you are on the Internet and leave your full e-mail address. This would look something like johndoe@aol.com.

Genie Goodies

Commercial services are more than on ramps to the Internet. They are self–contained entities of online information in their own right. For certain fees they offer you membership. Some of them offer a flat fee to access their information each month. Others charge a fee and give you a limited number of hours to use. Beyond that you are charged a per-hour fee to use their system. Talk to your friends to find out what they use and how they feel about them, and read the various computer magazines that include comparisons before deciding on one.

Commercial services like AOL and CompuServe offer significant advantages. These services are more like national ISPs, because the services' goals are to have lots of people sign up with them. As a result, the commercial services must strive to offer phone numbers in as many different places as possible—from a heavily populated place like San Francisco to a sparsely populated locale like rural Rush County, Indiana. As a result, you can usually use such a service as both your local and your traveling ISP.

The drawback to the commercial services is in the way the service accesses the Internet. When you want to visit a site on the Web, the service sends you through a gateway. If the term *gateway* is unfamiliar to you, picture it as a hotel's rotating doors. People are going in and coming out at the same time. With commercial online services like AOL, your PC and modem signal are transmitting signals out, and the commercial service is sending out information simultaneously with the incoming information. The data simultaneously traveling in and out can cause a major slowdown—a traffic jam of sorts. And on the Internet, a traffic jam is unacceptable. In fact, to many people, an Internet traffic jam is far less acceptable than a traffic jam on the way home from work.

Going back to our criteria of what to ask local ISPs before selecting one, let's look at what the commercial services offer in the way of monthly fees, available time, and Web page or home page space. Currently all of the major commercial services offer a monthly fee of under $25.00. That monthly fee entitles the member to unlimited hours on the service, which includes going out on the Internet. Members are also entitled to free Web page space, with the exception of MSN. MSN has not yet brought that capability onboard.

Libraries

Any public library today offers PCs for use. Some libraries have sign-up sheets for PC time, and others offer a more informal first-come, first-served basis.

You may wonder, however, if you can effectively use the Internet and not own a PC. Yes, if you plan your activities correctly, you can manage your own Web site by exclusively using PCs available in libraries. If you have control over your schedule and are organized in your approach to working on the Internet, this alternative might work for you.

Heritage Hints

Many online sites offer free e-mail. The e-mail recipient uses his or her browser to read and respond to the e-mail, rather than download it to a PC. Through such a free online option, you can even receive e-mail without actually owning a computer.

Using a local library computer to manage a Web site would probably require more advanced planning than I probably want to do, though I hate to admit it. You'd need to already have in mind the changes you wanted to make to your Web site, so that you could implement them quickly. Some libraries have limits on the amount of time you can spend online in any given session. Finding a library without any time usage limits would work better if you wanted to try to maintain a Web site without owning your own computer.

Educational Institutions

If you still have a child in school, you know that the Internet is everywhere in the education world. Instead of talking by phone with my child's teachers, I now e-mail. This technological innovation doesn't thrill my son, but the primary reason is because he is the one I need to talk about to his teachers. While the secondary schools are getting heavily into using the Internet, colleges and universities may offer you free Internet access. If you are a student or faculty member, you may also be able to access the Internet for free from home.

Genie Goodies

When you e-mail people, you can tell what method they are accessing the Internet by, and from what country, by looking at the end of their e-mail addresses. If the e-mail address ends in **.net**, then the e-mailer is accessing the Internet from an ISP. If the e-mail ends in **.com**, the user is accessing the Internet from a commercial account of some type. If the e-mail address ends in **.edu**, the e-mailer is accessing the Internet from a university or other educational account. When it comes to determining country of origin for e-mail, with the exception of the United States, all other countries have a two-letter code included in those countries' e-mail addresses. **uk** stands for United Kingdom; **au** means the e-mail came from someone in Australia; and so on. Remember, though, that with the Internet, e-mail addresses are not case-sensitive (meaning you can use upper- or lowercase letters).

Even if you no longer work at the university, you may still be entitled to the free Internet access. Some retired professors can continue to access the Internet from home by going through the university's Internet or e-mail systems.

So, how each person accesses the Internet is a matter of personal preference—and is sometimes determined by monetary issues and limits. Regardless of technology, I think our ancestors take great delight in leading us on a merry goose chase as we search for them. Even though the Internet wasn't around when our ancestors were, I swear that mine have been doing their best to hide themselves whenever I find Web sites where I know I should discover much about them.

Now, on to the world of online genealogy!

The Least You Need to Know

➤ To make surfing the Web easier, you will want to ensure your PC can handle the demands you'll place on it.

➤ Keep in mind that when surfing the Web, your phone line is busy to anyone who is trying to call you.

➤ You'll want to see which ISPs offer services in your area and what features they offer.

➤ Make use of some more creative ways to access the Internet that may cost you nothing but time.

Chapter 3

"Geek Speak" for Family History Hunters

In This Chapter

➤ Talking "techie" with the best of them

➤ Conveying emotional reactions online

➤ Discovering acronyms: the online genealogist's friend

➤ Mastering Internet etiquette

➤ Learnin' the lingo

Pick up any PC magazine, or tune in to any Web-oriented television program, and you'll discover the foreign language known as "Internet Speak." When you started reading this chapter, I'll bet you didn't realize you were going to visit a "foreign country" without ever leaving your comfortable couch. We are off to cyberland, where "Internet Speak" is the only language most of the "residents" understand.

"Techie" Terms

The Internet is a conglomeration of computers, which guarantees (more or less) that you'll encounter plenty of terms that make no sense whatsoever. Worse, 10-year-olds spew forth techie terms with total innocence in their eyes.

But the learning curve for mastering techie talk is small, so soon you, too, will not only understand the techie terms, but will be using these new words and expressions in your everyday conversations. The transformation from "normal" to "techie" happens so quickly, you don't even notice it, and I did not notice it as it was happening to me. Yes, my children call me a geek—a title I wear proudly.

Any Internet book should include some sort of glossary, as we have done in the appendix section of this book. However, the Internet itself also has some great online sites that can help you find definitions of various technical and Internet-specific terms.

Lineage Lingo

A **computer interest group** is usually a subset of a genealogical society that is devoted to the computer aspects of genealogy. At their meetings you will learn of new genealogy software and online sites devoted to genealogy.

Heritage Hints

You can find one of the best sites for learning Internet lingo at NetLingo (www.netlingo.com). This site offers a searchable dictionary of hundreds of everyday Internet terms.

Another great source of technological and genealogical terms can be found through your local *computer interest group* (CIG) of your genealogical society. Through your local group, you will get the chance to see new software in action. Very often these groups have a library of software and data CDs that you can use when you attend the meetings.

"Emoticons"—The Emotions of the Internet

Perhaps one of the hardest aspects to get used to when it comes to online communication is how two-dimensional it is. When you read an e-mail or are working in an online chat room, you can't tell very easily how the writer is feeling. As a result, some people become offended simply by the ambiguity of the written words. Because e-mail and chat communications can take place at such a quick pace, recipients are often offended, resulting in flaring tempers.

To solve the gap that comes with e-mail and chat communication ambiguities, the online world has come up with *emoticons*: icons that convey emotions. When they first appeared, emoticons consisted of straight text. A person telling a joke online might put <grin> after the message to let anyone else who read the message know that it was a joke.

However, the online community always strives to find ways to shorten the number of keystrokes necessary to send a message. So online communicators began to create via the keyboard little characters to use in place of words. These characters always looked like little, somewhat crude sideways pictures of peoples' facial expressions. Granted, you need to stretch your imagination a little as you look at these little faces, but soon you see that interpreting the meaning behind the little sideways characters is second nature.

You are likely to run across emoticons in every facet of communicating online. These little emotional messages work their way into e-mail messages, bulletin board messages, and chat rooms.

Sometimes, new Internet users refer to the emoticons as "smiley faces." This nickname started because the original emoticons were a form of a smiley face. The following table shows a very short list of these smiley faces.

Lineage Lingo

Emoticons are a way of using characters on the keyboard to denote various emotions including happiness, anger, surprise, mischief, and more.

Smiley Faces and Other Emoticons

:-)	Basic smiley
:-(	Frowning smiley
:-X	Lips are sealed
:-/	User is skeptical
;-)	Winky smiley
:->	Sarcastic smiley
:-C	User is really bummed
:-0	Uh-oh

Of course, there are some great Web sites that offer you complete lists of these little smiley face emoticons. Here's a list of these sites:

➤ The Unofficial Smiley Dictionary (www.eff.org/papers/eegtti/eeg_286.html)

➤ Smiley and Emoticons (www.netlingo.com/smiley.cfm)

➤ The Smiley Home Page (www.lib.utah.edu/navigator/email/emoticon.html)

➤ Smilies Unlimited (www.czWeb.com/smilies.htm)

Additionally, no computer book publishing world would be complete without an entire book devoted to the smiley phenomenon. Appropriately called *Smileys,* the definitive smiley book was written by Doherty Sanderson and David W. Sanderson (O'Reilly & Associates, 1993). *Smileys* is

Lineage Lingo

E-mail is a message that arrives in your e-mail program. You don't need to actually seek them out. **Bulletin board messages** are messages that appear on a site on the Internet in a linked format. **Chat rooms** are similar to the old telephone party lines. More information on all can be found in Chapters 10 and 11.

a short book (only 93 pages), and you can buy it at most local bookstores, including online at www.amazon.com.

Secret Codes—Genealogical Acronyms

Genealogists are major supporters of acronyms, second only to the military, I think. Read any genealogist's online message and it is likely to be fraught with acronyms. The preference for acronyms probably stems from the extremely long names of repositories, book and software titles, and other resources that we use. It takes so long to enter the entire title, we've developed a major set of acronyms to help conserve time and shorten messages.

Back in the "online dark ages"—about 10 years ago—we had no easy access to the Internet. At that time, most genealogists who were working online were either accessing electronic bulletin board services (BBS) or the early online commercial services, like CompuServe. Each of these online connections had its own unique situation. Calling bulletin board services usually required long distance phone calls. The early online commercial services had hourly charges, so the result was sometimes expensive. But the necessity of brevity sometimes sacrificed completeness; thus genealogists began popularizing acronyms.

Genie Goodies

A **BBS** or bulletin board service was an early online system. It required your computer to dial and connect directly to the computer that housed the BBS. The computer with the BBS usually had just a single phone line, so folks were encouraged to stay on for just a short time. A group of these BBS computers joined the *National Genealogy Conference.* This meant that they all carried messages from the genealogy groups. And despite the small number of genealogists who were using these groups, the amount of useful information that flowed back and forth was amazing.

While many of the genealogical acronyms frequently used are specifically in reference to genealogy, some are a general part of online communications. In the following table, I've listed a few of the more common acronyms you'll see online.

Genealogy and Online Acronyms

AFK	Away from keyboard
BRB	Be right back
BTW	By the way
FHC	Family History Center
FHL	Family History Library
FWIW	For what it's worth
FYI	For your information
GMTA	Great minds think alike
IGI	International Genealogical Index
IMHO	In my humble opinion
LOL	Laughing out loud
NGS	National Genealogy Society
OTOH	On the other hand
ROTF	Rolling on the floor (with laughter)
TTYL	Talk to you later

As I mentioned earlier, genealogists are great at coming up with their own acronyms, because when we name our societies and books, we appear to strive to come up with the longest name possible. Even the shorter names for societies aren't really that short. Take the *National Genealogical Society.* This name is really a reasonable one for the society, which is intended to be of use to genealogists nationwide, but write this name more than once or twice, and your fingers begin to rebel. So genealogists immediately shortened it to NGS. Of course if you tell a travel agent that you want to go to the NGS annual conference, you will want to be sure to stress what city it is in. Otherwise you may find yourself in need of your passport. NGS is also the airport code for the Nagasaki, Japan, airport. I include this example to illustrate that acronyms may not have the same meanings in all circles, so always remember your target audience when using acronyms.

The Internet features a wonderful site, the Acronym Finder (www.AcronymFinder.com), which currently features more than 85,000 cataloged acronyms. You can type into the Web site the acronym in question, and the Web site will display the results. When I typed in *NGS*, the Web site returned a list of nine acronyms, including the Nagasaki airport.

Cousin Counsel

Sometimes we get into the habit of using acronyms so frequently that we forget what the letters really mean. Depending on what words the letters represent, you might possibly offend someone. So be sure you know what the letters stand for before you use an acronym.

This database, however, is loaded with many genealogical acronyms, so I decided to give the Web site a little test. One of my favorite resources is the *American Genealogical Biographical Index*, which also happens to be rather rare. I recently discovered that there are only about 200 sets available in libraries in the United States. I have been quite fortunate to live near one of those libraries. However, many times when mentioning this source, in its abbreviated form, of course, AGBI, I would get many questions about what it was. So I tested the Acronym Finder site and typed in AGBI. I was tickled to discover that the site did indeed find this acronym, providing me with the name of the source. This example is a good one of an acronym that is strictly genealogical.

Mastering Cyberspace Etiquette

Most of us have been taught etiquette for the table, meetings, and when driving on the road. I can remember growing up learning which was the proper fork to use for my salad. And my kids can tell you that they are being taught to say please and thank you, though I suspect it is against their will at the moment.

When you consider the millions of people accessing the Internet, you should not be surprised to find rules of etiquette governing behavior and conduct for surfing the World Wide Web.

For me one of the most surprising aspects of getting online is to comprehend what I call the "Jekyll and Hyde" complex. Face to face, these people are very polite and congenial. Even if these people had disagreements, they would be able to handle the situation with control and understanding. But put these same people behind the anonymity of the keyboard and watch out! They almost seem to have split personalities, with the personality appearing at the keyboard combative and intent on tormenting the other people online.

Yet other Internet users walk into an online attack through naivete. Whether they don't understand the purpose of a message area they enter or they type their messages in all uppercase letters, they bring the wrath of other less-than-patient online users down on them. To keep peace throughout the online world, this section contains a few guidelines that I hope will spare you such a baptism by fire.

Watch for these items when you are sharing information through online messages:

➤ Subject lines

➤ Obsessive quoting

➤ Shouting in messages

➤ Signature lines

➤ Sending unwanted attachments

Heritage Hints

When you first join a mailing list or bulletin board, you will want to sit back and **lurk.** A "lurker" just reads the messages for a couple of weeks, to get the feel and tone of this particular Internet area. Once you become comfortable with an area, you have a much better idea of how to post acceptable messages.

➤ Using stationery

➤ Staying on topic

➤ Arguing

Before I discuss each of these subjects, I must add one important item: Always remember to ask nicely for things. "Please" and "thank you" go a long way—even online. When someone goes that extra step in trying to help you with your family history, be certain to show appropriate appreciation. Even if you are tempted to send the thank-you message to the public area so that others will know how appreciative you are and how helpful the other person was, it is usually best to send such comments in private e-mail. Many people see such messages as clutter even though that is not your intent. Of course, someone who has done an exceptional job does deserve the recognition of a public thank you.

Using Informative Subject Lines

Read through any genealogy messages for very long, and you'll find other onliners complaining about a few subject lines others are using for the messages. In general, using Genealogy as a subject line is not very informative or helpful. Since all the messages someone posts in a genealogy area have to do with genealogy, this subject line is assumed. When you post a message, the subject line should tell the reader at a glance what specific information you want.

For instance, when you post a query on a genealogical line on which you are stuck, always try to include the SURNAME of your subject, a year or period of years appropriate for your query, and a locality. The more specific the items, the better chance you have of getting the types of responses that will be helpful to you. Including this information will enable anyone reading messages to see in an instant if the query is of interest to him or her, and if he or she may be able to help you. Also notice that I have suggested putting the surname in all caps. This is to call attention to the surname in the subject line and is a standard method of recording surnames on charts and should be in corresponding online documents as well.

Refraining from Obsessive Quoting

When you send e-mail back and forth, your e-mail program may be set up to "quote" the entire message of the sender when you respond. Although this feature is nice, it eats up lots of transfer time and hard-disk storage space, if overused. In most cases, you don't have to quote the entire, original e-mail that someone sent you. When you respond to an e-mail, cut out those parts that do not apply to your response. Everyone who reads the smaller version of the message will be grateful.

Lineage Lingo

Cutting is the act of highlighting specific text with your mouse (or other pointing device) and then pressing the Backspace or Delete key to remove it.

The other problem with quoting occurs as an ongoing dialog develops between you and another party or parties. As your e-mail dialog goes back and forth, the quoted material begins to grow, almost exponentially. You write the message, the person responding quotes your entire message. When you respond back you quote everything from the other person's message, which includes quoting your original message. Pretty soon, you have your very own version of "he said, she said" going on.

I know you are sitting there defending this as an excellent way to retain everything for future reference. If the string of messages is that important, then you should save the individual e-mails, or print them out, or both. Printing and saving e-mail correspondence lets you retain the complete conversation thread, without causing problems for anyone else who may be picking up your e-mail dialog and is forced to download your ever-growing tome.

Lineage Lingo

SHOUTing is the term used for messages that are posted in all caps. While genealogists use capital letters to signify surnames, the rest of a given message should be in mixed case, with upper-case letters being reserved for emphasis.

Learning Not to SHOUT!

SHOUTing is probably one of the first mistakes made by newcomers to online messaging. They post a message and leave the caps lock on. The old-timers of the area then chastise them within seconds. Messages typed in all caps are construed as shouting. It is a major faux pas on the Internet, and perhaps one of the least tolerated. And of course, it is also one of the most heavily debated as well.

Genie Goodies

To write an effective e-mail message, you want to include the names, dates, and places about which you currently have accurate genealogical information. And when you are messaging about places, you should also include counties, provinces, or shires for each place you mention, if you know this information. You also want to let the e-mail recipients know of the research you've already done. If e-mail respondents know that you are new to genealogy or just new to online communication, they might change the content of the e-mail message they use to respond to you. Properly including information and formatting your message appropriately will also save any moderator of the message area from asking you what you may have already done and what you are currently trying to work on.

In genealogy message areas, uppercase letters are reserved for emphasis, and especially for surnames, making it easier for everyone to scan messages when the surnames appear in capital letters. When messages are particularly lengthy, effective use of uppercase letters can be very important. However, this preference can also be traced back to genealogy's original rules.

When genealogists fill out pedigree charts or family group sheets, they write the surname in all capital letters. This rule helps other genealogists with whom you are sharing, and it is particularly important for those surnames that are multiword, such as the surname DE LA VERGNE.

Controlling Signature Size

When you are ending a message, you should also always include your name and your e-mail address, which the online world refers to as a *signature*. Most e-mail programs allow you to create these signatures once and then just reuse it whenever you need it. Because signatures are so easy to create in the first place, online communicators often overuse them or include too much information. Your ideal signature should not be more than four lines long.

Many online communicators have also begun to include not only their names and e-mail addresses, but also the addresses for their Web pages. Some e-mailers will then add a tagline, and still others will add their surnames.

Large signature files increase the size of the e-mails you are sending and receiving. If you send out a message that has a 10-line signature, you could add as many as 700 extra bytes to that particular e-mail. Now, this extra length may not sound so bad, but don't forget that thousands of other online e-mailers are doing the same thing. If some service archives these messages, additional signature lines will just result in wasted bytes saved in the archive.

Finally, I do understand how tempting it is to include your surnames in your signature. We want every genealogist in the world to know for whom we are researching. We hope that someone out in cyberland has the family Bible of Uncle Pat and Aunt Rhody that will finally break open our genealogical search. Unfortunately, putting surnames in a signature file frustrates many others and may actually cause you to miss the very cousin for whom you are searching.

Archived messages are usually searchable. If you have included the surname ENDICOTT in your signature, then every time someone does a search of that archive on the surname ENDICOTT, he or

Lineage Lingo

A **tagline** is usually a one-line quote of some sort. You can consider them the bumper stickers of e-mail. There is an entire book of these quotes. The New England Historic Genealogical Society publishes *Everything's Relative*, compiled by Elizabeth Biggs Payne which includes such tidbits as "My family tree got cut up for firewood."

she will find your messages. Unfortunately, as individuals search these archives, they may not scroll down each message to see where the surname ENDICOTT is included. If your query or e-mail is about a surname other than ENDICOTT, the searcher may become frustrated at the apparent lack of the ENDICOTT surname in the message, when in fact they have just not read far enough to see the surname in the signature file. To eliminate this confusion, please leave surnames out of signatures.

And because people tend to be impatient, someone who has searched online and become frustrated with the confusion of surnames included in signatures will then post a caustic message for the manager of that archive. While the poor manager will understand what has happened, there's nothing they can do.

Keeping Your E-mail File Lean

Recently a fellow researcher and I were talking as she was downloading her morning e-mail. As she continued downloading her files, she finally realized that someone had sent her an extremely large attachment.

When you send e-mail through the Internet, you can attach files. These attachments are usually something someone has written in a word processing document, like an article, research paper, or longer document, that the sender wants someone else to see. Text files are generally small and not a problem to attach to e-mails so long as they are not 400-page books. But graphic files (pictures that have been scanned, for instance) can be extremely large files.

It's good Net etiquette to ask someone whether he or she wants the file attachment before you send it. Some e-mail accounts may not be able to handle such large files, resulting in locked e-mail accounts and calls to ISPs to help download large files. Be considerate and *ask* before you send that file attachment.

Lineage Lingo

Snail mail is the online term for mail sent through the regular postal system. While it may be faster now than in the days of the Pony Express, when compared with the speed of e-mail, it crawls.

Resisting Online Stationery

Just to show that I can be non-techie from time to time, I still think of stationery as the nice flowery paper that you write letters on to be sent to someone via snail mail. Now, though, you can create fancy-looking e-mail that features "electronic stationery."

To use stationery in your e-mail, you need to have one of the newer versions of the many e-mail programs. These newer e-mail programs allow you to use a graphic image as a background. When online e-mailers open e-mail that has stationery, they will perhaps see flowers in the background, and then the text will appear written over the graphic image. The overall effect is similar to looking at a Web page with pictures and text, but it creates some problems.

First, using stationery causes the e-mail to be much bigger in size, thus taking longer to download. Second, not everyone receiving the e-mail will have a program that can handle this fancier version of e-mail. In cases where a person's e-mail program doesn't support receiving stationery, that person gets something that looks like a mixed-up Greek alphabet soup.

I'm not saying you can't ever use this type of fancy e-mail. I am just suggesting that you reserve it for family and close friends. When posting e-mails requesting help on your research, be considerate of all the strangers that might access your messages.

Keeping Spaghetti Separate from Genealogy?

As this book's author, I'm afraid that I'm somewhat of a "topic witch" from long ago. I've already confessed to having been online for more than 10 years now. For a long time, I was involved with one of the commercial online services, and part of my job was to make sure folks in my online area stayed on topic.

Surprisingly, keeping online communicators on topic is no easy task. While keeping two genealogists on the topic of genealogy should be easy, it is surprising what else they can talk about. So, as part of my job, I had to guide the topic back on track. I learned that a few well-placed lightning bolts will do wonders; and this method is how I would get users in my area back on to the topic of genealogy. With tongue firmly in cheek, I would send a message that the "topic witch" was "circling overhead," aiming lightning bolts at the offenders.

Now that genealogy has found the Internet, more and more people gather there to talk about it. The stories and memories that one single comment elicits can quickly overtake an online message area.

As you write e-mail, don't fall into the temptation to dash off a note to an entire group of e-mailers. Instead, take a moment to ensure that your comment is going to the individual who posted the message, rather than an entire group. Not everyone in the group may appreciate learning that you and Clare both cook your spaghetti for three minutes. If you don't heed this warning, you might encounter that "Mr. Hyde" to whom I referred earlier in this chapter. Talk about another way to kill a good information exchange.

Keeping the Flames Comin'

Online arguments take on lives of their own. They erupt with such speed and magnitude they can easily overwhelm an online discussion area.

Because of the speed with which these arguments can burst forth, they have been aptly labeled *flame*

Cousin Counsel

If a flame war erupts in any discussion area that you are reading, it is best to just stay out of the fray. The moderator will get things under control. The fewer people who engage in the flaming, the quicker the discussion group can get back on the topic.

wars. Flame wars start when someone reads something and takes offense. Instead of taking a breath and counting to 10, he or she immediately dashes off a hotheaded response. Soon others are jumping on the bandwagon to agree with the hothead or defend the original poster.

Genealogists seem to be impatient types. Usually by the time the flames have cooled, the conflict has caused major damage. As a matter of perspective, I have seen online flame wars that were worse and spread faster than the fires we went through in Florida in the summer of 1998.

Learning Web Lingo

Launching yourself onto the World Wide Web is sort of like getting off a plane in a foreign country. To feel your most comfortable, you will want to learn the lingo. There are some great Web sites out there that can help you. Consider them your "Geek-English" dictionaries.

➤ Basic Internet Terms for Newbies (www.geocities.com/FashionAvenue/4869/desc.html)

➤ Glossary of Computer/Internet Terms (www.htmlgoodies.com/tutors/glossary.html)

➤ TechWeb TechEncyclopedia (www.techWeb.com/encyclopedia/)

➤ U-Geek Technical Glossary (www.ugeek.com/glossary/glossary_search.htm)

With each of these sites, you enter the term about which you are unsure. Each site has a slightly different interface and a slightly different set of definitions.

The Least You Need to Know

➤ Because computers are involved, you will have to learn some technical terms.

➤ Because communicating with people is involved, you can learn to convey emotion online through the use of emoticons.

➤ Because genealogists rely on acronyms, the Web features many sites to help you make sense of the genealogical alphabet soup we use.

➤ Because the Internet is a public forum, please show manners while online.

➤ Because the Internet doesn't seem to be a personal connection, yet it is, you should practice Net etiquette to keep the information flowing.

Putting That PC to Work for You

Many of us have had PCs in our homes for several years. Unfortunately, some of us still look at PCs as glorified game machines. Our children or grandchildren are more comfortable with PCs than many adults can ever expect to be. Truthfully, though, you can make your PC useful and the real workhorse of your genealogical research.

PCs Can Be Your Friends

If you've been frustrated to tears or insanity by your PC, grab hold of your remaining brain cells. In this chapter, I'm going to show you what your PC can do for you.

About 13 years ago, I discovered genealogy software, and at that time, I didn't even own a PC. My husband, though, actually purchased our first computer, and I suspect he now sometimes questions what possessed him. When I combine the time I spend using the Internet, researching, and writing, I must confess that I spend most of my time with my PC. More than eight years ago, my husband decided to purchase a second PC so he could spend some time on it. In previous years, the public judged family life by whether people had two cars. Now, we make the same judgment based on whether we have two computers.

Finding the right PC can be hard if you do not understand all the "techie-babble." If your children are old enough, though, they will be able to help you with this difficult purchase.

When my husband and I first began to look for a PC, he specifically wanted to get a system that would run the genealogy software I wanted. (I was not knowledgeable about PCs at that time.) PCs have changed a lot over the years, but finding a system that will run a specific piece of software designed to perform a specific task you desire is sometimes the best way to select your first computer. In short, select your most desired software and then buy a PC that will run that software. This criteria still seems the best method to select a PC system.

When portable PCs became available, I knew of a specific piece of Windows software that I wanted to be able to use when I visited Salt Lake City's Family History Library. I shopped around and made my decision based on the system requirements of that piece of software. I then proceeded to use that notebook computer for about five years. Today my son uses it for basic programming, because it isn't powerful enough for anything else.

Genealogy software can help you in many areas of your research. The software market-place now offers many good programs specifically designed for genealogy, but you can also use some more "regular" software programs you can tailor to help you with your genealogy research, like Microsoft Access, Excel, or even Word.

The following sections explain where you can use your PC to ease your workload as you conduct your genealogical research.

Genie Goodies

Spreadsheet software such as Excel, database software such as Access, and word processing software such as Word will become extremely useful as you work with your family history. You can use these programs to create indexes (of an unindexed book or other record), list details about your family tree, and extract, or pull out, pertinent data on your family from those hard-to-read deed and probate records. I encourage you, though, to get a genealogy program for handling your family tree, because it is specifically designed for handling family relationships.

Eliminating Repetitively Entering Data

Genealogy software helps researchers by eliminating the need for them to enter data repetitively. Before PCs, genealogists would have to write the same information at least three times for each ancestor. You would first write his name, date and place of birth, date and place of marriage, and date and place of death on the pedigree chart. You would then need to write this same information on a family group sheet where he was the father. Finally, you would need to write the very same information on a family group sheet where he appeared as a child. I don't know how you feel about repetitive writing, but just thinking about doing the triple-entry reminds me of the hand cramps I used to get from all that writing.

Genealogy software is designed to reuse the information you enter about specific individuals. For instance, when I begin working on my own genealogical information in today's genealogical software, I type in the information about myself only once. To expand my family's listing, I type in my spouse's name and data, and then to create a new family for us, I just pull up the record I created for myself from a list of previously entered individuals and create the marriage. I can then print out any number of reports that include me as a child, mother, or primary individual on a pedigree chart.

Each individual in the database will have his or her own record. This record will contain the events in his or her own life. You can then connect any of these individuals together through either family links (father to child, husband to wife) or through events (witness to seller of land, minister to bride and groom) depending on what type of software you elect to use.

Many of the currently available genealogy programs eliminate the need to enter duplicate data one step further. With these software packages, you can also type in a place or information on a source and just recall this information whenever you need it. No longer do you have to retype locations and places. I particularly enjoy this added feature because I happen to have in my family's history such lengthy places as Allentown, Merrimack, and New Hampshire.

Avoiding Human Errors

As human beings, we are not perfect. How I wish I could be perfect just once in a while. I usually discover my imperfections when I am making a presentation in front of an audience, and I discover a mistake in my presentation's overhead graphic, or realize I didn't grab the right overhead.

Fortunately for my genealogical data, my genealogy program helps me by checking what I am typing. Many of the genealogy software applications that

Lineage Lingo

User error is something that we as humans hate to admit. We will always blame the computer or program first before we admit that perhaps we didn't enter something quite right. User error generally means we didn't type something in correctly or accurately tell the computer what we wanted in the first place.

are currently available offer built-in features to help check for accuracy and spelling mistakes.

Good thing, too. I have had a few slips of the fingers. I have a friend from an online chat room, and he likes to blame any typos he makes on his keyboard. Assigning blame in a similar fashion works for me, too. If the keyboard's keys were in the right place when I pressed them, I wouldn't have had any problems.

Accuracy checks built into today's genealogy programs are a great asset. Because I usually am looking at the source of my information as I type, my fingers don't always hit the right keys, especially when it comes to numbers. If I slip up with a date, the program will let me know. In fact, a little warning window complete with an appropriate graphic opens up to point out that the information I have entered would make the person buried before he was born. The software allows the user to override the warning, but when the warning appears, I know I've made an error in typing.

Genie Goodies

Almost anyone who is a PC user knows about spell checker, because of their inclusion in all the popular programs. However, a spell checker doesn't actually tell you that a word is misspelled. Instead, it calls your attention to a word that is not in its dictionary. With spell checkers in genealogy programs, you could be alerted to many such words, especially surnames. When the spell checker encounters a word that is spelled correctly but is not in its dictionary, you can add the word to the dictionary. And with surnames like STANDERFER and SICKAFUS, you can bet I have words to add to my spell checker's dictionary. You'll have many words to add to yours, too.

Now, sometimes when errors occur, it isn't my fault. I have found information recorded where the date of a child's baptism is before his birth. I carried the error with me when I extracted the information from the original source. Not until my genealogy program pointed out the error did I realize the problem. Once I was aware of the problem, I returned to the source, and discovered that the dates were entered into the source incorrectly, as well. Further sleuthing supplied me with the correct information, but I might have never caught the error if my PC hadn't identified it. More and more genealogy software programs now include free-form text windows in which you can enter data like notes, anecdotes, and reminders—anything you feel is important. You can include the exact text of a will or land deed, a family story, or any other type of story. As with typing dates and names, however, the more you type, the more chance you have for an error, including spelling. So, the more fully featured genealogy programs have spelling checkers built in so that you can double-check your spelling.

Extending Your Contacts

The more you get involved in genealogy, the more you realize how important it is to find other people who are researching the same surnames and localities. In the past, this idea of finding others who are pursuing the same information as you seemed best accomplished by joining genealogical societies, reading those societies' periodicals, and other general periodicals, as well.

I have traced much of my maternal ancestry to New England, primarily Massachusetts. Of course, I wasn't swift enough to get involved in genealogy when I lived in Massachusetts. I waited until after I moved some 1,200 miles away and married before I got interested. My excuse, however, is that I was only a child when we moved away. Regardless of my excuses, as a result of my relocation, I spent a great deal of time writing letters to request information from my grandparents, who were still living in New Hampshire. I also wrote more letters to town halls requesting vital records, and still more letters to join genealogical societies located in that area. And what did I have to do after doing all this writing? Wait. And wait. And wait some more.

I have often questioned the impatience of genealogists. Let's face it: We are searching for information about people who have been dead for 50–300 years, so it's not like these dead relatives are going anywhere. And even though genealogists are the ones searching for information about these long dead individuals, they are also some of the most impatient people I know, including myself. When it comes to researching our heritage, we want it all, and we want it now. Of course, if we ever discovered all the information about our ancestors, we would also be some of the unhappiest people, with no one left to chase down.

However, before the Internet, we all had to use snail mail (the postal service), so once I'd sent all of these letters, I had to wait. And while I would wait for answers to these letters, I would begin writing queries for genealogical periodicals, or magazines devoted to the researching of family history, like *Everton's Genealogical Helper*.

Online areas allow me to extend the number of people who see my queries as well as the number

Lineage Lingo

Queries are requests for help in researching a particular family line on which you are having problems. Before PCs, genealogists put all these queries into genealogical periodicals. Now, we still put these queries into genealogical periodicals, but we also post them on online genealogical bulletin boards and other genealogically related message areas.

of queries I see. Think about it, people from around the world can access the Internet. This means that I have the potential to reach the rest of the world with my query. Through the search capabilities of the Internet, even people who are not aware of a specific Web site or online bulletin board may possibly come across my query by searching on a surname I have listed in the query. These capabilities far exceed the possibilities of printed genealogy magazines where my query reached only those who subscribed and those who took the time to check the magazine, if their local genealogy library even subscribed to it.

In fact, I get most of my successful responses from queries I place online.

So, put your computer to work for you, and let it begin making the copies for you, catching your errors, and extending the reach of your queries.

Selecting the Right Genealogy Program

For most genealogists, the first entrance into online genealogy begins with the innocent purchase of a genealogy database program. As I've already discussed in this chapter, these programs help you avoid having to do duplicate information entry and help you catch errors. Once you enter the information into the genealogy program, you can then print appropriate reports to share with family and fellow researchers. However, the number of genealogy programs from which you can currently select is amazing—more than 35 separate programs. Some of these programs are for PCs not running Windows, some are for Windows users, and others are for Macintosh users. You can buy some programs at the computer stores, while others are only available through direct mail. Each program has its own set of features and benefits, as well as its own price tag.

While I might be tempted to tell you about all the different genealogical programs currently available, I fortunately don't need to. Marthe Arends has written an excellent book available on this very subject: *Genealogy Software Guide* (Genealogical Publishing Company, 1998), which can be purchased from Amazon.com and through a variety of genealogical booksellers.

I will, however, provide you with an overview of the most popular and easily accessible genealogy programs. As I discuss each software product, if the program has a Web site associated with it, I have included that information. You can visit each site to find out even more about the product. Most Web sites also post messages from other users and you can use this information to more fully evaluate features and benefits as you select your genealogy software. Here is a list of the genealogy programs we'll take a look at in the remainder of this chapter:

➤ Family Origins (Parsons Technology)

➤ Family Tree Maker (Broderbund Software)

➤ Generations (Sierra On-Line)

➤ Personal Ancestral File (Latter-day Saints Distribution Center)

➤ Ultimate Family Tree (Broderbund Software)

Family Origins

Family Origins is available from Parsons Technology (P.O. Box 100, Hiawatha, IA 52233-0100; 319-395-9626; info@parsonstech.com). The software company makes available a demo version that can be downloaded from its Web site at www.parsonstech.com/genealogy/index.html. The following figure shows Family Origins' Tree View.

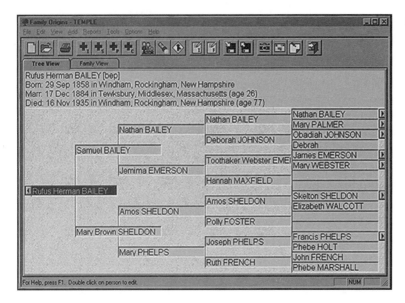

Family Origins, Tree View.

Family Origins comes with some 50 predefined event fact types, like the basic ones of birth, marriage, and death. The program, however, features a number of others such as occupation, religion, divorce, and probate. You can also create new fact types.

Family Origins has a number of ready-to-print reports, so you can satisfy everyone in the family, even those that don't seem to be interested in the family genealogy. (You know, the ones whose eyes glaze over every time you open your mouth to speak. They are so sure you are about to talk about the latest quest for Aunt Julia.)

If you are interested in the World Wide Web, you can create the necessary files to upload a Web page. Family Origins' fully featured options also make this selection a great program for Latter-day Saints (LDS, or Mormon) individuals. In fact, of the genealogy programs I discuss in this chapter, in addition to Personal Ancestral File (PAF), Family Origins is the only program certified to use with the TempleReady system.

Lineage Lingo

Event fact types are the terms used by Family Origins for the method in which it allows you to record a given event in a person's life, such as birth, marriage, graduation, death, or burial.

Genie Goodies

To those of the LDS faith, the researching of their family history is very important. They believe that the ties that bind a family together are not just limited to their time here on earth. They believe that family ties are binding for all eternity. So in order for their family to be complete, they need to research the family lines back as far as they can go and then complete certain sealing ordinances in their Temples. It is the "sealing" that binds the family together for eternity.

Family Tree Maker

Family Tree Maker is available at many computer stores, as well as many discount stores with software sections. You can also get the program from the developer, Broderbund Software (Banner Blue Division; 39500 Stevenson Place, Suite 204; Fremont, CA 94539-3103; 510-494-2754 for voice or 510-794-9152 for fax; info@familytreemaker.com).

To try this company's software, you can download a demo version from the Web site at www.familytreemaker.com. The following figure shows the main screen of the Family Tree Maker.

Family Tree Maker,
Archive Viewer.

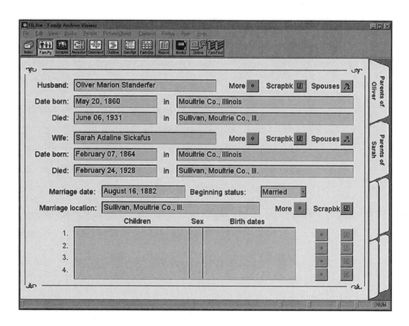

Family Tree Maker is a very popular program for many genealogists. For some time, this program was the easiest one to find at the computer stores. Many individuals also find this software easy to use. The program offers a wide variety of predesigned charts to print for sharing with relatives and other researchers. You can also create some of the charts as Web pages, which you can then post on the Family Tree Maker Web site.

Depending on whether you need the Windows-based or Macintosh-based version, you might also get some additional database CDs which Broderbund has released, including a set of lineage-linked CDs called the World Family Tree. The Deluxe version comes with five volumes of lineage-linked CDs and an index for them on a separate CD.

You can scan in images (photos) and link pictures to specific individuals and to marriages. When you have completed a significant amount of genealogical research, you can print a "book" about family lines that is created by the software. The program will include those images you link to individuals in the printed book.

Generations

Generations is available at many computer and discount stores, and is manufactured by Sierra On-Line (3380 146th Place SE, Suite 300; Bellevue, WA 98007; 425-649-9800). The software manufacturer offers a downloadable demo version of the Generations program. You can learn more about Generations by visiting the Web site at www.sierra.com. The following figure shows Generations' Grand Suite's main screen.

Heritage Hints

TempleReady is a special program available for Mormon individuals to compile the work they wish to do at their local Latter-day Saints Temples. The program is available at local Family History Centers.

Cousin Counsel

The information that you find on CDs is a wonderful tool, but just keep in mind that the information is only a tool. You need to work further on discovering information on those individuals you locate in CD databases to verify that the information is accurate.

From the Generations' main screen, you can enter information about relatives, along with text and images. You can alter this screen depending on what you feel is the most important information to be viewed, either the relevant life event dates or the free-hand notes for that person. Like the other, more powerful programs, you can enter unlimited life events for each person. Generations also features a list of set, predefined events, and you can also create new life events as you need.

Generations' Grande Suite, Main Screen.

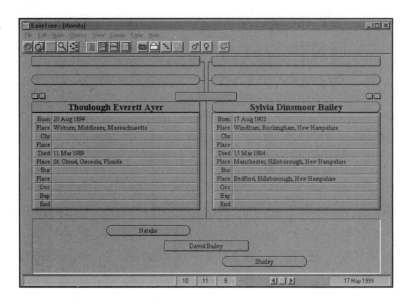

Generations' biggest strength, though, lies in its amazing chart features. In addition to featuring the standard family group sheet and pedigree chart, Generations provides a method for you to manipulate many of the charts to include graphics. You can change the shape and focus of any Generations-created chart by adding color, and the program also features the ability to drag information from the predefined charts to new locations.

Additionally, you can use Generations to create Web pages. Once you've created your Web page, you can then upload them anywhere you want.

As we mentioned earlier, when shopping around for your ISP, it is possible that you have Web space available to you. Once you have created the files in Generations, you can then upload them to this area, as opposed to an area specific to the software program.

Personal Ancestral File

Personal Ancestral File (PAF) is available from the Latter-day Saints Church Distribution Center (1999 West 1700 South, Salt Lake City, UT 84110; 1-800-537-5950). You can also order this program online by visiting the FamilySearch Web site at www.familysearch.org.

PAF is one of the few DOS-based programs still available, meaning that you do not have to own a PC capable of running Windows. With PAF, you can enter basic information about each relative, but it limits the life events to only birth, baptism, marriage, death, and burial dates for any individual. You can also include notes and source information for each relative as a whole or for individual events. You can link stories and notes to the individual (by adding notes when in the name field) or to each specific event (by adding notes when in the event field).

If you have visited a Family History Center, you already have access to this program—at least to see what it can do. Most local Family History Centers feature this program at their locations.

The Church of Jesus Christ of Latter-day Saints has also recently released a version of PAF for Windows. Although the Family History Department said it will not release this program on disk until the year 2000, you can download PAF version 4.0 for Windows at the FamilySearch Web site at www.familysearch.com/OtherResources/paf4/.

While PAF for Windows still limits life events to basics (birth, baptism, marriage, death, and burial), you have more power with other aspects of the program. With this program, you have better control over source output, and you can now use the software to create family history Web pages.

Lineage Lingo

A **Family History Center** or **FHC** is a branch of the large Family History Library located in Salt Lake City, Utah. Through your local FHC, you can search their databases on CD and request microfilms from the main library, which currently has some two million rolls of micro-filmed records. FHCs are found in local Mormon chapels and are usually listed in the phone book.

Ultimate Family Tree

Ultimate Family Tree is available at various computer software and discount stores. It is manufactured by The Learning Company (88 Rowland Way, Novato, CA 94945; 415-895-2000). You can also download a demo version that will run on PCs only at the Ultimate Family Tree Web site at www.uftree.com. The following figure shows the Ultimate Family Tree main screen.

Ultimate Family Tree, Main Screen.

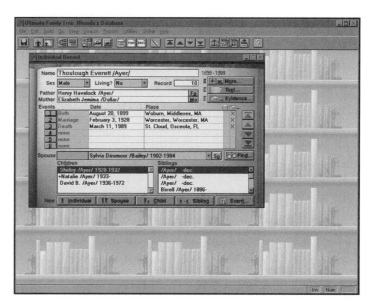

Ultimate Family Tree is one of the more powerful genealogy programs currently on the market. With this software, you can enter unlimited life events for each relative. You can also enter three different types of notes (text, footnotes, and research notes) for each relative, pertaining to that relative's entire entry or individual life events.

One of the Ultimate Family Tree's greatest strengths is in its source citation capabilities. By using templates especially created to work with the different types of records genealogists are most likely to use, the Ultimate Family Tree can provide you with "fill-in-the-blank" ease. With this program, you can be assured that you are creating proper source citations. Ultimate Family Tree's source citation templates were created by Elizabeth Shown Mills, a well-respected individual in the genealogy field.

Lineage Lingo

A **source citation** is an entry that states where you found the information about the life event. Sources can be books, land records, vital statistics, and so on; and each type of record will have a different citation form.

Genie Goodies

Elizabeth Shown Mills recently wrote a book on the subject of source citations. *Evidence! Citation and Analysis for the Family Historian* (Genealogical Publishing Company, Inc., 1997) includes a chart of about 100 different source citations. The first part of the book looks at the fundamentals of citing sources. While we all learned source citation in our high school term paper projects, many of us have forgotten the basics. This book should be in every genealogist's library.

Like several other programs mentioned, Ultimate Family Tree has Web page creation capabilities, as well. You can include scanned pictures of family members, and add your own graphics to give your Web page its own flair.

For each program that I have mentioned there are about 10 others that I didn't and there are more than 30 genealogy programs available right now. Some of the others that you are likely to see at genealogy conferences and online are:

➤ Ancestral Quest

➤ Legacy

➤ Parents

➤ The Master Genealogist

Trying Software Before Buying

Up until now, I have discussed commercial software that you purchase, take home, and load onto your system. At that point, if you decide you don't like it, you either have to chalk it up to experience, or you have to contact the company to see if they offer any type of money back guarantee.

However, there is another type of software that lets you try before you buy. You may have already used some of these types of programs without even realizing it. They are called shareware or freeware, and you can try out the programs before you commit to the purchase.

Here is a short list of currently available shareware programs:

➤ A-Gene

➤ Brothers Keeper

➤ EZ-Tree

➤ Family Matters

Don't automatically cast off shareware just because it isn't in a fancy box sitting on the computer store shelf. Oftentimes, shareware programs offer significant options, with one of the best being technical support. The developer doesn't stay in business if he doesn't listen to those who have supported him with their shareware payments.

The shareware program Brothers Keeper, for instance, offers reports and entry in multiple languages. Even some of the more powerful and expensive software programs don't offer this type of option.

Heritage Hints

With shareware, you can try the software before paying for it. In most cases, shareware authors rely on your honesty to pay them if you decide to continue to use their products. Once you have decided that you will continue to use shareware, then you are ethically bound to send in the shareware program fee. Freeware, on the other hand, is just that: It's free.

You can download most shareware and freeware programs from Web sites. One easy way to find many genealogical shareware packages is to visit Cyndi Howell's site at www.cyndislist.com, and select her software section option.

What's More Personal Than Your Ancestors?

I have given you a taste of what is available in dedicated genealogy software packages. Now the hard part for you is to decide which program is best for you. If you ask other genealogists, you'll find that most software users will defend their favorite programs to their dying breath. I have seen terrible arguments erupt over which genealogical software program is best. Get two genealogists together who each use a different program, and look out! They are more likely to agree on who their ancestors are than about the benefits and values of the other's genealogy program.

Everyone always asks me what I think the best program is. My answer is always the same: It's the program that does what's important to you. Many feel I am trying to be diplomatic, but it is just the way I feel about selecting and using software. Each of us gets interested in genealogy for a different reason. As a result, our goals are different. A feature that I feel I just can't live without may not be of interest to you. I may feel that properly citing my sources so I can publish in one of the scholarly journals is important, whereas you may value the ability to put up your family information Web site as quickly as possible.

Decide what your goal with your research is, and then purchase your program accordingly.

Learning about Other Programs You'll Find Irresistible

Genealogists don't just collect ancestors. We also collect software. We see one program that will help us with our census research, and we grab it. We see another program that will help us with the weird land descriptions in the land records, and we just can't live without it. And, then, of course, we must have another program to help us keep track of all the research we have done. If you have a notebook PC, you really want all this software loaded on it, because they can be great assets when you are traveling.

Some of the types of genealogically related software with which you are likely to become obsessed (er, I mean have an interest in) are:

➤ Census programs

➤ Cemetery programs

➤ Database programs

➤ Mapping programs

Census Programs

Just what is a census program? It's a program intended to help you keep track of information you find in census records. These programs generally have a "fill-in-the blank" approach, because the census itself is a form. By entering information into such a program, you are able to search and otherwise manipulate the data. Working with the data is not always so easy when it is simply a paper version of the record.

One census program that you might want to learn more about is Design Software's Family Census Research. You will want to visit their Web site at www.dhc.net/~design/fcr30.htm.

Lineage Lingo

The **census** is a recording of information that is going to be used by the government. Census results may be reported in tabular format with very few names, or the report may list the names of everyone in the household. You will come across several different types of census reports: agricultural, population, and military. Each will offer you a different slice of information about your ancestor.

Census database programs assist you in transcribing the families you find in the census.

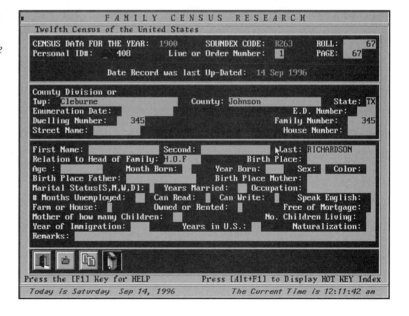

Cemetery Programs

Searching for your family history will take you to many interesting places, including cemeteries. Additionally, some software programs are designed to help you organize the information you find in cemeteries. Generally, when you visit a cemetery, you'll discover more than one grave of a deceased relative in which you will have an interest. (After all, families are generally buried together.) If on your visit you discover enough graves of individuals that are somehow related to you, either by blood or by marriage, you will generally want to get that cemetery's information into some sort of database.

However, as a beginning researcher, or when you are just learning how to do research in cemeteries, you will probably overlook some critical pieces of information. If you put all your relevant discovered cemetery data into a cemetery program, you are more apt to get all the vital, necessary information on your first visit to that cemetery location.

To learn more about cemetery programs, you may want to check out Genealogical Cemetery Database, which is available from Design Software. You can visit their web site at www.dhc.net/~design/desig1-4.htm.

X WWW.DESIGNSW.NET

Database Programs

Database programs differ from genealogy programs in that their primary focus is to keep track strictly of the data, rather than linking the individuals in the data together through a familial relationship. Some of these database programs can combine the features of other utilities, including the previously mentioned cemetery and census programs.

If you have a database program such as Microsoft's Access, and you are comfortable with it, you can create databases for census, cemetery, family photo collections, or anything else you may be interested in keeping track of.

Using a database even as user-friendly as Access is something, I confess, I leave for the technical types. Learning to effectively use a fully featured database software package can be confusing and time-consuming, especially if you have no previous experience with programming. However, one particularly useful database program is Clooz by Liz Kelley Kerstens of Ancestor Detective. With this database program, you can keep track of records, photos, and other documents. What makes this program more useful to genealogists is the capability to link relatives to various records. You can then extract the pertinent information from the record into the database about that relative.

Clooz, a database pro-gram, offers you a way to track the records you have searched and the results of those searches.

To find out more about Clooz, visit the Ancestor Detective Web site at www.ancestordetective.com.

Mapping Programs

A plethora of mapping programs are currently available. One type of mapping software helps to show you changes in states or counties over the years. Another draws a map of the land that your ancestor bought and sold. Both types of programs are valuable to your research.

AniMap is one of the mapping programs that show how an area has changed through the years. Currently, this software is only available for the United States. You can see how the western migration affected the shape of the United States from 1776 onward, and the program will show you the changes to all the states from the earliest known date to the most current date. So, for the first 13 colonies, you can follow the growth from the early 1600s to today. Of course, some of the Western states began their transformation more recently (California in the late 1800s, for example). To find out more about AniMap, visit the software manufacturer's Web site at www.goldbug.com/.

Heritage Hints

You should plan to plat the land owned by your ancestors. **To plat** means to draw a graphical represen-tation of the land based on the land's description. To plat the land, you'll need protractors (and you thought you only needed them for school) and rulers to figure out the shape of the land your ancestors owned. This graphical representation will help you get a feel for the amount of land and how it changed if portions were sold off.

Trying to plat the land that your ancestors bought and then sold can prove interesting. Historically speaking, surveyors and land records don't always measure the land in ways that we can easily understand today. However, by platting the land, you can see how it changed or create a map that includes the surrounding land of other owners, who may turn out to be related. Reading early land records is an adventure, so I enthusiastically selected my first mapping software. With the program called DeedMapper, you can enter a land description and create an image of the property as it would have appeared at that time in history.

One of the great features of this type of software is that you can better see if there was a piece of land that your ancestor hung on to. As you begin to create plats of all the land transactions, you will begin to see patterns. And through these patterns, you might pick up a clue or two to help you reach back further into your ancestry.

Cousin Counsel

As you research your family's history of land and property ownership, who knows—you may discover unclaimed estate items that descend to you!

The Least You Need to Know

➤ Learn to use your PC as a helpful tool to ease all phases of your genealogical research—from generating correspondence to tracking complicated cemetery data.

➤ Genealogy software developed for dedicated genealogical use is intended to help you avoid having to enter duplicate information and to eliminate errors.

➤ Many fully featured, dedicated genealogy programs are commercially available direct from the software manufacturer, your local computer or retail store, or online.

➤ The genealogy software you select should fit your research needs.

➤ In addition to dedicated genealogy software programs, genealogists also find cemetery, census, and database software—along with other types of software—to be helpful with genealogical research.

Part 2
Genealogy 101

The word genealogy *can be intimidating. What we seek, however, is not simply genealogy, but family history. We want to know who has lived before us. However, like most hobbies, unraveling family history still requires that you learn a few new rules and guidelines specific to the genealogical quest.*

Part 2 will start you on the right foot, as you begin researching your family's history. For your family history, you must begin at the beginning—which starts with you—and trace your family's past back as far as you can. Unraveling this life-story ultimate mystery provides you a wonderful trip back through history.

To keep you from having to "cut off" a family limb or two (in the figurative sense), Part 2 will teach you the basics of recording and evaluating your introductory genealogical information.

Beginning at the Beginning

Because genealogy is the process of researching of our ancestry, we tend to want to jump back to begin our research with relatives who are already deceased. However, if you do start at this point, you will be frustrated very early in your genealogical research. In genealogy, you need to know a little something about the person you are trying to research beyond just a name. If you have nothing but a name, you have no way to tell just which John Smith is actually your ancestor.

When I first got involved in researching my family tree, I was given wise advice: Work from the known to the unknown.

Is this advice some cryptic secret axiom that only genealogists know? In a way it is. So, what does it mean to work from the known to the unknown?

What it means is that you need to gather some records on the individuals for whom you already have some information. This might mean gathering birth certificates for your parents or grandparents. Even if your parents and grandparents are still living and you can ask them any questions that you may want to know, it is still important to gather records on them, ranging from birth certificates, marriage records, and other records of their life.

While all this questioning and record gathering may seem like a duplication of effort, think of this opportunity as training for when you do research on those generations when you no longer have someone you can ask questions of.

And the best way to work from the known to the unknown is to begin at the beginning, which means beginning with you.

I'm Born—Beginning with Myself

"To begin my life with the beginning of my life, I record that I was born (as I have been informed and believe) …" These lines from Charles Dickens's *David Copperfield* have stayed with me. Even before I was a genealogist, this opening from the book fascinated me.

Probably the first time I heard the David Copperfield words, I was about 12, and my mother had taken me to see the movie *Gone with the Wind*. At that time, I never could imagine that I would end up so involved in genealogy. Perhaps even at the age of 12, I was a genealogist without realizing it.

Of course the line from the book shows just where a genealogist should begin. I cannot stress how important it is to begin with yourself. As David Copperfield said, he was "informed" of his birth. Most of us have been informed of our births as well. Although we were there, few of us can remember what happened when our births took place. Our parents usually share our births with us through birthday parties, birth videos, baby books, and mementos when we are older.

Genie Goodies

In the case of marriage records, you may have a large variety. You may have a copy of the church certificate, or the actual marriage certificate. However, you may also get a copy of the marriage application as well. Usually, the application will have information about the parties getting married and may include the names of parents and other vital information important to genealogists.

However, the genealogist in you should not be satisfied with this beginning collection of information. You should get a copy of your birth certificate. Usually, if you are an adult you already have a copy of your birth certificate. But, have you bothered to look at it? What information is included on that piece of paper that defines your birth and specifics about your parents? Do you have a copy of your marriage certificate? Have you looked at it to see what it tells about you and your spouse?

So, even though your main genealogical goal is to find out about your ancestors, the best way to begin that research is to start gathering information about yourself. Although you'll need help for those times when you don't already know everything, you are, in fact, the first piece of the genealogical puzzle. After all, this is your family history.

Interviewing Yourself

We've all read interviews in magazines and newspapers. We have also seen many television interviews. The best part about interviewing yourself is that you don't have to put yourself in the "hot seat." You can be gentle and understanding, and you can be assured that you won't turn your own words around in print or take quotes out of context.

By interviewing yourself, you can begin to create questions to ask other living relatives later on in your genealogical quest. Put a cassette tape recorder inconspicuously in front of you, and become familiar with the feeling your other relatives are going to experience when you interview them. If you find that you don't like the interview process, you can guess that other relatives won't like it either. From your own personal interview, you can consider other ways you can record the information that relatives might have to share without making them feel self-conscious or uncomfortable.

So, sit down, pull out a pen and paper, take out a cassette tape recorder, and officially begin your own family's genealogical research. What are some of the questions you should ask?

➤ What is your name?

➤ How old are you?

➤ When were you born?

➤ How long have you been married?

➤ When were you married?

➤ What are your parents' names?

➤ Where did you live when you were a child?

➤ What is your occupation?

➤ Why did you pick that profession?

Once you have answered these questions about yourself, you will already have some events on which to get vital records. You could even write a

Cousin Counsel

Remember in your enthusiasm to gather information on the family that not everyone *is* as excited about digging in the family past as you. There will be times when family members will be hesitant to share family stories, especially if there are scandals in the family closet.

very simple narrative about yourself that contains the answers to these questions. In fact, when you document your parents' names, you have already added a generation to your family tree. Now, from a genealogical standpoint, you're on a roll.

Writing It All Down

When you first begin to research your family history, you can lull yourself into a sense of false security. You can convince yourself that you can remember everything without needing to write it down.

Sure, you can remember things about yourself, and perhaps even your parents. But you need to realize that as you move further back into your family's generations, you are doubling, and then quadrupling information with the addition of each family generation. At this point in your research, this information stream doesn't even include the children of each generation.

So, you will want to get into the habit of writing down everything as you learn it. Consider yourself a detective. Your notebook is your collection of clues and evidence in the case, and the case is your family tree.

Heritage Hints

With each generation that you locate, you automatically need to look for two more individuals. The family tree grows exponentially as you go back through the generations.

Lineage Lingo

A **repository** is any building that houses records for safekeeping. It could be a state archive, a library, a museum, or a historical or genealogical society building.

When you first get started, a simple spiral notebook will work just fine. I suggest that you include the following information on each page, or with each entry that you make:

➤ Name of person or resource from which you are getting the information

➤ Date you received the information

➤ Address of the individual or repository from which you received the information

➤ The information itself

Using the notebook method, as you turn the pages, you can follow the trail from you to your parents and grandparents and beyond, watching your knowledge of your family tree grow.

In this world of PCs, you may be asking yourself just why I am suggesting that you use a spiral notebook at the start of your research. That one reason is *portability*. Although you have a desktop PC, not everyone has a notebook or laptop PC to take with them, whereas a spiral notebook can go anywhere and never needs batteries or a wall outlet for power. PCs have drawbacks that you have to deal with—along with getting started in your genealogical research.

Eventually, you will do something with the notes that you've entered in the notebook. You might transcribe them to your PC, or make photocopies of them to file away as archive material. Over the years, I have gone through a number of notebooks, filling each with the research I discovered at the repository or a relative's house. If you continue your genealogical research, you'll no doubt fill a number of notebooks, too.

Eventually you will get enough information to put on charts. It makes it easier to understand how the various people are related to you and each other.

Learning to Use Family History Forms

If you use genealogical software, you will most likely be entering the information you find into one of the programs that we discussed in Chapter 4. Using your PC makes everything easier—both in time and putting to work what you need to know right away. You may have instances, however, when you need to use one of the genealogical software's forms, especially if you are using resources at a library or other archives location. Regardless of when you begin to use family history forms, you need to know how to fill out these forms correctly. The following section will provide a primer for you on family history forms.

Filling Out the Forms Yourself

The two most likely family history forms you will work with are the *family group sheet* and the *pedigree chart*.

Genie Goodies

You can purchase a number of genealogical forms from libraries, genealogical publishers like Evertons, and through your local Family History Center (FHC). In fact, FHCs offer a number of excellent forms. If you have already selected a software package, it is very likely that you can print out the basic **family group sheet** and **pedigree chart**. And included in Appendix D, you will find many forms that you can photocopy to get you started.

The family group sheet includes information on a single family unit that covers a father, mother, and their children. While the family group sheet concentrates on this single-family unit, it can also include the names of the parents' parents, too. The form usually has a space for the names of the children's spouses. The family group sheet is intended to give you a family "at-a-glance." The following figure shows a typical handwritten family group sheet.

Family Group Sheet

Husband's Full Name ROBERT McCLAIN   **Chart No.**

Husband's Data	Day Month Year	City, Town or Place	County or Province, etc.	State or Country	Add. Info. on Husband
Birth	14 DEC 1780			PENNSYLVANIA	
Chr'nd					
Marr.	abt 1813				
Death	1864		ORANGE CO.	INDIANA	
Burial					

Places of Residence

Occupation   Church Affiliation   Military Rec.

Other owners, if any No (1) (2) etc. Make separate sheet for each marr.

His Father DANIEL McCLAIN   Mother's Maiden Name NANCY

Wife's Full Maiden Name ELIZABETH VAN ZANT

Wife's Data	Day Month Year	City, Town or Place	County or Province, etc.	State or Country	Add. Info. on Wife
Birth	abt 1796			KENTUCKY	
Chr'nd					
Death					
Burial					

Places of Residence

Occupation   Church Affiliation   Military Rec.

Other husbands, if any No (th 5th etc. Make separate sheet for each marr.

Her Father   Mother's Maiden Name

Sex	Children's Names in Full (Arrange in order of birth)	Children's Data	Day Month Year	City, Town or Place	County or Province, etc.	State or Country	Add. info on Children
M	1 WILLIAM McCLAIN	Birth	1814			KENTUCKY	
		Marr.	10 MAR 1834		ORANGE CO.	INDIANA	
	Full Name of Spouse	Death	1 SEP 1870		ORANGE CO.	INDIANA	
	MARTHA IRVINE	Burial					
M	2 JOHN McCLAIN	Birth	1818			INDIANA	
		Marr.	bef 1845				
	Full Name of Spouse	Death					
	CHARLOTTE J.	Burial					
F	3 JANE McCLAIN	Birth	18 JUL 1820		ORANGE CO.	INDIANA	
		Marr.	12 NOV 1840		ORANGE CO.	INDIANA	
	Full Name of Spouse	Death	14 FEB 1879	SULLIVAN	MOULTRIE CO.	ILLINOIS	
	JESSE LOCKE	Burial					
F	4 MARGARET McCLAIN	Birth	1825			INDIANA	
		Marr.	18 AUG 1848		ORANGE CO.	INDIANA	
	Full Name of Spouse	Death	27 JUL 1894		ORANGE CO.	INDIANA	
	WILLIAM G. BAKER	Burial					
F	5 ELIZA McCLAIN	Birth	1828			INDIANA	
		Marr.					
	Full Name of Spouse	Death					
		Burial					
F	6 EMILY McCLAIN	Birth	25 SEP 1830			INDIANA	
		Marr.	4 JAN 1849		ORANGE CO.	INDIANA	
	Full Name of Spouse	Death	8 JUN 1860		ORANGE CO.	INDIANA	
	WILLIAM CHISHAM	Burial					
F	7 SARAH ANN McCLAIN	Birth	abt 1833			INDIANA	
		Marr.	23 OCT 1851		ORANGE CO.	INDIANA	
	Full Name of Spouse	Death					
	WALTER MOODY	Burial					
M	8 ISAIAH McCLAIN	Birth	25 FEB 1837			INDIANA	
		Marr.					
	Full Name of Spouse	Death	17 NOV 1873		ORANGE CO.	INDIANA	
		Burial					

Compiler		Notes:
Address		
City, State, Zip		
Date		

Form A500, Family Group Sheet by The Everton Publishers, P.O. Box 368, Logan, UT 84321. Publishers of The Genealogical Helper. Send for a free catalogue with list and full description of many genealogical aids.

Family group sheet.

In a perfect world, all of our family group sheets would have no empty boxes. But, if that were the case, we wouldn't need to be researching our family any further. All our work would most likely be done. Thankfully, in most family histories that won't happen. However, you do want to be as complete and accurate as possible when you fill out this form, or any of the other family history forms.

The other form, the pedigree chart, is a road map to your family tree. Beginning with you, the pedigree chart then lists your parents, your grandparents, your great-grandparents, and your great-great-grandparents. Standard pedigree charts contain either four or five generations. If the chart were five generations old, then it would also include your third great-grandparents. The screen below shows a handwritten pedigree chart.

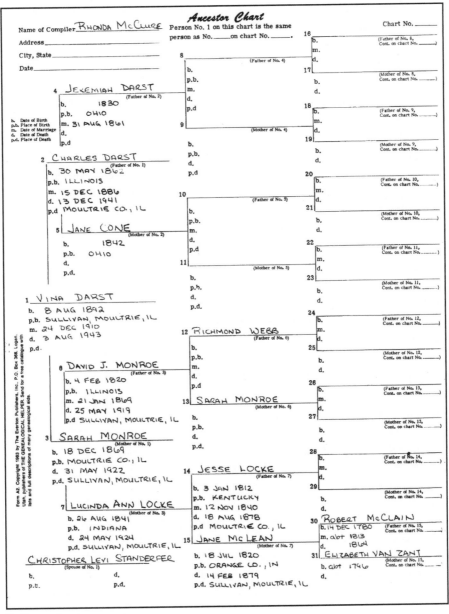

Pedigree chart.

When you have to fill out these forms by hand, you'll want to follow some guidelines, because genealogists handle names, dates, and places in specific ways.

Names follow this pattern: Enter first the given name(s) and then enter the surname in all caps. When writing out a female ancestor's name, you will always list her with her maiden name. So, my name, when written on any forms, appears as:

Rhonda Renee STANDERFER

The surname is capitalized so that it stands out easily from the rest of the names. Some surnames, such as DE LA VERGNE, are more than a single word, so capitalization also signifies exactly what parts of the name are the surname.

Genealogists also give dates a very specific format. You want to write them as DD MMM YYYY. So the death date of my father would be written 11 JUL 1995. While the genealogy police won't come after you if you don't write your dates in this manner, you will find this standard method to be the most accepted, regardless of country or language. And if you were ever in the military, this date format will be "old hat" to you.

Cousin Counsel

When you are filling out any genealogical forms by hand, you'll always want to fill them in using a pencil. Genealogists realize that the information they have at any time may not be completely accurate. When you fill out the forms in pencil, then you can easily correct and make changes.

Genie Goodies

European and American dating formats are the opposite of each other. Europeans put the day first, then the month, followed by the year. Americans usually put the month, then the day, and then the year. So, if you were to come across a date of 6/8/87 would you think it was June 8 or August 6? Thus we use standard genealogy dating formats. If you always put the first three letters of the month in uppercase, then you will never have to guess.

Why genealogists use a four-digit year is not always clear to genealogical newcomers. Usually when you first begin genealogy, your dates are all in the twentieth century, so you feel silly about writing the year as 1995. However, as you work back through the centuries, you will soon find yourself doing research in the 1800s, then the 1700s, and eventually even the 1600s and 1500s. If you don't include all four digits of the date, you won't know what century the information you have comes from.

Yes, if genealogists have conventions for names and dates, they have guidelines for places, too. When you are writing a place name on one of the forms, you will want to include all the jurisdictions from the smallest to the largest, including:

➤ town or parish

➤ county or shire

➤ state or province

➤ country

Why do genealogists follow this convention? Well, as our ancestors moved from civilization to the wilderness, they often brought one of the few things they had to remind them of where they came from, the name of the town, province, or country which they'd left. If you look at the names of the towns in Massachusetts, you will find many of them carry the same names as English towns. Considering that most of those early settlers were from England, this naming of the new with familiar names from home makes sense. Even that group of northeastern states carries the nickname of New England.

So, because immigrants loved to remind themselves of their roots, you as a genealogist need to know just which Gloucester or Orange City is appropriate in which instance.

Using Your PC As Scribe

As I mentioned in Chapter 4, you probably have purchased or acquired by some other means a genealogy program, which makes genealogical research much easier. Entering the names of relatives, and following name, date, and place conventions can be handled by your software.

Most genealogy software uses a specific system to identify surnames. You don't type them in using all uppercase letters. Some genealogical programs use slash marks (//) to surround surnames. These programs recognize the last word in the name field as the surname and automatically surround it with the slash marks. If you have a surname that is more than a single word, you will want to type in the slash marks around the appropriate words, but

Heritage Hints

An important reason for always including all jurisdictions is to know where to look for records. Some will be found in the town records, whereas others may have been recorded at the county courthouse. If you don't have the complete place name, you will waste time determining what county to work in.

Cousin Counsel

Not all genealogy programs handle surnames the same. You will want to pay close attention to this aspect of any genealogy software you use, especially if you have surnames that are more than a single word. How you enter them could affect your reports later, and definitely any indexes you have your genealogy program create.

I offer it as an example of a variance from the norm. Different programs will handle identifying surnames differently.

As for conventions dealing with dates, you can select a set format for your dates' appearances within many of the currently available genealogy programs. If you are accustomed to spreadsheet programs, you can set the format of a date in a cell. Most genealogical software lets you select the same date formatting as those options available with spreadsheets. When you select a date format within a genealogical program, your selection will select all the dates you enter from that point on, instead of affecting only that single cell that you format in spreadsheet use.

As for the conventions of the names of places, the only thing you have to worry about is if you don't know the county or other civil division. When you are handwriting the names of places, you can be a little more lenient in how you enter them. However, if you want your PC's genealogical software to accept names according to that software's conventions, you'll need to enter them according to the PC software's preferences.

For instance, you discover that your ancestor lived in Sullivan, Illinois. Unfortunately, you don't know what the county for Sullivan, Illinois, is when you are typing this information into your genealogy program. You still need to tell the genealogy program that there is a missing civil division. You can indicate this omission by using commas.

Many genealogy programs will recognize a change in a place or location division when the software encounters a comma.

So, when you enter Sullivan, Illinois, into your PC, you will want to type it in as Sullivan,,Illinois. (Yes, with two commas.)

Heritage Hints

When working with genealogy software, remember that software does just what you tell it to do. So, to be able to make the most of your PC software, you must learn how your software handles idiosyncrasies in your data.

With genealogy software, you can often alter the printed forms the software creates. Instead of printing a report with the surname in all uppercase letters (as you would a form you filled out by hand), you can direct the software to print the surnames in a bold format. This change in print format has a neater appearance, and works well with the more narrative reports that most genealogy programs generate. The following figure shows a PC-printed family group sheet.

Computer-generated family group sheet.

Congratulations! You Are Now a Genealogist!

Well, you have now interviewed yourself, and written down the important information you got. You've filled out a family group sheet for your immediate family and entered the first couple of generations onto your pedigree chart.

Guess what? Completing these processes so far makes you a genealogist, or, if you are wanting to include more family stories, a family historian. Although you can take classes in your area from which you can benefit greatly, once you begin the genealogical hunt, you are officially one of us.

So, what does it mean to be one of us? Well:

➤ People will give you "Warning! I Brake for Cemeteries" bumper stickers.

➤ Your nice tidy house will quickly be filled with stacks of papers that cannot be moved under any circumstance.

➤ The letter carrier will begin to curse you, as he delivers more mail to you than anyone else on his route. (I did warn you about this problem earlier in the book.)

➤ You will remember the death date of Great-Great-Grandfather Rufus and forget your spouse's birthday.

These are just a few of the symptoms. You should realize, however, that genealogy is not an illness; it's an addiction—one for which there is no cure. So, sit back, relax, and have the time of your life digging through your family's history.

The Least You Need to Know

➤ You should start your genealogy research with you.

➤ Although you may find it silly, practice interviewing by interviewing yourself several times.

➤ Using a notebook is a good place to start taking your notes.

➤ Although genealogy software is available, you still need to know how to fill out, by hand, preprinted blank family group sheets and pedigree charts.

➤ If you have gotten to the end of Chapter 5 (this far in the book), you are hopelessly hooked and are now an addicted genealogist.

Chapter 6

Hello Mom?

Families Are Forever

In This Chapter

➤ Interviewing family members

➤ Contacting family by phone and mail

➤ Gathering the family papers

➤ Using modern technology to help

When I think of families, I think first of my own husband and children, then my mother, and then inevitably of those who have come and gone before I had my turn on Earth. Regardless of your religious beliefs, if you are researching your family history, then your family will live forever. Many ethnic groups believe that to remember your ancestors is to show them respect. And considering the hardships many of our ancestors endured to bring forth the next generation, we certainly owe them that respect.

Talking with Family Members

Okay, now that you have interviewed yourself and begun to write everything down, it is time to turn yourself loose on your unsuspecting family. Some of the family will happily answer your probing questions and offer you pictures and family papers. Others will not be as thrilled. In many families there are those who feel strongly that the family history should be left as just that—history.

When I first got involved in genealogy, my grandmother very kindly shared a copy of her Daughters of the American Revolution (DAR) application. From this, I began to re-create that part of my family tree. A few years later, as my grandfather began to go through the house in preparation for selling it, he was thrilled to realize he could box up any pictures, family papers, and other "junk" and send it to me. Although Grandfather found it a great way to clear out all that paperwork, I could also tell he was very happy that I was helping the past stay alive. He was always interested in my latest finds. Grandfather was not one of those family members who looked high and low for a way to get out of listening to me go on and on about my latest family heritage discovery.

However, when I interviewed him, I discovered that I had to ask Grandfather very specific questions. Ironically, if you ask people to tell you everything they remember, they will tell you they don't remember anything. But if you ask specific questions, you'll be surprised when the stories come spilling out.

Sometimes you will find time to sit face to face with family members. Other times, though, you might have to rely on the telephone or letters. Each method requires a slightly different approach.

Talking to Relatives Face to Face

By far, the best way to interview a relative is when you can sit down across the table from that person. Not only do you have the advantage of being able to just go along with the flow of the discussion, but you can also see the animation on your relative's face. If your relative doesn't object, I encourage you to videotape these interviews.

Usually, you should reserve these types of interviews for older relatives. If the older relative dies, you'll have a special archive of his or her thoughts, stories, expressions, and his or her voice to last for many additional generations. What a special relic.

As I said earlier, you don't want to just ask your relatives to tell you everything they recall. Remember that you will need to guide them with direct questions. Additionally, remember to ask each relative the same questions you asked yourself, but also ask them about their schooling, jobs, and other memorable events in their lives. Asking these questions will help them recall other stories. Remember to record as much information as you possibly can, and also, that audio- or videotaping the

Heritage Hints

Families are not perfect. Sometimes babies came too early, and not from being premature. Other times, divorces ripped families apart. Ours is not to judge, just to find the pieces and put them together. However, in finding those pieces, we often upset those who had to live through the more embarrassing or unhappy events in our family history.

Lineage Lingo

DAR is the abbreviation for the **Daughters of the American Revolution**. This organization is a lineage society—a society that admits individuals only when they have a proven family connection to a qualifying ancestor, one who either fought for the colonies in the American Revolution, or offered aid in some other way, such as food or horses.

interview works best, if the relative doesn't mind. However, if the relative prefers not to be taped, take care to accurately write down everything that relative tells you—including the most important aspects of any of their stories:

➤ Who is mentioned in the story?

➤ What event is the story about?

➤ Where did the story take place?

➤ When did the story take place?

➤ Why did the event take place?

➤ What happened?

Cousin Counsel

In your attempt to record everything accurately and thoroughly, don't forget that you have a real person sitting in front of you. Remember to keep eye contact and to show that you care about their stories for more than just the names, dates, and places you will extract later.

And don't forget to include information about the person that you were interviewing.

➤ What is his or her name?

➤ When did you interview him or her?

➤ Where did the interview take place?

➤ How old was he or she when the interview occurred?

➤ Was he or she present at the events being described?

Genie Goodies

You can find many books to help you master techniques for interviewing relatives. Some books are designed to be given to that person for them to fill out as best they can. (I've seen such books for grandmothers, grandfathers, mothers, and fathers.) Although using these workbook-format books can give you some great results, I prefer the personal method of interviewing relatives. If, however, you want help on which questions to ask, try a resource text called *To Our Children's Children, Preserving Family Histories for Generations to Come,* by Bob Greene and D.G. Fulford, published by Doubleday.

Let "Ma Bell" Help

Yes—historically speaking—we all had one telephone company, which everyone affectionately called "Ma Bell." For talking with relatives, Ma Bell—generically speaking because we don't have just one telephone company anymore—can be a great asset. Although you can't see the person's face (at least, not quite yet), you can still hear voice inflection, letting you share the same emotions the relative on the other end of the phone line is experiencing.

You should always make an appointment to talk on the phone with your relatives. Whether the interview is done on the phone or in person, please keep the interview time short. You could always plan several short interviews and conversations with the same relative over an extended time. This way you don't overtire any relatives, and they are likely to remember more after their initial interviews, as they reflect on the questions you asked during your first conversation. If you can remind them to keep a list of stories or items they might recall from the time you first talked to the next, this little "cheat sheet" can assist them for their second conversation with you.

Also, please remember time zone differences as you use the phone. Take into consideration relatives who get up early, sleep late, and whether you're calling at lunch or dinnertime. Of course, if you have arranged the time in advance, as I suggested earlier, these additional time constraints won't even be a problem.

When you call someone on the phone, be sure that you have a notebook and pen handy. Always ask the person if you can record him or her; your answering machine may be able to handle this task. Oftentimes, people in phone conversations will forget that you're recording them, because they don't actually see the tape recorder. To them, they are just talking on the phone.

Before you call, make sure to have some prepared questions ready to ask. Having a family group sheet and pedigree chart will be handy, too. This will help you identify names and information the relative is likely to share.

Let Uncle Sam Deliver

Another way to get information from living relatives is through the art of letter writing. Granted, in this world

Cousin Counsel

When you call a relative for genealogical information on the phone, don't surprise him or her. If you call a total stranger, you'll discover that he or she generally will not be too forthcoming with the information you hoped to get. Try to contact the stranger in some other way first to "break the ice."

Heritage Hints

One trick that some genealogists resort to in an effort to guarantee a response to their mailed out family group sheets is to add a few years to the age of the woman you are mailing to. While this is pretty sneaky, you will be surprised at how quickly they are likely to respond.

of e-mail, many of us have lost touch with this fine art. Regardless of your writing skills, take time to sit down and write a nice letter to request genealogical information, and if you are writing to a relative you do not already know, please introduce yourself.

A friend of mine has taken letter writing one step further, and he has found his system to be quite successful. He writes a nice letter to the relative, and includes family group sheets, pedigree charts, and other pages of interest, and includes a *self-addressed, stamped envelope* (SASE). He then puts this all in one of the U.S. Postal Service's Priority Mail envelopes. This method does cost him a little more than a regular letter, but he feels that it's worth the results. And, he gets a high percentage of responses with this method.

Lineage Lingo

SASE stands for a **self-addressed, stamped envelope.** Whenever you are contacting anyone and requesting information from him or her, you should always include an SASE. You are more likely to hear back from the mail's recipient.

Family information shared through letters.

73

Including a family group sheet and pedigree chart is also important. Once relatives have these forms in front of them, you can ask them to share what they know. Sometimes when someone sees these family history charts, he or she can recall more memories of family stories. Oftentimes, relatives will share these with you, the family historian.

While most people now use their PCs to type letters, I love to pull out the handwritten letters I have from my aunts. They were so happy to share family information whenever I would ask. And now that these dear relatives are gone, I take out those letters to conjure up memories of my aunts. The figure on the previous page shows an example of how family history can be shared through letters, either handwritten or PC-created.

Heritage Hints

While the audio or video recording will be an excellent source, you may want to be sure to write down at least some of the names, dates, and places that Uncle Bud shares with you. With the recorder you won't have to be as meticulous with your notes, but having it in print as well as on tape is a good practice.

Heritage Hints

Family traditions and the family stories that have been passed down through the years are great sources for clues. These stories generally do not prove to be 100 percent true, but usually each story has a grain of truth. The trick is weeding out the truth from the embellishments that have been attached to the stories through the many retellings.

Interviewing Uncle Bud

Uncle Bud is coming for a visit, and you're going to finally get a chance to talk with him about the family tree. You want to make sure to be as prepared as possible. Make sure that you have a family group sheet with Uncle Bud as a child. And have a pedigree chart on hand, too. The one included in Appendix D will be perfect for your talk.

If you have any relevant photographs, bring those along as well. Photos are a good resource for jogging memories from cobwebs of the brain. And, you never know, Uncle Bud may be the only one who can identify those other three people in the picture with your grandmother.

As you visit with Uncle Bud, try to be as inconspicuous as possible with your notes and audio or video recorder. And, if Uncle Bud lets you tape him, you can just sit back and relax, enjoying his recollections.

Start Uncle Bud's interview by asking him some basic questions about himself, including some about his wife and children. Although your primary goal is gathering family history information, you'll want to keep Uncle Bud at ease.

If you know of specific family stories you want Uncle Bud to recall, ask him about them. He might very well add a new perspective to what you've already been told by others.

Be prepared for Uncle Bud—and other relatives, as well—not wanting to discuss some stories. Many times our relatives don't wish to speak ill of the dead. So, usually, living relatives perceive that if a particular family story puts a dead relative in a bad light, or if the dead relative was just a colorful character, Uncle Bud may not want to talk about this particular person. That's okay, just move on to another question or story.

In addition to the names, dates, and places that you are hoping Uncle Bud can share, you'll find it fun to ask him about other people. You may want to ask Uncle Bud questions about his favorite colors or favorite sports. You can ask about endless topics, and here are a few:

➤ Favorite color

➤ Favorite food

➤ Favorite holiday

➤ Special quiet place

➤ Favorite pets

➤ Special school memories

➤ Best friends

➤ Favorite subjects in school

➤ Least favorite subjects in school

➤ Special activities in the town where the person grew up

Lineage Lingo

Family traditions are more than the activities repeated each year on given holidays. In family history, a family tradition is the story passed down through the generations. It is these stories that may hold the clues you need to pursue a particular family.

Asking relatives about the previous list of favorites usually brings out even more stories. While not all the stories will help you with family history, they can help you get a better sense of what growing up was like for Uncle Bud.

Whether you can interview relatives in person, or must call or write to them, don't delay. I always hear stories of big regrets that beginning genealogists no longer have older relatives to question. Although you can conduct genealogy research without relatives' help, I firmly believe that you miss something extremely special when you can't personally talk to older family members.

If we take the time to get off this busy merry-go-round of a world in which we all have gotten caught, we won't miss the chance to talk with those who may not be around much longer.

Raiding Grandma's Attic

As I mentioned, my grandfather was very good about sending me pictures and papers. As he worked on cleaning out his house, he would box up anything he thought I might want or need. And if he wasn't sure, he would still send the stuff to me anyway. As a result, I am the proud collector of family photos, old-fashioned photo albums, land deeds, wills, and even deeds to cemetery plots. I have significant historical documentation in the form of letters from family, businesses, and doctors.

Genie Goodies

If you can convince your family, you might want to establish yourself as the family archives keeper. Most of the time, people don't really care about old papers, but they can't bring themselves to throw them away, either. So, if you can encourage them to send family papers to you, you may become the caretaker of a wealth of family history. Diaries, family letters, and newspaper clippings all help to give you clues about your ancestors, and these items give you an insight into the lives your relatives lived.

One of the eeriest items I have in my possession is a letter from a doctor that was written on December 12, 1922. On September 24, 1922, my grandmother, 19, was standing along the roadside, waiting for a trolley car when a car struck her. My grandmother spent a lengthy time in the hospital, and based on this doctor's letter, I know she was still in the hospital almost four months after the accident. The doctor's letter says my grandmother's prognosis was not good, and that the medical profession has done all it can do for her. The letter also says the attending staff will make her comfortable, but she will most likely die. Boy, am I glad she was a tough fighter, or I wouldn't be here. The figure following shows this letter from my grandmother's doctor.

Heritage Hints

Newspapers from the town in which your family lived can be very informative. While your family may have saved select clippings, you might want to consider visiting the local town library or the archives of the historical society to see what was going on in the town.

In addition to that letter, my grandfather sent me two newspaper clippings that gave me the date of the accident. With headlines like "Worcester Girl Dying of Injuries" and "Girl Critically Injured …," I read with astonishment the extent of her injuries. I was surprised to learn the details of this car accident.

Preserving these tidbits of history from my family is important to me. Because they are letters and newspapers, they run the risk of deteriorating because of the paper used and the effects of the current environment. It is important to preserve your valuable family papers. Currently you can find acid free paper and archive boxes to help you in the preservation. Such items can be found in some stationery stores, or better yet, through your local Creative Memories distributor. They specialize in these papers and other tools to help you in preserving paper and especially your photographs. I know I would be heartbroken to discover in a few years that these special memories have disintegrated.

```
TELEPHONES                    WYMAN WHITTEMORE, M. D.              PATIENTS SEEN
BACK BAY  3209                   199 BEACON STREET                BY APPOINTMENT
                                   BOSTON, MASS.


                                              December 13, 1922.


         Dr. Ernest L. Hunt
         Worcester City Hospital
         Worcester, Mass.

         Dear Dr. Hunt :

                 I saw Miss Sylvia Bailey with you in consultation
         on Dec. 6, 1922 and believe her condition to be as follows:

                 The right chest showed a pneumothorax with a
         right lung largely collapsed.  On the left side I could find
         nothing except exaggerated breathing in my physical examin-
         ation.  But from the x-ray and sputum examinations I believe
         that she has a septic condition in this lung.  I consider
         that this condition is due to a direct extension from the
         sepsis in the region of the mastoid and the sinus thrombosis.
         I believe the pneumothorax on the right side is due to a
         perforation of the abscess situated in the periphery of the
         lung and that following this there was some pleuritis but
         not an actual empyema as there were no organisms.

                 I consider her present condition a very serious
         one and do not feel that one can give a definite prognosis.
         In this disease there are multiple minute abscesses scattered
         through the lung and it is my opinion that many such cases
         die.  On the other hand, there is some reason for hope in her
         case on account of her general condition being better than it
         was previously and on account of the fact that the blood cul-
         ture was negative showing that she did not have a general
         septicemia.
```

Letter from doctor detailing condition of my grandmother.

Sometimes raiding the family attic won't be an option. For whatever reasons, the person who keeps the family documents just isn't ready to part with them. However, if you can convince him or her that you will share information—or not, as the case may be—hopefully you will be able to raid your grandmother's (or great-grandmother's or aunt's) attic. Most people have trunks, hope chests, boxes of photo albums, mementos of bygone eras, school publications, and other bits of history, all hiding under the dust of an attic or basement. If you can get to these mementos, they will become some of your most prized possessions.

While the letter and newspaper articles didn't really supply me with anything on my grandmother's parents or their ancestry, they did establish where she was living in 1922. And the articles gave me insight into that time with trolley cars (or electric cars, as one newspaper called them).

Cousin Counsel

If you have put your photographs in those binders with the "magnetic pages," get them out immediately. The glue used to hold the pictures to the page is not safe for your photographs. You will ruin the very items you were trying to preserve. Archival quality photo sheets can be found at many photo specialty stores and will not damage your photographs.

Lineage Lingo

Photo quality paper looks and feels like the paper your photos are printed on when you take a roll of film to be developed. When used with high-resolution color printers it offers you the chance to recreate the photograph for yourself and others in the family.

One of the best finds that may show up in the family attic treasures are diaries, which are a wonderful window to the past. I have been fortunate enough to have four diaries of my grandmother's. Now that I'm an adult with children, reading my grandmother's diaries brought back not only memories from my childhood, but a better understanding of my family's life then.

Even if your other family members aren't willing to give you their family papers, perhaps you can convince them to let you copy them. Today copiers are easily available in office supply stores, libraries, post offices, and copy stores. Once you have the copies, transcribe the letters and diaries and abstract the vital records. Then preserve the original copies. Another option is to scan the family papers into your PC, if you have a scanner. Copy shops usually have scanners available for such purposes.

Scanning photos and family papers allows you the ability to include them in any books that you publish or in a Web page that you create. Scanning allows you to preserve photos and documents that may already be falling apart. With the currently available technology, the scanned images are very clear. Sometimes you can even repair some damage to a photograph. Graphics software programs allow you to alter brightness, increase the sharpness of an image, and take out red-eye in color photographs. Photo quality papers even give you the ability to recreate the photo for yourself and others should there be only one copy of a given photo.

I like to scan documents that have signatures of my family members. Then I include the document, and a zoomed-in copy of the signature, as it really helps to remind people that those who are now dead were actually alive and living their lives as we are doing today.

Begging Aunt Ruth for the Family Bible

As I mentioned earlier, sometimes the family keeper of a given record isn't ready to give up that item yet. You can use several techniques to overcome this problem, but you might have to travel to see Aunt Ruth.

Modern technology offers us many new gadgets that genealogists can put to good use, including scanners and digital cameras. If Aunt Ruth doesn't want you to physically take the family Bible anywhere, first see if she will let you copy the family record pages.

If Aunt Ruth won't let you copy the important pages, and you can convince your spouse to purchase a new electronic toy, you could purchase a scanner or a digital camera. You might even be able to rent such an item through a PC rental firm.

While most scanners have to be attached to a computer when they are scanning, Hewlett Packard recently released one that is actually a portable scanner that doesn't require you to immediately save each individually scanned image to a PC. The HP CapShare 910 can store up to 50 letter-size pages of images at one time; this can be the text scanned from a family history book, or a photograph from Aunt Ruth you scanned.

Purchasing a scanner need not be daunting. If you are planning to print out what you scan, especially photographs, you will want to purchase a scanner that has a 300 dpi (dots per inch) resolution. That means for every inch of the picture, there are 300 dots to make up that part of the picture. Generally, the higher the number, the clearer the picture as you do not actually see the individual dots. While there are many high-end scanners with very high dpi numbers, these generally only result in really large graphics files on your hard drive. A 200 dpi scanner will give you a good quality printed image from the scanned image.

Another option is a digital camera. Again there are different brands and each has different capabilities. It is a good idea to get one with a flash. If you are hoping to take pictures of photos or documents up close, then you will want to make sure that the camera has a *macro* feature.

Of course, if you use a scanner or a camera to document family records, be sure to force yourself to do something right away with those captured images. If you use a regular camera, get the film developed right away. If you captured the images with a scanner or digital camera, download the images to your desktop PC as soon as you can, and then print them out. Make necessary notes below the images (or on the back with an archival quality pen), so you don't forget the documents' significance or where the original source documents are located.

Cousin Counsel

If you have a regular camera that has the ability to take pictures of items that are extremely close up (known in photo lingo as a **macro** capability), you may not need to buy a new digital camera. Your current 35mm camera may be all you need to photograph the important pages of the family Bible.

Lineage Lingo

A **macro feature** in a camera allows the camera to be extremely close to a given document. With my Sony Mavica digital, I can take pictures of a document within half an inch, if I need to, without losing the image's clarity.

When Is a Letter Not a Letter?

When is a letter not a letter? When it is a source.

When I refer to letters right now I am not limiting myself to those that are handwritten or even those that are sent through the postal service. Even e-mail can be considered in this category, if you are corresponding with relatives through the Internet.

Letters become sources whenever they contain information about any of your family or ancestors. You will not want to throw these letters away. You will want to hang on to them so that, if ever necessary, you can refer back to them.

The Least You Need to Know

➤ If at all possible, interview older relatives soon.

➤ If you can't visit your relatives, call or write to them.

➤ If possible, try to get copies of the family papers.

➤ If you use a scanner and/or digital camera, you can help preserve your family's records.

Chapter 7

Organize, Organize, Organize

In This Chapter

➤ Making copies of important documents saves you time, and perhaps money

➤ Piling or filing: Make sure you have a system

➤ Keeping track of your research eases your workload

➤ Marking important Web sites

When you first begin your family history research, you think you'll always be able to keep track of your gathered records and documentation. However, from the very beginning of your research, you can set up some good organizational practices to completely avoid that sick, overwhelming feeling of trying to tame the wild paper beast later on in your genealogical research.

Paper beast? Some of you—office workers, insurance adjusters, editors, and authors, as well as genealogists—will know exactly what I mean. Others of you may not understand the paper beast. (You're lucky if you've never encountered it!) I am sure you are wondering just what I am referring to. If you ask my husband, he will tell you that I have more paper than the Library of Congress. He would, of course, be exaggerating. I only have as much paper as the local library. All that paper becomes a beast when you can no longer find information quickly.

Genie Goodies

The Library of Congress is a major repository and one that genealogists will often make a pilgrimage to. When a new book is published, a copy is sent to the Library of Congress. And, if you have been to a bookstore recently, you know just how many books are being published each year. The Library of Congress has a large variety of books useful to genealogists, including family histories, county histories, cemetery records, and vital records.

Copies, Copies, and More Copies

When I first got involved in genealogy, I was encouraged to make copies of any records I used. By doing this, I always have copies of the original document to check back to see whether I've made any errors. Sometimes, when you research a family, you will find data that conflicts with data you already have. When this occurs, you need to return to your previous research to see whether you can figure out how the discrepancy occurred. One quick and easy way to make this fact check is to refer to the copies you made whenever you located source material in a library or other genealogical facility. If you failed to make copies, you will have to return to the location where you discovered the information. But, on the other hand, if you religiously make copies of all relevant paperwork, you've saved yourself time, trouble, and sometimes money, if returning to the source location is more than a simple trip.

Now, mind you, I spend significant time at many, many libraries. But if I'm working on a family history and I used the records at the Family History Library in Salt Lake City, I can't just hop in my car and head to that library. To check the discrepancy, I would either have to order the film to be sent to my local Family History Center, assuming the record I needed was on film, or I would have to shelve that research until I could return to Salt Lake City.

Getting back to the discrepancy mentioned above, neither waiting to revisit the library nor ordering the microfilm is an option that works for me. Remember, genealogists are impatient, and I am no exception. By

Heritage Hints

One of the most important aspects to making copies is to be able to properly cite your sources. You must write on the copies exactly where the information came from. And the best time to write down all your source citations is when you make the copy.

copying the records the first time I discover them, I guarantee that I can find the copies whenever when I need to verify the information I took from them. By photocopying all records and writing the source citation on the back, I have ensured that I will not later have to waste time redoing the research.

What Source Documentation Should You Keep?

As you read this book, you may from time to time question my sanity. If I really do copy everything, then perhaps I do have as many papers as the Library of Congress—but every piece is important to my research.

Just because I have seen a record and written down the information on a family group sheet or typed it into my genealogy software does not mean that it is the best source or the most correct. The source, however, is the best for the moment. It may be the source on which your family history may be based.

Earlier I described a letter from a doctor about my grandmother. Would I get rid of that item? Not on your life! It's an important piece of my family history. The records I come across at libraries and archives, whether they are census records, published family histories, or vital records, are also part of my family history. I want to keep them all.

Genie Goodies

In genealogy, we use different levels of sources. **Primary sources** are usually the most reliable. An example of a primary source would be someone who was in attendance at an event such as the parent at a birth, who would then fill out the information for the birth certificate. A certificate was created at the time of the event by someone who was present at the birth, wedding, death, and so on. **Secondary sources** are those created later on, not necessarily by someone who was present when the event took place. An example of a secondary source would be a published family history. As a result, secondary sources can actually do more harm than good by passing along inaccurate information.

Look at it this way: If your ancestor's name appears on the page, or someone with the same surname that you suspect may be related to you, then you want a copy of that record. You don't want to be merrily progressing with your research only to realize months later that you now desperately need a copy of that page.

Heritage Hints

Very often our time at a library or other repository is limited, usually by the hours of operation. If you are staying for a few days, have a plan in place for the records you want to copy each day. Make your copies, then take time to study them back at the hotel room and make your plan for the next day.

Recently, when I was traveling to a genealogy conference, I took a list of important items for which I was searching to a public library renowned for its genealogical department. As I found each item I needed, I happily headed to the copier to make my photocopy. As my friend watched me, she laughed, even though she understood why I was going to all the trouble of copying each item. I couldn't guarantee I could ever get back to that library, and I didn't want to overlook anything. And in some cases, I wasn't taking time in the library to really read and study my much-sought article or record.

While I was at this library, I was in what I call the "copy now, read later" mode. With this mode of operation, I can make all the copies I need, and then carefully read each of them when I have more time. This method also allows me to compare the information with what I already know. I tend to stay in this copy mode, regardless of what library or repository I am at, even those close to home.

Avoiding the Paper Trap

Well, now I've confessed to being a photocopy fanatic. So how do I keep track of all these papers? After all, I have to be able to find what I need when I need it! When you are doing genealogical or any similar type of research, you have to have a system for keeping track of your copies and research documentation. You need to be able to find a certain piece of paper right when you need it, not waste a half hour searching for it.

Cousin Counsel

If you have an organizational system that works, there is really no right or wrong way to keep track of your data. The most important aspect of any system is that you use it. If you begin with a system and find it too time-consuming to maintain, then quickly find another one. Once you get too far behind in organizing your data, you may never get caught up, and you'll be stuck in a paper trap forever.

Genealogists and other detail-oriented researchers use any number of systems. Some use notebooks, others use 3" x 5" index cards, and still others use file folders.

When genealogists find a good organizational method, they usually write books outlining their methods. The books below, available at your local library, might be helpful to you:

➤ Dollarhide, William. *Managing a Genealogical Project*. Baltimore, Md.: Genealogical Publishing Company, 1991.

➤ Jaussi, Laureen R. *Genealogy Fundamentals*. Orem, Ut.: Jaussi Publications, 1994.

➤ Whitaker, Beverly DeLong. *Beyond Pedigrees, Organizing and Enhancing Your Work*. Salt Lake City, Ut.: Ancestry Publishing, 1993.

The organizational system I actually use does not appear in these volumes. I learned my filing system from a course I took through Brigham Young University. This system consists of file folders for each couple on my pedigree chart. The file folders are given the name of the husband and are filed alphabetically first by surname and then by given name. I also took this system one step further, by using the colored file folder labels. Each lineage is assigned a color. This became important to me when I discovered I had three different unrelated SMITH lines and two different BAILEY lines.

To find out more about this particular system, you may want to read "Avoiding the Paper Trap: Setting Up a Genealogy Filing System," which appeared in issue no. 28 of *Heritage Quest,* May/June 1990, pp. 17–18.

By using research planning sheets to track my day-to-day research and an index sheet to see what is found in each folder, I can determine what research has been done, as well as the results that pertain to a particular family. I file all my research information into file folders for the family I am working on.

Lineage Lingo

Research planning sheets are designed to record pertinent information about a research problem. You include the name of the ancestor, the source information, the date of the search, the goal or problem you are trying to solve, and the results of the search. These research planning sheets are then filed in the folders along with any copies that might have been made from the source. The figure that follows shows a practical example of a research planning worksheet.

RESEARCH PLANNING SHEET

ANCESTOR _____

PLACE _____   RESEARCHER _____

SOURCE _____   DATE OF SEARCH_____

CALL NO._____

Definition of Problem
_____
_____
_____
_____
_____

Information Found
_____
_____
_____
_____
_____

A research planning sheet helps to focus your research on a specific goal.

Following the Genealogical "Bread Crumbs" Trail

Part of avoiding the paper trap and staying organized is to meticulously keep track of where you've been. You need to leave a little bread crumb trail, so you can then follow it back should you need to do so. Of course, librarians would frown if we came in carrying a bag full of bread crumbs, so instead we have to leave a paper trail.

Later in this chapter, I'll explain about the various logs you can create to help track your information. However, just as you need to keep up with your filing system, you also need to keep up with whatever system you decide to use to track the resources you've used.

The tracking method for resources you've used differs from the filing system you'll use to keep track of your entire research effort. Genealogy filing systems are very often designed to just keep track of a given family's or surname's research.

Keeping Track of Why, When, and Where

Another black mark against using bread crumbs to mark your genealogy research trail is that they are not date-stamped. So, if by some miracle the librarians did let you leave your trail, you would have no idea of when you were last there. I suppose you could check to see how stale the bread crumbs were, but somehow that just doesn't seem like the most reliable method.

Heritage Hints

Any system for tracking your research should include information on when you did the research, what you researched, where you found the information, the information you did or didn't find, the surnames you checked, and whether you made copies.

Regardless of which systems you use to organize your paperwork and keep track of where your genealogical search takes you, you also need to include the sources you used and the repositories you visited. And, you need to keep track of when you last visited each genealogical repository.

Genealogy is ever-changing. The same can be said for the holdings of most libraries and archives. As you progress with your family research, you'll always add new surnames and flesh out others in your family tree. Because of this constant change, you may not have known about your relationship to the MOON family, when you last checked that book on Essex County, Massachusetts. However, if you didn't document the date when you looked at the book on Essex County, you may not know whether you need to recheck your newly discovered MOON family link.

Learning to Use Family History Logs

You can use many forms to track your research. And, as we have already discussed, you can start with a notebook. However, if you learn to use family history logs, you will be able to index the wide variety of research information you've already completed.

Mastering Research Logs

One of the easiest forms for tracking family history research is called the Research Log. You can buy pre-formatted research logs from many genealogical suppliers. Some of these forms are quite simple, while others are extremely elaborate. One good way to see several different forms is to attend a genealogy conference. Because conferences have vendor halls, you'll be able to go from vendor to vendor, looking at each one's forms to determine which one is the best for you. Some of these genealogical suppliers are:

➤ Everton Publishers

➤ Heritage Quest

➤ Skeleton Closet

In addition, your local genealogical society may have designed some forms. You shouldn't overlook your local sources.

Lineage Lingo

A **research log** is a pre-formatted page that allows you to track research. Most of these forms have columns for important items like search date, call number and repository, source title, and research results.

Genie Goodies

Genealogical societies are a major asset to any researcher. Even if your ancestry is not in the area where you live, you will still want to join the local society. Your membership provides you a chance to get together with others who share your interest. And generally, the invited lecturers talk on a variety of subjects. You can find a listing of local societies in Elizabeth Petty Bentley's *The Genealogist's Address Book*, published by Genealogical Publishing Company.

Of course, if you are of a creative nature, you might want to take a stab at designing your own customized form. If you do create your own forms, remember to include spaces for the following:

➤ surnames researched

➤ localities researched

➤ search date

➤ repository

➤ library call number

➤ full source title

➤ search results

You may already have access to a research log without even realizing it. The Family History Library has designed a number of forms, including a research log. Your local Family History Center may have some for sale. If not, you can order this form directly from Salt Lake City. The staff at your local Family History Center can supply you with the necessary order form. The order form will include a phone number, if you wish to call and charge the order. The figure that follows shows a research log, which is necessary for keeping track of your research.

Research logs are important for keeping track of your research.

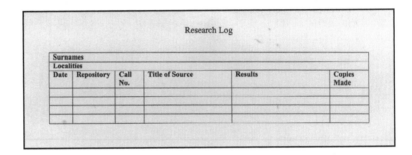

Date	Repository	Call No.	Title of Source	Results	Copies Made

Mastering Electronic Logs

I recently wrote an online article about research logs, and my audience chastised me for using a manual form (one that is filled out by hand) as a basis for my discussion. While I practically live in front of my PC, we still have to endure times when our computers can't go with us. So, if you are new to genealogy, you should know how important it is for you to be aware and capable of using both manual and electronic methods.

If you don't want to go to the trouble of locating genealogical forms, you probably already have some programs on your PC that you can tailor to track your research. You can use any spreadsheet program to create a research log. Just remember to include the necessary columns to hold every piece of vital information as I discussed earlier in this chapter.

Lineage Lingo

A **spreadsheet** program is often used for the recording of data in rows and columns, much like the old-styled ledger books used to track finances.

One way that you can guarantee you have the best possible electronic log is to create one on your PC using a pre-formatted log as your guide. If you follow the information requirements of the pre-formatted log, you'll be sure to include all the important information columns.

If you would prefer to use a database structure for your electronic log, you can create your genealogy forms in a database program, such as Microsoft Access.

Electronic logs are a great opportunity for you to play around with software that you wouldn't normally use.

Try taking a small sampling of your research and designing different electronic logs to accommodate your data. When you've created a few genealogical form variations, see which one offers you the most flexibility and contains the most information.

Electronic logs have one major benefit that the printed copies don't. You can search the file for specific items. If you have a file that includes a column for surnames, you could have your spreadsheet or database program do a search for a certain surname for you.

Another feature found in the electronic log is the ability to alter the listing format. One day you may want to look at your log in chronological order. Another day, you may want to have your log show localities in alphabetical order.

You may not even need to use a separate program to keep your electronic log. There are a couple of genealogy software programs available that will allow you to include your research logs and have to-do items built into the program for this very reason. Both Family Tree Maker and Ultimate Family Tree offer such features.

PCs and paper don't have to be mutually exclusive, despite what PC advocates say. I use both to keep track of my research in the most effective manner. Remember that any system is effective only if it works for you—and if you actually use it. And if your system doesn't work for you, or you don't use it because of whatever reason, you need to revise your system until it works appropriately and suits your genealogical research needs.

Lineage Lingo

A **database** program is designed to store, retrieve, and organize information. For genealogists this could be information about those interred in a cemetery or those you are extracting from a census record.

Cousin Counsel

When you are working in an electronic file, you will want to be sure to keep backup copies of the file every time you enter new data. I encourage you to not only keep your electronic files on your hard drive, but to also save the file to a floppy disk or some other medium. In addition, you should always print a version of the file as a last-ditch fallback should your hard-disk version and backup fail for some reason.

Returning to the "Crime Scene"

Research logs are as important to genealogy as the actual research you do online or in the library. In some cases, you should take more care to track online information because the Internet is ever-changing. The page you viewed last week may have been updated this week to include additional information.

Your browser software has options built in to help you keep track of what sites you have visited on the Internet. Considering how much Net surfing one can do when hot on the trail of an elusive ancestor, you need to be able to use your Internet browser to track the important Web sites you've visited.

Relying on Bookmarks, Web Style

We've all been there: It's midnight, and you've been surfing the Web for the past three hours. Your eyes have that eerie red tint to them and your hand is only capable of clicking on the next link. Suddenly, with the next mouse click, you find the number one, best Web site you have ever seen for your family. This site has everything you ever wanted to know, and better still, the Web site has included documentation. This triumphant moment is usually when your spouse will "pull the plug," figuratively speaking, of course.

You're certain you can easily find that hot Web site again, so you agree with your spouse to log off the Internet for the night. You want to be able to devote extensive time to studying the site at a later time when you are more rested. So you close your browser, and shut off your computer for the night.

You've just committed the unthinkable online crime: You didn't bookmark that important Web site. Will you really know how to return to that Web site again?

Anyone who surfs the Net is guilty of this "online crime." In fact, we usually fail to mark our most sought-after site. The next night, when we get back online, we may spend as much time finding that hot Web site as we did the first time. Bookmarking takes only a few seconds, so don't forget about this time-saving feature. As you surf the Net and discover a Web site that interests you, make it a habit to bookmark that site. You can always delete the bookmark later, if you discover that the site really isn't of interest to you. Deleting bookmarks is much simpler than trying to relocate some important Web site.

Lineage Lingo

With Internet browser software, you use an electronic **bookmark** to record the information necessary for the browser to return to that particular Web site. When you bookmark a Web site, you don't have to follow the links you did when you first discovered the site. Your Web browser remembers the URL, or Internet address, of that Web site location. To access that site, just access your browser's bookmarks and select the Web site you want. With Netscape's browser, you use the term **bookmark;** with Explorer, you use the term **favorites,** but they both mean the same thing.

Maintaining Your Internet Travel Log

Earlier in this chapter, I discussed how important it is for you to keep a log of the resources you check. Keeping a log of your Web site visits is doubly important. Although you still need to bookmark the important Web sites to which you'll want to return, you should also keep a running log of the Web sites you visit.

The paper trap mess is nothing when compared with the Web trap mess, and the World Wide Web itself is the source of the problem. You can easily get caught in the Web, and find yourself constantly and repeatedly returning to the same Web sites.

While you are working with your browser, you should also have an electronic log ready to access. You can then copy and paste the URL from your browser window to your electronic log. You can also make notations, including the date you visited the site and the information that you did or didn't find at that site.

Genie Goodies

One of the benefits of the new computers that run Windows is the ability to have more than one program running at the same time. In fact, when I am online, I often have my electronic log open, the browser open, and my genealogy software running. By using the ALT-TAB key combination, or clicking on the names of the programs in the task bar at the bottom of the screen, I can switch back and forth between the various programs that I have running. Don't be afraid to try this out. Start your genealogy software, then start your browser, and finally the program that has your electronic log in it.

You can use any program that works for you. Most people tend to create logs in spreadsheets or database programs, as the columns are a set format and offer sorting features. You simply need a way to create different columns for the pertinent information, including one column for the URL of the Web site.

The best way to create an electronic log is to pattern it largely after the research log we described previously. However, instead of having a repository, you would instead have a Web page and the address for that site. I prefer a database program for creating such a log as I can control the length of any given column in the database. When first creating the necessary fields, I tell the program how long I want each one. Then the program creates my document with those items in mind. This usually means that I don't need to go back and resize any columns later on as I would have to do with a spreadsheet program.

When entering the URL to the Web site into your electronic log, be sure to copy and paste from the browser window to the electronic log for accuracy. Those URLs are sometimes long and you can easily get a typo when typing it in by hand.

Lineage Lingo

A **URL** or **uniform resource locator** is the address of one Internet page. Just as you and I rely on addresses to find our way as we drive around town, we also rely on URLs to locate Web pages. Without URLs, we could not access any Web sites.

Genie Goodies

To **copy** the URL from your browser window, click inside the address field (where the URL is located) and notice that the URL is highlighted. You can now pull down the Edit menu and select Copy (or use the CTRL-C key combination). Then switch to your electronic log and place the cursor where you want the URL to be listed. Then pull down the Edit menu in the new program and select **paste** (or use the CTRL-V key combination). The URL will now appear in your electronic log.

If you don't have a specific software program to create an electronic log, another option is to use WordPad or Notepad or some other word processing program. You can include the date, then the title and URL for the Web site. Then I suggest you make some notations as to the information on that site.

If using WordPad or Notepad, you will not have columns. So an entry should have the following lines:

1. Search date
2. Web site title
3. Web site URL
4. Notations as to surnames searched and information found

If you are going to be using another word processing program, you have the ability to work with tables. This allows you to set up columns, similar to those used in the spreadsheet or database program. Each column could be labeled with the headings listed above in the steps for using WordPad, but instead of having each item on a separate line, you would get to work across a row, putting the information into specific columns.

Why notations in your electronic log? I suggest including comments for the Web sites that you visit simply to help refresh your memory. After months and months of Web surfing, you'll find that you have 54 log entries that all share the same title of "My Family." This title is not too helpful, if you can't remember to which family you were referring. Helpful notations include of these suggestions:

➤ surnames
➤ localities

➤ type of information available

➤ whether sources are cited

➤ the data's reliability

Using Your Browser's History

If we revisit our nightmare example where we could not re-find our "dream" family Web site, you might be able to find it even if you didn't bookmark it.

Browser software can currently be used to keep track of the sites you are visiting. The browser software refers to this process as maintaining your Web surfing "history." In theory, these browsers should list all the sites that you've visited, but the lists browsers maintain don't always show up in my browser history. Sometimes sites I visit via hot links rather than by entering the URL fail to show in my history file.

Internet browser history files have another problem, too. The history feature relies on the Web page's title, which may or may not be the actual Web page's title. When someone designs a Web page, the creator needs to include a special code to give the page a title. If the Web page creator didn't give the page a title, then your browser cannot enter that Web site into the history feature. This technological oddity really frustrates me.

So, although current browsers offer these history features and can hold anywhere from a few days to a couple of weeks worth of history links, the feature still has some drawbacks. If you are desperate to find that special Web site, you may be able to locate it in a pinch. However, you should develop a more reliable system for tracking your visited Web sites, as well as forcing yourself to save bookmarks.

Lineage Lingo

Hot links refers to the active links you see in Web pages. Usually they are a different color than the rest of the text on the Web page and they may be underlined. Your cursor will also change as you pass over them, usually from a pointing arrow to a pointing hand.

Heritage Hints

When you open the **history** section, you may have to open subfolders to see some of the sites that you have visited. In Netscape Navigator, you will need to pull down the Window menu and select History to view the history of links visited. In Microsoft Internet Explorer, you see a button on the tool bar that says History.

Drowning in Bookmarks?

Now that I've gone on and on about bookmarks, you know that creating them is something you should do. If you have already gotten into the habit of creating bookmarks, you may reach a point where you spend more time looking through them than you'd spend returning to the main Web site and following links to your desired location. This problem occurs when you save Web pages individually in your bookmark or favorites areas, and you don't organize the bookmarks in files or folders by topic. Imagine an old-fashioned filing cabinet, but each paper had its own storage slot and there was no order to the papers. No one would be able to find anything without spending lots of time and effort. But by adding topic file folders to store individual papers, some sense of organization begins to appear.

Folders Are Your Friends

Earlier in this chapter, we discussed organizing family record copies in notebooks or folders. With your browser, you can use electronic folders to organize your bookmarks or favorites.

Although you can set up file folders within your browser, the easiest way to get your bookmarks organized is to set up main folders for your major research headings, like:

➤ Surnames

➤ Localities

➤ Societies

➤ Libraries

➤ Archives

Once you've set up these main folders, you can then create subfolders within the folders. For instance, in my Surname folder, I have folders on the surnames which I am working, BAILEY, DAVIS, MOON, SICKAFUS, STANDERFER, and WEBSTER. In my Localities folder, I have folders for Illinois, Indiana, Ohio, Massachusetts, and New Hampshire.

Heritage Hints

Don't be afraid to change the "title" of a Web page as it appears in your bookmark folders. If the creator called the Web page "My Family," but the page is all about the MOON family, I might rename the site in my bookmarks to "MOON Family," for example.

By organizing the Web sites in such a way, you can easily return to them.

When you are working with your PC, remember that you are the one in control. You will want to learn all the ins and outs of your browser software. One good way to learn more about your browser is to visit that browser's Web site. At that site, you can read up on the tricks shared by other users. Using all your browser's capabilities will make you a stronger researcher and a better genealogist.

To create new folders in Internet Explorer:

1. Select the Favorites menu.

2. Select Add to Favorites.

3. In the window that opens, click the Create In button.

4. Click the New Folder button.

5. Name the folder.

6. The URL reference will be saved in this folder.

When working with Netscape, create folders for your bookmarks as follows:

1. Click the Bookmarks button that appears next to the URL field.

2. Select Add Bookmark

3. Click the Bookmarks button again.

4. Select Edit bookmarks.

5. Pull down the File menu.

6. Select New Folder

7. Name the folder.

8. Highlight the title of the Web page you just added.

9. Pull down the Edit menu and select Cut.

10. Click on the newly created folder and pull down the File menu and select Paste.

If you are concerned about these steps, I encourage you to visit the Web site for the browser you use. Very often they have detailed tutorials, complete with screen captures showing each step of the process.

Cousin Counsel

When using the Create In option, be sure that you have highlighted the folder in which you wish to create the new sub-folder. Otherwise, the new folder you are creating will appear in whatever location is highlighted at that moment.

Names of Places?

When it comes to putting Web pages into folders, do you file a certain Web page in the Surname folder or the Locality folder? When you first visit the site, ask yourself whether the site is geared toward the surname research or the locality research. As you look at a number of sites useful to genealogists, you'll begin to understand how the focus is obvious. Most researchers gear their focus toward either surnames or a locality.

So, if I bookmark a site that's all about MOONs in Illinois, I will put that site in my Surname folder. Although the site also mentions a location, its overall emphasis is on the MOON family.

But keep in mind that the organizational methods that work for me may not be the best for you. Experiment with different organizational approaches to see what techniques make you feel most comfortable and provide you with the most organizational firepower.

The Least You Need to Know

➤ Always make copies of any records where you find family information.

➤ A good filing system is important for keeping track of what you know and where you are going with your genealogical research.

➤ Keeping track of when you searched a source is as important as what you searched the source for.

➤ You will want to organize your online bookmarks in the same manner you use to organize your research files.

What's Next for the Genealogist on the Hunt?

Once we have gone through significant preparation, including talking with relatives, we need to take the information we have and begin working with other records, taking trips, and going to the libraries.

Later in this book, we will look at many of the record types you are likely to use as we investigate what types of information you can get online. First, let's look at how to get prepared for your search.

Planning for the Future

Whether you're going to your local library, or logging on to the Internet, you need a plan. Without a plan, you will quickly find yourself floundering in a wealth of research materials, and you will easily grow frustrated with your research.

Use your research planning sheets to help prepare for research trips. These sheets also help you focus your research on a specific problem or goal.

I always know when I have lost my focus or sight of my goal. I basically start jumping from my chair, grabbing book after book, or microfilm after microfilm. I skim these items quickly and then move on to the next. And while I'm in this mode, I never seem to find anything. Not surprising, since I am just jumping from name to name and place to place. When I have a goal in mind, I am much more likely to make some progress.

And no, the goal cannot be so encompassing as to be something like "get all my genealogy." Your goal should be something reasonable, like finding proof of a birth, or finding the marriage license for your great-grandparents. You want your goals to be attainable.

Research Trips

Once you have exhausted the records that your family is willing to share, then it becomes necessary to take research trips. I have a little secret: Every time I go to my local genealogical library, I consider it a research trip. Research trips can be halfway around the world or just around the block. Following are some places you might look:

➤ Your local library's genealogy section

➤ Major libraries like the Family History Library or the Newberry Library

➤ The town where your family settled and raised children for three generations

➤ The family cemetery

The Local Library

Why on earth would I consider the local library to be a research trip? Anyone with small children can give you the answer to that question. Planning the local library trip, kids in tow, takes as much energy as planning a cross-country trip. Once you've made an initial visit, you're never sure when you'll get back to that research location.

While my children are no longer infants, I can still vividly remember the hassles of getting all of us out the door for a brief four- or five-hour trip to the library. Convincing my husband that it was absolutely necessary to go hunting for these lost ancestors was the hardest part. He just didn't understand the urgency. His point was that they were dead, so they weren't going anyplace. But when you get a new clue or a vital record arrives giving you a new name to add to the tree, all you want to do is hit the library and see what else you can find out.

If you can get your spouse as addicted to genealogy as you are, then the two of you have a really binding hobby. If your spouse is addicted, he or she will always overlook the number of hours you are putting into this hobby. In fact, if spouses are really excited about genealogical research, they'll even encourage you. After all, for every hour you get to search for your ancestors, that's an hour spouses can search for their ancestors as well. Unfortunately, this doesn't always happen. Usually you are the only one interested in hunting down the family history. So when you finally do get to hop in the car and go to the local library, make sure that your trip will be a successful one by planning ahead. Later on we will look at how the Internet can help you with regards to searching the library catalog before you actually go to the library.

Lineage Lingo

Vital records is a term used to refer to those certificates recorded by civil authorities. Generally this category includes birth records, marriage records, and death records.

Major Libraries

Family history–starved researchers from near and far are anxious to visit several special large-scale libraries located all over the country. Although we have many great libraries, some are so spectacular that visitors naturally drool when they think of them. Here is a list of major libraries:

➤ Family History Library, Salt Lake City, Utah

➤ National Archives, Washington, D.C.

➤ Allen County Public Library, Ft. Wayne, Indiana

➤ Newberry Library, Chicago, Illinois

➤ DAR Library, Washington, D.C.

➤ Library of Congress, Washington, D.C.

Getting to these libraries usually requires some time and effort, unless you are lucky enough to live close to one. This means taking some kind of trip, which costs time and money. When you do visit one of these major libraries, you'll definitely want to be prepared to get the most from your research time.

Now let's look at what you'll want to have with you when you visit a major library:

➤ Family group sheets

➤ Pedigree charts

➤ Research planning sheets, or some list of goals

➤ Research logs to record the progress of your research

➤ A spiral notebook or other means for taking copious notes

Obviously, if you have a lot of family group sheets, you won't be able to take them all. If you have a notebook PC, don't worry about taking lots of paperwork with you, because your PC will have your entire database on your hard disk. However, if you have your family history written on forms, then you may need to select only certain families on which to concentrate.

If you do have a notebook PC, you will still want to select specific families to research. Remember that if you haven't set specific goals, you might accomplish very little on your visit. You might even begin to understand how a hamster feels as he runs on that little wheel, never really getting anywhere.

Family Locations

Libraries and archives won't be your only destinations on research trips. You will often find yourself visiting cousins, taking road trips to family cemeteries, or just visiting the town where your family grew up.

Visiting the family homestead or touring the local haunts are fascinating experiences. Once in a while, you can bribe other family members to accompany you. If you have small children, you can sometimes turn these research excursions into fun family outings. There is nothing like discovering pieces of the past, especially when they were part of your ancestors' lives.

As I mentioned earlier, my grandmother joined the DAR. Her primary reason for joining was to be able to volunteer at the General John Stark House, which is located in Manchester, New Hampshire, just down the street from my grandparents' home. When my grandmother would go there to clean, she often allowed me to accompany her. I always enjoyed going because I felt a connection with the children of a bygone era. And at one point I remember fulfilling a school assignment by writing about General Stark, which seemed like writing about an old friend.

Not all DAR chapters have such a responsibility as the Molly Stark Chapter did in the preservation of the house. Because the house was maintained by the chapter, it was necessary for those who wished to volunteer there to be members of the DAR. I don't know if that is still a requirement today.

Heritage Hints

Joining a lineage society offers an evaluation of your research as well as the support of fellow genealogists who have gone through the same process. Most lineage societies require that you prove descent from a given individual, and generally their required sources are rather stringent.

Genie Goodies

When you visit your cousins, see if you can get copies of whatever family-related material they have. Usually, no one is eager for you to even borrow his or her originals. But, as with Aunt Ruth's family Bible, if you can take pictures or scan the memorabilia, you can have quality copies of these items, too. If your cousins have a local photocopy store, you might ask them to accompany you to the store, so you can make copies. With today's high-resolution color copiers, I have seen some copies that looked better than the originals.

Cemeteries

Family picnics aren't always in parks—some families opt to have their family get-togethers in family cemeteries. One of my friends took her children, even when they were small, on many family outings to cemeteries. Because my friend was a conscientious mother who realized that small children would need to eat, she always prepared a picnic lunch, which the family would very often eat in the cemetery. Later, when her children were grown, my friend invited her daughter's fiancé to a family picnic. The daughter piped up to warn her intended that he must first verify where the picnic would take place, because her mother had a propensity for picnicking in cemeteries. Over the years, my friend merely proved that fresh air, food, and family history can go together.

Heritage Hints

Not all cemeteries are fit for having picnics. Many times the cemetery you will need to plow through will be heavily overgrown. It is a good idea to dress accordingly in long pants and boots that go up to your ankles.

Cousin Counsel

When you visit cemeteries, please do not put shaving cream on the tombstones. Some genealogists suggest using shaving cream to bring out the features of a tombstone so it will photograph better. Unfortunately, shaving cream is very damaging to these stone memorials.

In addition to being great picnic locations, cemeteries offer much information about the people who are buried there. In addition to noting headstone names and dates, be sure to pay attention to the epitaphs because they give you insight into the deceased's attitudes and those survivors who may or may not have cared for them.

Where graves are located in the cemetery, and who is buried nearby, offers clues to relationships and intrigues of the family. Please be sure to keep an eye out for freshly dug graves. These can be hazardous to your body. And, yes, I know someone who has personal experience with this issue.

Evaluating Your Research

You've interviewed relatives and acquired some records. Before you pat yourself on the back, take some time to carefully look at those records and recognize just what they can tell you. Before you scrutinize your records, you must understand that different types of records may have different degrees of reliability. Some sources are considered primary, while others are considered secondary.

Primary sources include:

➤ Birth records

➤ Christening records

➤ Marriage records

➤ Death records

➤ Family Bibles

Secondary sources include:

➤ Census records

➤ Obituaries

➤ County histories

➤ Family histories

➤ Passenger lists

Sometimes a record can be both a primary and a secondary source at the same time. A death certificate, for example, is a primary source for the death and burial information. However, it can only be considered a secondary source for any other event or relationship information it might contain.

Genealogists should apply the same principles of information analysis as those used by detectives. Each record must be carefully examined and honestly evaluated within its frame of reference.

Family Bibles, while very often a primary source, are also secondary sources. When you look at the lineage information recorded in a family Bible, you must also look at the Bible's copyright date.

For instance, if your family Bible has recorded family events dating from the early 1700s, but the Bible was not printed until 1892, then you must treat the information contained within the Bible as though it came from any other secondary source. Such information is subject to error, so you will need to verify the information with other records.

A family historian's goal should be to seek out the very best records available, relying more heavily on primary sources than secondary sources, when possible. However, sometimes you won't be able to locate primary sources, or perhaps no such records exist, or they cannot be located or obtained. In such instances, you will need to piece together the threads of your family history in order to weave your ancestors' stories.

As Sherlock Holmes said " ... when all other contingencies fail, whatever remains, however improbable, must be the truth." Sometimes, you will have to eliminate all other possibilities in family history. Usually whatever information is left will turn out to be the correct lineage.

Lineage Lingo

The records that result from eyewitnesses typically are **primary** sources, as they were present at the time of the family history event. **Secondary** sources are typically created at a later date and are based upon hearsay. The following figure shows a copy of a vital record, which is considered a primary source.

Vital records are primary sources for the genealogist "on the hunt."

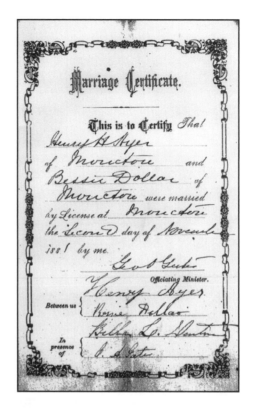

Building on Others' Research

You've begun to grow your family tree with the sources you have already collected. Now, you must enrich your small family tree with the results of others' compiled work.

Cousin Counsel

You will want to be careful when trusting the work of others. Humans compile family histories, and discrepancies do pop up. After all, we're not perfect.

As you begin to venture forth into the libraries and archives, you will find many treasures:

➤ Published family histories

➤ Biographies

➤ Histories

➤ Lineage society records

➤ Abstracts

➤ Compiled works

As you begin to work with these resources, you will want to apply the note-taking methods we discussed earlier in this book. Through this method, you will begin to add new leafs, twigs, and branches to your family tree.

Like all trees, some branches will grow faster than others. Do not get discouraged if you cannot fill all the branches equally at once. When you first begin genealogical research, you'll find it more important to have sturdy roots than flashy branches. Otherwise, you run the risk of inadvertently adding someone else's branches to your family tree.

As you are taking your notes, remember that you need to include details as to the source from which you get your data. While few of us remember how to cite sources from our high school term papers, I suggest you brush up on citation methods, and I recommend a great book that takes all the guesswork out of recording your sources. Elizabeth Shown Mills's *Evidence! Analysis & Source Citations for Family Historians* offers you a chart of more than 100 citation examples to follow.

Just as important as recording your source information is making notes about how you discovered the source in the first place. Writing down your thoughts as you began to build on the family tree will show you a road map of your thought processes.

Heritage Hints

Always give credit where appropriate. This way, if there is a mistake in the research, your source citations will point to the originator of the mistake.

The Least You Need to Know

➤ Plan your work and work your plan.

➤ Information can and will come from many different places.

➤ Evaluate carefully the information you discover.

➤ Always take notes and always cite your sources.

➤ It's okay to work slowly and methodically.

Part 3
Surf's Up

In Parts 1 and 2, we looked at PC basics and the fundamental requirements
of getting hardware to access the Internet, and the basics of beginning genealogical
research. Now, you need to get your feet—er—your fingers—wet. Surf's up!

In Part 3, I'll gently guide you into the World Wide Web. But, fear not, because I've
made certain no spiders are laying in wait to trip you up. You will begin to learn how
the Internet catalogs online information, and how you can sort through it. I'll also
introduce you to various ways of communicating with other online genealogists
through bulletin boards, mailing lists, and newsgroups. You'll also get a look at
various Web pages that other genealogists are creating and posting on the World
Wide Web.

Chapter 9

Surfing—
Genealogy
Style

In This Chapter

➤ Saving time searching the Internet

➤ Learning how directories categorize sites by subject

➤ Searching many sites with metasearch engines

➤ Searching for genealogy sites only

Pick up any magazine or ad, even in the genealogy community, and you will see e-mail addresses and URLs to Web sites. In a relatively short time, we have truly become an online society. We rely heavily on this technology to communicate with friends, family, and colleagues around the world. For genealogists, this new medium is a wonderful way to meet other genealogists whom we otherwise would never meet.

What's in Your Beginner's Basket?

First-time Internet visitors are often disappointed because their preconceived expectations of the online experience are easily dashed. This disappointment occurs usually because they are unaware of how to find the sites they want. We have the misconception that literally everything is available on the Web. True, the Web currently offers a great deal of information, and every day new sites appear and more information is added. However, if you cannot find the information you need, or do not know how to look for it, you may decide that the Internet offers nothing for you.

Perhaps one way that WWW novices can begin to understand what the Web offers and how it is organized is to think of the Web as being similar to a library. A library shelves books using a system of numbers. For some libraries this is the Dewey Decimal System; however, the Family History Library has its own system, as do some of the other larger repositories. Knowing about this numbering system is the key to being able to find the book you want. When you go to a library, you will most likely search for books in one of two ways:

➤ Searching the library's catalog

➤ Walking among the aisles of books

Heritage Hints

There are times when you are searching through the library's card catalog and you just don't know what to look under. This is often true with the newer computerized library catalogs. If you keep your search as general as possible, you are more apt to see what you are looking for.

Lineage Lingo

Directories offer you a list of Web sites. Many times these lists are organized alphabetically or under subheadings to make it easier to find a particular subject.

Both methods will result in finds. Searching the catalog is generally going to save time and find more titles than walking among the shelves of books. When you search the library card catalog, the catalog tells you what books the library has and supplies you with the call number of where the book is shelved.

The up side to walking among the bookshelves is that you sometimes see a book that you would not have thought to look up in the catalog.

Each method—searching the catalog and scanning the shelves—has its benefits. Time, however, will usually determine which method you choose. If you are in a hurry, you are much more likely to head for the catalog, so that you can go directly to books you know will help you. If you get to spend all day at the library, you probably will also spend some time just scanning the bookshelves looking for useful books.

You can also approach the Internet in similar fashion. You can either choose to use various search sites, or you can begin your research by visiting a directory. Both offer you a way to focus your initial Internet search launch. Similarly, you will sometimes start your Internet work at a particular site, and then begin to use that Web page's links to surf from Web site to Web site.

Sometimes you will combine both strategies—using searches or linking from site to site. First, you will find a page using a search site or directory. Then you may wish to surf the various links made available by the person who created the page. Web page links are very often related, so it's like walking along the books and eyeing a book you hadn't known about.

Link to Link

Surfing the World Wide Web can feel overwhelming. You can get carried away as you discover all the pages available to you. Some of them will be easy to read, and you will be thrilled with the information found on them. Others will make you wonder why the person created the page.

Most of us usually know the address of at least one Web site we want to visit when we log on to the Internet. For genealogists, they may find these Web page addresses in a genealogy periodical, or perhaps a fellow researcher has provided them. Many times, friends and other researchers will send the URLs of the better Web sites to you via e-mail. Regardless of how you get hold of the better URLs, you'll be eager to log on to the Web and find some information on your own.

If you don't already know of some sites that you want to visit, and you just want to find out what Web sites are available for genealogists, then using an Internet directory may be helpful to you. Directories are an efficient way to get started moving around the Internet. Here's my list of favorite directory sites primarily geared to genealogists:

➤ Cyndi's List (www.cyndislist.com)

➤ Helm's Toolbox (www.genealogy.tbox.com)

➤ Genealogy's Most Wanted (www.citynet.net/mostwanted/links.html)

➤ The Genealogy Home Page (www.genhomepage.com/full.html)

Lineage Lingo

Surfing is when you go from a link on one Web page to another Web page. From page to page, you move through the Internet, hopping from one Web site to another.

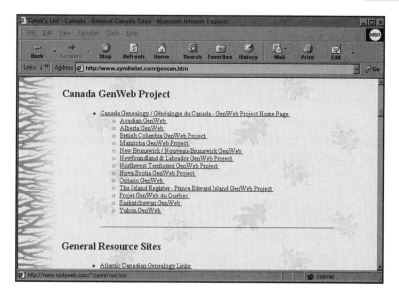

Cyndi's List groups Web links under subjects.

All these sites feature directories with lists of links for genealogists. However, not all Internet directories are the same, and some are better organized than others. Some will offer you a way to search their links and others will have more links to begin with. You'll want to visit many different directory sites, so that you know you've reached as many genealogical sites as possible.

Heritage Hints

Humans usually compile directories. A **bot** or other automated computerized finder searches the Internet for the various Web sites that will appear in the directory. However, some directories, including Cyndi's List, are organized and categorized by the human compiler of the site. Many times, the compiler will elect to include comments to define the site in an effort to give you a better idea of what that site contains.

Yes, directory sites overlap their listings of potential Web sites. However, the way in which each directory gathers its information on the Web sites it lists affects the Web site listings you find. Also, how the directory's compiler arranges its links is another factor affecting how the directory displays its listings.

If a Web site has its links arranged alphabetically, hope that the Web page creator gave the site a descriptive title when he or she designed it. Unfortunately, not all Web site developers keep this design aspect in mind, so Internet surfers often get nondescript pages with titles such as:

➤ My Home Page

➤ Family History Page

➤ My Family

➤ John's Family History

Of course, some title is better than no title at all; and, unfortunately, some designers don't give their Web pages titles at all.

If the directory arranges the links by subject, it works similar to a library where you can select the book you want from the shelf of books on that subject. This method works especially well when you have a specific subject in mind to research. When you have a specific site, but one for which you do not know the URL, then finding the site is more difficult. If you and the directory's compiler have different ideas about the purpose of a particular Web site, locating the site again becomes more difficult.

When you are working with URLs, there's no rule that prohibits you from experimenting by guessing the URL. If you wanted to see whether there was a Web site about the HORRIGAN family, you can always enter into your browser's URL locator something like www.horrigan.com or www.horrigan.org. If the Internet has no such Web site, then your browser returns a message that tells you it cannot find that Web page. If by some chance, the Horrigans have an official family Web site, and you guess the URL correctly, your browser will take you right to the site. This URL guessing game works especially well for retail sites. For example, www.evertons.com will take you directly to the Everton's online store, where you can purchase genealogical supplies and search online subscriber databases.

The Cream of the Crop

Just as people will ask what the best genealogy software is, many will also ask what Web sites I consider to be the best. My answer is very much the same. The best Web site is the one that gives you what you need. When you are beginning your work on the Internet, you might experience a great deal of frustration because at first you won't know exactly what you need.

Directories

Many beginning genealogists have discovered and use Cyndi's List as their Internet starting point. This vast directory lists the various links by subject. At last count, the site had more than 100 subjects from which to select. Many genealogists consider this Web site to be the best genealogy site on the Internet.

Another directory is Helm's Toolbox. This directory of genealogical sites currently claims over 70,000 links. Actually Helm's Toolbox combines a directory with a search engine. The search engine found on this site will search the directory of Web sites and display those that fit your criteria.

You will use different sites for different purposes. Sometimes, you'll search for sites, and sometimes, you'll use links to move from site to site. Sometimes, too, you'll need to begin your work from one of the Internet's many directories. It's great to have so many ways to find the same information!

Another good Web site directory is Yahoo (www.yahoo.com). With the Yahoo directory—as with most Internet directories—you can search the directory's entire listings to see what Web sites Yahoo can link you to. Yahoo also offers many more features than just searchable links to genealogy sites. You need to visit Yahoo when you begin working online.

When you are working with an Internet directory, you will more likely get results if you conduct your online search with a specific goal in mind. You'll find it simpler to find some bit of information when you have a sense of what information you want.

Cousin Counsel

When looking through directories, keep in mind that the compiler may have felt the purpose of the given Web site applied to a different subject than you did. It is a good idea to keep an open mind when looking for a Web site by checking multiple subjects in the directory.

Cousin Counsel

Directories do not include links to all of the Internet's genealogy Web pages. Each day, new genealogical Web sites pop up. If you don't find what you are looking for listed on a directory page, don't give up. You may need to use another method to locate the site you want.

Recently, I searched for some Web sites that might have information on my McCLAIN family from Orange County, Indiana. As I started my search, I went to a directory site and began to look for Web sites devoted to Indiana, and also to Orange County, Indiana. Once I was at a Web site devoted to records and genealogy of Orange County, Indiana, I then concentrated on the McCLAIN surname. Through this search, I was able to determine from what county in Kentucky my McCLAIN family migrated to Indiana. I was just a little excited. My kids would tell you I was jumping off the wall. But we all know that children exaggerate.

Heritage Hints

While you need to have a plan, don't make the plan so narrow in concept that you cannot find anything. If you search for sites on a given surname and come up empty-handed, rethink the search by looking for information on the localities from which that family came.

Search Engines

In addition to directories, I mentioned that search engines can be of use to a genealogist. There are a number of useful search engines. I include a list of just a few of them here:

➤ AltaVista (www.altavista.com)

➤ Hotbot (www.hotbot.com)

➤ Excite (www.excite.com)

➤ Infoseek (infoseek.go.com)

➤ Ask Jeeves (www.askjeeves.com)

Genie Goodies

A **search engine** is a site designed to help you search for specific pages on the Internet. By typing in certain key words, the site displays a list of Web pages that meet your search criteria. Some of them will even include a probability rating. The higher the number, the more likely the search engine thinks it has met your criteria. The probability number does not necessarily mean you are guaranteed to find what you want, but generally the higher the number, the more likely the site will be one that you were hoping to find.

Just as directories are different, search engines are different. Each search engine conducts its searches a different way. However, the one constant factor with the different search engines is that they are all computers—meaning that they are extremely logical and just as literal.

Because computers are so logical and literal, using them can be frustrating. I keep waiting for someone in the computer industry to invent a DWIM button (the Do What I Mean button). But until someone does perfect the DWIM button, I'm left having to conduct my searches in a logical fashion. The following figure shows Excite!, one of the Internet's many search engines you may want to visit.

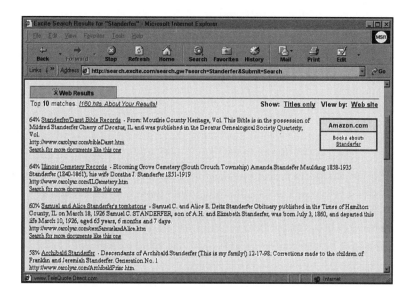

Excite is one of the search engines that you'll want to investigate.

Some of the computer logic comes from the mathematics on which they are built. When computers conduct searches, they rely on Boolean logic, named after the mathematician George Boole, to set the search criteria. These search criteria rely on three parameters:

➤ AND: Search reveals only those sites that contain *all* of the keywords.

➤ OR: Search reveals those sites that contain *any* of the keywords.

➤ NOT: Search excludes *any* sites that include those keywords.

By working with these three parameters, you can manage to narrow down your search. A friend of mine was recently teaching a class on how to search the Internet, and she offered me one of the most perfect examples of how to use these Boolean search parameters. Here's my friend's example:

An Internet researcher was looking for the surname MALLARD. Now, I am sure you can imagine what happens when he types in the word mallard *and tells a search engine to initiate a search. Yep, he discovers every site in the world ever devoted to the mallard duck. Of course, because he is interested in*

Lineage Lingo

Boolean searches are based on the mathematics of inclusion and exclusion, depending on which of the search terms (*AND, OR, NOT*) that you use.

humans with the Mallard name and not ducks, he can use the NOT command to exclude all those Web sites about Mallard ducks. By typing in "mallard NOT duck" into the search engine, he excludes all those unwanted duck sites.

While many of the search engines rely on some form of Boolean searches, many of them handle the searches differently. The following table shows you a list of some of the more popular search sites and how each one handles these Boolean search criteria.

Genie Goodies

Inclusive and exclusive can be a little confusing if you are not familiar with them. The trick is to include the terms that are important to you, and to exclude those that have nothing to do with what you are looking for. In the story above, the researcher was **including** the word MALLARD to search for his family history. However, since he found many sites devoted to a Mallard of a different kind, he also had to **exclude** sites that referenced ducks.

Search Engine Capabilities

	Alta Vista	Excite	HotBot
Default Setting	OR	OR	via menu
Exclusion	– or AND NOT	via menu	via menu
Inclusion	+ or	AND	+ via menu
Phrase	"quote marks"	via menu	via menu
Proximity	NEAR	N/A	N/A
Wildcards	* N/A	N/A	N/A

In addition to handling Boolean searches differently, each search engine handles such things as phrases and *wild cards* (the inclusion of a character to represent multiple letters) differently. Wild cards are extremely useful to genealogists. If a genealogist discovers that a name being researched is spelled in many different ways, he can use a wild card (a *) to automate his search. For example, I know that when I am researching STANDERFER, I must also keep a look out for STANDFER and STANDIFER. By using a wild card, I can tell the search engine to search for STAND*. The wild card will include all the other spellings I mentioned. Of course, it will also include some surnames that may not be related, like STANDFORD.

How you use the different search engines will depend on:

➤ What you are searching for

➤ Which of the search engines you use

➤ What requirements the search engine has for Boolean and phrase searches

Metasearch Engines

You may be thinking to yourself that there ought to be a better way of searching the Internet. Having to visit a number of different search sites and then figuring out how each search engine works is time-consuming.

Other Internet users feel the same way, so a new type of search engine is evolving, called the *metasearch engine*. With metasearch engine sites, you type in your keywords and the PC meta-searcher generates searches in a number of the different search engines that we discussed earlier in this chapter. Metasearch engines do much of the work for you, and then display the results.

When you do a search using one of the new metasearch engines, the results help to drive home the point that not all search engines are created equal. I am always amazed at the disparity in the results. Most metasearch engines, when showing the results, will also show you which of the many search engines actually found the site.

Some of the currently best-known metasearch engines are:

➤ ByteSearch.com (www.bytesearch.com/)

➤ Dogpile (www.dogpile.com)

➤ Google (www.google.com)

➤ GoPortal.Com (www.goportal.com)

➤ Highway 61 (www.highway61.com)

➤ MetaSearch (www.metasearch.com/)

➤ MyGo (www.mygo.com/)

Genealogy-Specific Searches

Wouldn't it be great to be able to search just on genealogical sites? And such search sites are now beginning to pop up. This allows you to eliminate

Heritage Hints

Whenever you are using the various search engines, you should start your search efforts with your most uncommon word first. So, searching for **Standerfer + genealogy** will result in a more concise results list than if you were to reverse the two-search line to **genealogy + Standerfer.**

Cousin Counsel

The metasearch engines are for simple searches, like searching for genealogical societies. Whenever you create complicated searches for the metasearchers to handle, some of the search sites they query will be eliminated because they cannot handle the search in the form the metasearch engine presents to the searcher.

Heritage Hints

Remember that the Internet is always changing, so sites get added to search engines continually. A search that yields negative results one week may show a couple of sites a week later, and tens of sites a couple of months later.

non-genealogy sites that get added to the list simply because something on one of the pages fits your search criteria. Genealogy-specific search sites allow you to look for only those sites that have to do with family history.

When you work with these search sites, remember to continue to search for the same information in the future. The following figure shows the Web site GenealogyPortal.com (www.genealogyportal.com), which is dedicated to the topic of genealogy.

A couple of genealogy-specific search sites are:

➤ GenealogyPortal.com (www.genealogyportal.com/)

➤ Internet FamilyFinder (www.familytreemaker.com/allsearch.html)

Search engines devoted to genealogy sites can save you time.

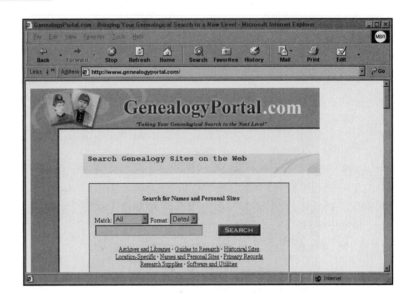

What's Really Out There?

After all our discussion about the Internet and the WWW, just what is on them to help you with your genealogical research? Can you download your entire family tree? Probably not. Can you access vital records and other information? In some instances, yes. Will you come into contact with other genealogists? Most definitely.

As you surf the World Wide Web, you'll find pages devoted to many of the records and types of information which family historians are eagerly searching, including

➤ Vital records information

➤ Census information

➤ Compiled family information

➤ Queries

➤ Biographies

➤ Land records

➤ Advice and articles from professionals

Information can vary greatly depending on who put the information online and what the person or entity has as a goal in making the information available. An individual information provider's familiarity with the Internet itself, and how much the person creating the site knows about creating Web pages will also affect how the Web page(s) looks and what data you can get from that site.

While much of the Internet is available for free, you will find that some areas are commercial. Commercial sites usually charge for you to access their compiled data. They may offer some free areas also.

Lineage Lingo

Queries can be found both offline and online. They allow you to post a question about a certain individual or line of your family tree. They are a request for assistance from your fellow researchers.

Genie Goodies

With regard to commercial sites, many people are afraid that if they do any searches or select links from a commercial site that they will be charged. Unless the site asks you for your credit card number, you can rest assured that you are not being charged for what you are doing. The commercial sites are very upfront about charging their patrons. In fact, if you do come across a subscriber site, you will generally be blocked from viewing any information that is available only for a fee unless you pay.

The vast majority of the genealogical sites found on the World Wide Web are free. Those who just wish to share information upload these sites. Some genealogists put in countless hours to design pages devoted to specific surnames or localities. These people do not see any payment for the efforts they extend on behalf of the online genealogical community. If you find one of these contributors' sites useful, take a moment to drop them an e-mail to say thank you. They will appreciate it.

Cousin Counsel

Remember when you are viewing Web sites that in most cases they are secondary sources. Someone had to sit at his or her PC and type in the information. This exposes the data to possible typos and other errors from misreading of the original data.

Beware: Addiction Imminent

When you first venture on to the Internet, you'll find it fascinating. You'll get excited about the sites you find. But somewhere after your Internet introduction, something else takes over. Each night, you find yourself searching more and staying online longer.

As you begin finding data, you will soon have sites that are your favorites. You don't think I mentioned bookmarking sites with your browser for nothing, right? You will soon have a whole list of favorite sites and bookmarks.

But, don't worry. This addiction won't hurt anyone, including you. You will be growing your family tree and learning from other genealogists, including professionals. You will be able to take pride in seeing your family history come together through your efforts and determination.

So, enjoy yourself as you begin to visit some sites in cyberland and see how these sites can help you with your genealogical research.

The Least You Need to Know

➤ You can directly search the Internet or just wander from site to site.

➤ Some Internet sites are directories of sites to help you as you get started.

➤ The Internet features different search engines, and each has its own idiosyncrasies.

➤ Some search engines search genealogy sites only.

➤ Online genealogy can be addictive.

Chapter 10

Wanted: Great-Grandma Bertha

In This Chapter

➤ How bulletin boards and newsgroups connect you with other genealogists

➤ Letting your PC search for relevant messages for you

➤ How to use "chats" to share your information with other family history lovers

➤ Learning to verify the information shared by others

Although it is tempting to want to immediately hit the various Web sites that you can find quickly, please don't overlook some of the valuable newsgroups and other message boards that aid genealogists with their research. Talking online with others who share your interest in a particular surname, locality, or ethnic group is extremely beneficial.

Learning to communicate on bulletin boards and in chat rooms is an important part of being in the online genealogists' "community." In this chapter, we'll look at how to avoid some mistakes commonly made by new online genealogists.

There are many ways to communicate online. This chapter is devoted to discussing:

➤ Bulletin boards

➤ Newsgroups

➤ Chat rooms

We will talk about mailing lists in the next chapter.

Let's Hit the Boards

Bulletin boards have been around for a long time. Most of the early commercial online services, including CompuServe and AOL, had bulletin boards. In fact, this was where most of the genealogy discussions took place. People would share their questions and information via these bulletin boards.

My first experience in online genealogy was with one of the early commercial services, Genie, back when General Electric owned it. At that time, all the Internet carried was text—there were no pretty pictures and moving graphics—it was just plain text. Also, the online genealogists of that time displayed tremendous give and take. People were always willing to help each other out.

Lineage Lingo

Bulletin boards are online message areas. The messages stay at the site where the bulletin board is located. If you want to respond to a message, you must do so online.

Today, many Internet sites offer bulletin boards for discussion of topics pertinent to that site. With genealogy sites, the bulletin boards featured may be specific to a program, or locality, or they may be more general in nature.

Bulletin boards are effective only if the messages posted are of both the asking and the answering types. As genealogists, we all have a different level of understanding and knowledge of the various aspects of family history. Through contact on the bulletin boards, we can learn from each other.

Here are just a few of the more popular Internet sites that feature genealogy-related bulletin boards:

➤ GenForum (www.genforum.familytreemaker.com)

➤ GenConnect (cgi.rootsweb.com/~genbbs/qindex.html)

➤ Irene's Genealogy Post Forum (www.thecore.com/~hand/genealogy/post/)

➤ YourFamily.com Genealogy Bulletin Board (www.yourfamily.com/bulletin.cgi)

Heritage Hints

Threaded conversations on a bulletin board indent each "response" from the original. Many times, you'll find multiple threads as someone responds to another's response. When you read threaded conversations, start at the beginning because not everyone participating in the message thread flow quotes from previous messages. This sometimes makes following the threaded messages difficult.

Bulletin boards allow people to communicate at any time. When a person discovers a bulletin board, he or she can post a message, and then, when you or I discover the bulletin board, we can read the posted messages and post our own responses. Unlike other online features, you do not need to agree to meet online at a certain time. You can just stop by, read, and respond at your leisure.

There's Thread on that Board

Many of the available bulletin boards now are *threaded*. Threading is an excellent feature because you can use it to follow a discussion from beginning to end. The figure that follows shows how a threaded message uses indents to help readers follow the online discussion.

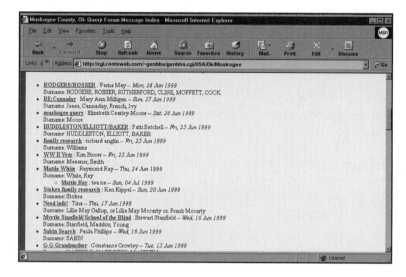

Threaded boards indent responses, making it easy to follow the discussion.

Bulletin boards are another avenue to help you reach fellow researchers. With threaded boards, you can follow a research problem from the beginning. Very often, you can find no better learning experience than watching another researcher resolve her problem. Reading suggestions from fellow researchers and seeing how they attack the problem can sometimes be more beneficial than sitting in a classroom.

Avoiding Common Board Mistakes

Of course there are some important tricks to posting messages on a bulletin board. Some have to do with the information you share and others with how you present your material.

Bulletin boards put you in touch with cousins and fellow researchers who can help learn information about another generation or two. However, if you don't post your message in a way that others can easily read, they will tend to ignore your message. So, keep these following tricks in mind:

➤ In the message's subject field, be sure to include the surname, a year, and the state, province, or country of interest.

Heritage Hints

While I have included some suggestions to help make the most of your queries, please don't think that if you do not follow all of these guidelines that your queries will be ignored. The important point is to get your information out there on the Web.

➤ Always include full names, dates, and places.

➤ Remember that in most places, counties are important because the records are kept at that governmental level.

➤ Leaving white space around your message is important. Write small, concise paragraphs.

➤ Don't ask for "everything" on a given surname.

➤ Sometimes asking for help on the locale rather than the surname will generate better responses.

➤ Always say please and thank you.

➤ Don't be afraid to say you are a beginning researcher.

➤ If you have been researching for some time, give an overview of the records you have already searched.

While you were reading the preceding list of message-posting suggestions, you may have thought they were fairly obvious. You will be surprised to learn how many online communicators fail to follow any of the above suggestions.

Cousin Counsel

When you correspond with fellow researchers, don't be afraid to ask them for sources when they share something of which you weren't aware. They shouldn't be offended, and that very source may help you even further once you view it yourself.

If you ask people to correspond with you via e-mail, you will find that you don't get much response at all. The biggest reason is that everyone assumes that someone else has responded to you. Others think that you aren't willing to put effort into returning to the bulletin board. Genealogists don't mind sharing, but they prefer to share with someone they know is going to then help someone else in the future. So, if you ask for "everything" to be sent to you via e-mail, fellow researchers assume you aren't planning to return to that bulletin board. The genealogical online community is one based on sharing, so showing that you will reciprocate is important in establishing your credibility with these folks.

Requests for Clarification

One of the hardest things for online genealogists to grasp is that others reading their messages cannot see the records they are using. As a result, messages posted often require some form of clarification, and those who are trying to help will ask you questions.

Don't be offended. These respondents are not questioning your research or your methods. They just do not have the benefit of looking at your notes. The only way they can figure out how you have come to the conclusion you posted electronically is by asking questions about the records you have.

Genie Goodies

When writing e-mail messages, we tend to elect to keep them too short. I suspect it has something to do with the speed with which we type those messages. When we write a letter to be mailed, we take time and use descriptions and include copies of family group sheets. However, when we dash off an e-mail, that is what we do—dash off the e-mail. It is a good idea to take a deep breath and think out your e-mail before you let your fingers touch the keyboard. This way you are more likely to offer a clearer description of either your question or your research.

Sometimes asking questions can actually spark interest from another person. Remember, the more people who read the messages you're posting, the better the chance of making a connection with a cousin.

Connecting with a cousin is a very possible occurrence. For a long time, I was convinced that I was the only person in the world researching the STANDERFER line. It is my maiden name, and the only other person that I discovered was my aunt, who had already died. I assumed I was destined to find the STANDERFER family by myself. I was greatly excited when I read a message from a new member of the old Genie online service some nine years ago. He saw my messages on STANDERFERs, and we were working on the same line. Nine years later, we are still working together, but instead of just the two of us, we have grown to a group of four. I enjoy no longer being alone in researching this family line, especially after having spent much time beating my head against that brick wall.

So, whenever you are posting information and you are drawing a conclusion of any kind, try to show the readers how you got from "what you know" to "what you suspect." Mention in your messages the records in which your ancestor appears. This way, anyone reading your posted message will have better insight into your research, as well as understanding what records have led you to the conclusions you are now sharing with them.

Heritage Hints

There are many standard abbreviations such as **b.** for *born* that can help to cut down on the amount of typing and the length of your messages when you post information on bulletin boards and in other similar areas.

Newsgroups Abound

Another area in which genealogists get together in a message format is through the various genealogy newsgroups. In the online world, there are more than 30,000 newsgroups currently available. And, only a small percentage of those are devoted to genealogists. Right now, there are only about 60 newsgroups for genealogists.

Like bulletin boards, you need to electronically "visit" newsgroup areas to read the messages. And like current bulletin boards, newsgroup messages are threaded.

However, unlike bulletin boards that someone maintains on a server that anyone can access, your Internet service provider must carry newsgroups. In other words, your ISP needs to receive those newsgroups for you to read the messages. Most ISPs do carry them; however, which newsgroups your ISP carries is something to keep in mind when you compare ISPs.

Lineage Lingo

Newsgroups are electronic message areas where people "gather" to discuss a given topic. Newsgroups require a newsgroup reader to view and respond to the messages. Both Internet Explorer and Netscape Navigator have these newsgroup readers built into them.

Another way that the newsgroups differ from bulletin boards is in their format. Bulletin boards rely on HTML, the language used to create Web pages. Newsgroups, however, are more closely related to e-mail messages in both substance and form.

Additionally, you can very often download newsgroup contents and read the messages offline. By reading offline, you are able to spend more time reading the messages, and concentrate more on what the messages say or ask. You can also better frame your own thoughts before you post your messages to newsgroups. That way you can reread your message, making sure that your intent is clear. The following figure shows a Newsgroup reader.

Newsgroups are another way to correspond with genealogists.

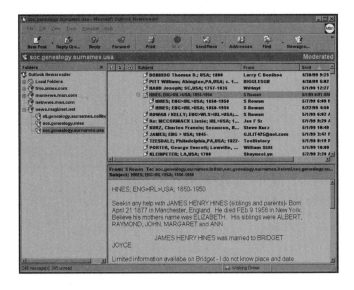

Cutting Through the Static

Because there are so many ways for genealogists to contact each other, researchers sometimes feel overwhelmed at the amount of message traffic. Even with the narrowest of topics, you'll still have to read some messages that don't apply to your research, or that don't interest you. I do have some suggestions on how to minimize these problems, though.

Searching Your E-mail

With most all of the currently available e-mail programs, you can search your messages in various folders. The most popular versions of e-mail readers all support this feature, including:

➤ Microsoft Outlook

➤ Microsoft Outlook Express

➤ Eudora Light

➤ Eudora Pro

➤ Netscape Messenger

If you wanted to search the previous list, you would use the Find from the Edit menu. Include the word for which you want to look, and scan the messages you've received.

With some of these e-mail programs, you can create different folders in which to file your e-mail messages based on *filters*. When your PC downloads your e-mail, the e-mail program will search for specific items or topics that you have preset, and the e-mail program will sort the mail in the folders, accordingly.

Lineage Lingo

A **filter** is a method of automatically sorting your incoming, unread e-mail into specific folders or files, based on specific criteria that you can preset with a selection of options that are part of your e-mail program.

Cousin Counsel

When you are working with filters, keep in mind what your PC is doing. PCs are very literal and will do exactly what you tell them to do. Most filters can read each part of the e-mail, so you can sort the messages by text displayed as part of the e-mail address, subject line, or something in the body of the message.

Searching the Newsgroups

When you read through your mail, you can sometimes feel that all you get is static, or unwanted messages, and with newsgroups, you often get an even higher ratio of static. This is due to the nature of the newsgroup "beast." Newsgroups bring into contact those who share an interest. However, that interest may be just broad enough that you find yourself reading a number of messages that don't apply to what interests you.

Depending on the newsgroup, the number of messages that don't interest you can be frustrating. For instance, if you read the soc.genealogy.computing newsgroup, the discussions deal with genealogy software, but the messages very often have nothing to do with the programs you use. So, how would you find the messages that pertain to yours without having to read all the others?

One way is to read the subject lines of the messages. It is hoped the message authors have put descriptive subjects for their messages. However, this still requires you to view the list of the current messages to scan the subject lines. There has to be a better way, right? After all, PCs are supposed to simplify our lives, not make them more difficult.

With newsgroups, you can have your PC search and find only those messages in which you are most likely interested. One such program is News Rover. You can even try this program before you purchase it. You can download a trial version of News Rover by visiting their Web site at (www.newsrover.com/).

Programs like News Rover are designed to search the newsgroups for terms you select. In some ways, programs like News Rover replace your newsreader, because these programs download the messages, too. The big difference with these as opposed to regular e-mail programs is that you can tailor your messages more closely to your desired subject.

Genie Goodies

If you want to search for messages online, then you will definitely want to check out deja news (www.dejanews.com). They archive many discussions from newsgroups. Archiving of the messages is the only way for those who are new to the Internet to see past discussions. Messages in newsgroups cannot remain on the newsgroup indefinitely, they scroll off when they get to be a week or a month old to make room for the newer messages.

For instance, within any genealogy newsgroup, the STANDERFER surname is rather rare, so the alt.family-names newsgroup will have many messages that won't apply to me. If I use News Rover to search the newsgroup for only those messages that include the surname STANDERFER, or whatever other surnames I specify, I will be able to view only those messages relevant to my name specifications.

Of course, you can experience a downside to excluding messages. When you set up filters and take advantage of autoscan programs, you exclude messages that might have held information for you. Even though the message may not have had anything to do with the surnames or localities on which you are concentrating, the research method mentioned in the message may have introduced you to a new resource or avenue for your own research.

Genie Goodies

Much of what genealogists get from each other is the "how-to." Although you'll discover a cousin or two online, the real benefit is the chance to read and learn from other researchers. Watching how these genealogists approach their research from the known to unknown will help you with your own research. Sometimes you don't even realize that you are learning, until months later when you apply something you learned online.

Getting Along with the Rest of the Group

For me, the major drawback to online communication is the inability to read emotions and inferences into the messages. Sometimes you just can't tell if someone is being funny or trying to offend. And when you begin to combine people from different backgrounds into faceless online communications, it's easy for people's beliefs, manners, and nationalities to clash.

One of the best ways to get along with the group is to read the messages for a few days before you jump in. This way, you can get a feel for the group as a whole. You can see if the participants like the messages to look a certain way. Does everyone put surnames in uppercase letters? Do certain people offer to do free lookups? Is the group overall friendly? You won't know these answers until you have read messages for a few days, at the very least.

Here are some thoughts on how to get along with the rest of the group:

➤ Make your first requests simple. Don't ask for the moon—only a ride to it at first.

➤ Don't get embroiled in other peoples' arguments. Disputes get settled faster without everyone joining in.

➤ If a message angers you, don't shoot off a response. Take some time to calm down.

➤ Remember the slang terms that you use may be offensive to others—especially to those from other countries. Stick with your best English, and avoid using slang terms or expressions.

Heritage Hints

When you are reading the messages posted to the newsgroup, don't just read them for content. Notice what is included in the subject lines and how the authors of the messages list their dates and names.

➤ If you do have a disagreement with someone else online, don't take the agreement public. Contact the person with whom you have the disagreement via e-mail and resolve your dispute privately.

➤ If someone "flames" you in public, just shrug it off. Chalk it up to a bad day.

Cousin Counsel

Any time you post a message in public, you take the chance that you will be misunderstood. Before you push the e-mail **send** button, reread your message. Make sure you were as concise as possible. Look for passages that could be misconstrued or misunderstood.

Unfortunately, public communication forums suffer from personality clashes and some public disagreements. After all, the newsgroups and bulletin boards bring together total strangers. Families, who have known each other forever, have disagreements all the time. It's only natural that conflicts will arise with people who know each other only through online communicate.

Someone has a bad day. That person comes home and reads the board messages or newsgroup, and his messages show his frustration with the day. Others read his posts and shoot off their own angry messages. What results is a "flame war." The disagreement will blow over, if others who are reading the heated messages don't feel compelled to take sides and feed the flames.

Joining the Party

When I try to explain an online chat room to someone who has not experienced one, I describe chat rooms as parties. When you enter the electronic chat room, many conversations are going on between the various other participants. Folks can choose to follow a single discussion or jump into each one.

Lineage Lingo

A **chat** can be equated with the party lines that were available through the telephone company. Many people have access to the conversation. In a chat room, everyone present in the room can see the messages you post.

As you are typing your message, the messages from other participants keep scrolling along. When you press your Enter key, your message is inserted into the scrolling text, so that everyone can see it.

Chat rooms bring you into contact with other genealogists. Sometimes, a chat room features a guest speaker or a theme on which to chat. Or, you can use the chat room as a way for you to get together with others who can appreciate your latest find, or commiserate with your current research problem. Sometimes, you will find someone who is familiar with a particular locality or surname, and be able to get lots of information from them.

Chat rooms differ from bulletin boards and newsgroups in that everyone has to agree to meet at a certain time.

For instance, if a chat is scheduled for 10 P.M. eastern time, those wishing to attend need to translate that time into their own time zone. The following table will help you with that task.

Time Zone	Chat Time
Greenwich mean time (England, Scotland)	3 A.M.
Atlantic time (New Brunswick, Nova Scotia)	11 P.M.
Eastern time (New York, Florida)	10 P.M.
Central time (Illinois, Tennessee)	9 P.M.
Mountain time (Utah, Colorado)	8 P.M.
Pacific time (Washington, California)	7 P.M.
Alaska time	6 P.M.
Hawaii time	5 P.M.

As you can see, getting folks together for a chat can take a little planning. And when things like daylight savings time get thrown into the mix, it can further confuse things. I have a friend who lives in a place that does not recognize daylight savings time. Therefore, when I am turning my clock forward or back an hour, he has to rethink what time the chat will be for him.

While chat rooms abound, finding those that have to do with genealogy can be a little taxing. Here is a list of some of the sites that offer chat rooms for genealogists. The following figure shows a chat room where genealogists gather.

➤ AGI Chat Room (agi.hypermart.net/ chat2.htm)

➤ The DALnet Genealogy Channels (www.geocities.com/SiliconValley/1641/ genechat.html)

➤ GenForum Chat Room (www.genforum.familytreemaker.com)

➤ Genealogy's Most Wanted Chat Page (www.citynet.net/mostwanted/prechat.htm)

➤ The International Internet Genealogical Society (www.iigs.org/)

➤ TalkSpot.com (www.talkspot.com)

Heritage Hints

Even if you arrive at a chat after it has begun, don't hesitate to enter. Usually chats carry on for an hour or longer and the door is always open.

Lineage Lingo

Real audio is a way of listening to interviews, music, and other sound from the Internet on your PC system.

Each chat room offers a little different entrance into the world of online chatting. However, TalkSpot.com has taken the chat world one step further. By marrying chat software and real audio, you get the chance to hear an interview while chatting with others listening to the same thing.

Chat rooms allow you to meet other genealogists.

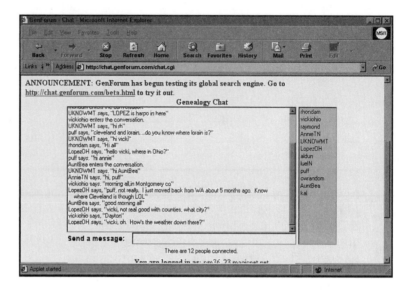

Because chatting takes place in real time, it is possible that someone you are talking to will request an e-mail address if he is going to check on something for you.

I've been attending chats for 11 years, and I have been moderating them for 10 years. This means I am there to answer people's questions and keep the room on topic. (Yep, I am still a topic witch.) Because of a chat room's fast pace, I have often not had the chance to search my resources for an answer to a person's question. When that problem occurs, I ask that person for his or her e-mail address, so that I can later e-mail the requested information.

Sometimes, a chat area will also archive chats. If you are planning to attend a chat for the first time, perhaps a specially scheduled one or one with a guest speaker, you will want to visit the chat site a day or two ahead of time. I suggest visiting the chat site because you might have to download a file or register a user name before you can become part of the chat activity. By visiting the chat site a day or two ahead of time, you won't have to rush to meet your chat appointment.

Heritage Hints

Depending on what type of browser software you use, you may have to download a **plug-in.** Plug-ins are add-on utilities that work with your browser so you can run video or audio clips or enter certain chat rooms.

Letting Your Fingers Do the Talking

I have described a few of the ways in which you can reach out and converse with other genealogists. And I have already admitted to contacting other genealogists this way for more than ten years. In fact, I probably communicate to more people online than I do face to face—certainly a greater number of different people. And, this type of communicating is a great experience.

Using What You Find

Of course, aside from creating a closer relationship with your PC, don't loose focus of the reason you are doing all this online communicating. Remember that you are trying to gain information either on your ancestors, specifically, or on records that can help you in your research. So, what should you do?

When I work with a bulletin board or a newsgroup, I print out the pertinent messages. If the message is about a specific family or ancestor, then I file it away in the appropriate family folder. If the message is about a resource that might be of use to me, then I put it in my research folder. I also make notes in my database about that resource and what I might find from that resource. If I enter information in my database, I can guarantee that I'll always have it with me, because I use a notebook PC. If I didn't have my notebook PC, then I would need to make notes on the printed message to document the surnames and families I might find from that resource.

Depending on how many different messages you post on the bulletin boards and the newsgroups, you have the potential to drown in information, leads, and potential information. Remember that you need to make goals for your online research just as you would if you physically visited a resource location, like a library. Begin your genealogical research by posting queries and messages about only a few specific family lines. Try to restrict your messages to those lines that you are currently actively researching.

Cousin Counsel

If I receive information from a fellow researcher about my ancestry, I always cite that message as my source. Then I make plans to independently verify the information.

The Least You Need to Know

➤ You have several different ways to communicate online with the genealogical community.

➤ You should check out the general feel for messages in chat areas and on bulletin boards before you post your first message.

➤ You can access message areas anytime.

➤ You usually access chat areas at preset times.

➤ You have several ways to search for messages that interest you.

➤ You should double-check any information you receive online from other sources.

Chapter 11

Worldwide Pony Express at Mach 4

In This Chapter

➤ Using mailing lists—the resource that comes to you

➤ Researching names, places, history, and other aspects

➤ Don't worry, you can always unsubscribe

➤ Creating your own mailing lists

We have already looked at some ways that you can communicate online with fellow genealogists. They all require that you go to a particular place to either find the messages or attend a chat. But we still have another, and in many ways more popular, method to get in touch with other genealogists.

It's a Small World

Mailing lists come to you, at least once you have subscribed to them. When people write to a mailing list, they use a special address to access the site. This address is actually housed on a powerful computer, known as a server. The server keeps track of everyone who has subscribed to the mailing list, and when it receives a new e-mail message for that list, it forwards it to all those people. Then, when you go to pick up your e-mail, you will find that you have messages from that list.

Nowadays, you can find thousands of mailing lists, with anywhere from a few to hundreds or thousands of people subscribed to them.

Genie Goodies

For as complete a listing as possible of genealogy mailing lists and other sites of use to genealogists on the Internet, check out *John Fuller's Genealogy Resources on the Internet* (members.aol.com/johnf14246/gen_mail.html). Please note that his address is **johnf** followed by the number **14246**.

Lineage Lingo

To **subscribe** to a mailing list means to have your e-mail address added to the list of individuals who receive any messages sent to the mailing list's main address.

Heritage Hints

When you subscribe to a mailing list, you should make sure that nothing else is included in the message, like a signature file or other additional words in the message. When you subscribe to a mailing list, a computer will be reading the message. The computer is designed to look for a certain format. If you do not follow that format, you will not be successfully subscribed to the mailing list.

For genealogists, there are mailing lists for

➤ Surnames
➤ Counties
➤ States
➤ Provinces
➤ Countries
➤ Ethnic and special interests
➤ Genealogical computing

To begin receiving a mailing list's messages, you need to *subscribe* to that list. Usually, when you find a list you are interested in subscribing to, you'll have to follow that mailing list's instructions.

Subscribing usually requires sending e-mail to a specific address with the word *subscribe* in the message's text body. If you found the mailing list at John Fuller's site, you'll see he has been very good about including the address you need to subscribe and the information you need to include in the subscription e-mail message.

Mailing lists can have just a couple of messages, or they can have 100 messages a day. So when you first discover mailing lists, don't subscribe to every one available for your surnames and localities. If you do subscribe to a number of mailing lists, you could have problems. Among them:

➤ Receiving hundreds of e-mails each day
➤ Overloading your ISP's system
➤ Filling up your mailbox

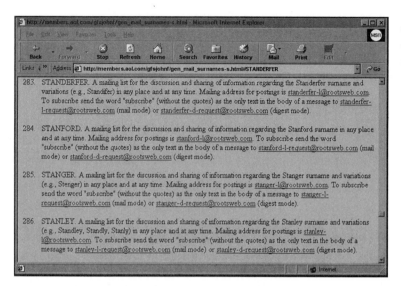

John Fuller's list is the place to start when looking for a mailing list.

If you receive hundreds of e-mails each day, you will not like trying to wade through these messages. Because you'll get so many messages, you are more likely to skim rather than read them, and you may overlook the very message that has the useful information you need.

If you overload your ISP's system, the service provider may take measures at the ISP's end. After all, the ISP needs to protect its hardware. And most ISPs usually have limitations built in regarding the number of e-mails any single subscriber can receive. If your ISP has an e-mail limit, then when you reach that limit, your ISP will respond to the mailing list that your mailbox is full. The ISP will send the message back to the mailing list owner.

Each mailing list has a moderator or list owner. The moderator's job is to make sure that the discussion remains on topic and that no one is insulting others or breaking other Net etiquette rules. This person also receives the error messages, such as the "mailbox full" ones.

When a person's e-mail address *bounces* with "mailbox full" error messages, or the e-mail server can't find the subscriber, the server housing the mailing list will track these problems. When the e-mail server reaches a specific number of problems with a specific subscriber, it automatically unsubscribes that e-mail address from the list. The list owner can also unsubscribe people, if there are other problems.

Lineage Lingo

A **bounce** is when a message does not get to its intended individual. Instead it bounces back or gets sent back to either the originator of the message, when sending personal e-mail, or to the list owner, in regards to a mailing list. A message can bounce because a mailbox is full or there was a typo in the e-mail address.

Help, I Want to Get Off

All right, so you didn't take my advice about the number of mailing lists to which you should subscribe, and now you have hundreds of e-mails flooding your mailbox each time you pick up your e-mail. You are beginning to pull out your hair, as you attempt to regain control of the e-mail monster. Well, take a big breath and begin to unsubscribe from those lists.

Cousin Counsel

When you subscribe to a mailing list, you will receive a welcome letter. Print out this letter, because it also has the directions for unsubscribing from the list. This unsubscribing information is important, so if you don't keep the letter, you'll find later that you wish you had. You will have times when you will want to unsubscribe, such as when you go on vacation.

Lineage Lingo

The **list** format of a mailing list sends each message posted to the list as a separate e-mail message. The **digest** format puts together anywhere from five to 30 messages into a single e-mail message.

When you feel a need to unsubscribe to a list, don't send that message to the list itself. You need to follow the unsubscribe directions from the welcome letter, because the address to unsubscribe is almost always different, and because that is the only way for you to unsubscribe. If you write to the list owner demanding to be unsubscribed, please keep in mind that list managers are volunteers. They agreed to monitor the mailing list because of their interest in the subject. Unfortunately, they usually have day jobs and families who insist on having a life, so it may take them a day or two to unsubscribe you.

If it becomes apparent that you need to cut back on your lists, look at each one and evaluate the information and knowledge you are getting from it. If you get one message out of 200 that is useful, then that may be a criterion for unsubscribing from that list. If you find that you are learning a lot from a list, only unsubscribe from that one as a last resort.

Don't forget you can use the features of your e-mail software to search for key words. You can always use that method as a way to scan the messages for information of interest and use to you.

If you don't really want to unsubscribe completely from the list, another option to consider is to change from the *list* to the *digest* format.

If you elect to receive the digest format, you may want to use your computer's copy-and-paste functions. You can then copy an entire week's worth of digests into a word processing document. Then use the word processing program's search function to look for the surnames and localities of interest to you.

```
Date: Tue, 13 Apr 1999 04:50:35 -0700 (PDT)
From: UFT-D-request@rootsweb.com
Subject: UFT-D Digest V99 #110
X-Loop: UFT-D@rootsweb.com
X-Mailing-List: <UFT-D@rootsweb.com> archive/volume99/110
To: UFT-D@rootsweb.com
Reply-To: UFT-L@rootsweb.com


UFT-D Digest                    Volume 99 : Issue 110

Today's Topics:
  #1 RE: [UFT-L] Upgrade to 2.8? No way   [Barbara Dooley <dooley@wcu.campusc]
  #2 RE: [UFT-L] Upgrade to 2.8? No way   [Richard Cleaveland <cleav@erols.co]
  #3 [UFT-L] Platinum Upgrade UFT        ["Alan J Goehle" <alger@ctaz.com>]
  #4 Re: [UFT-L] Platinum Upgrade UFT     [DCamp70537@aol.com]
  #5 Re: [UFT-L] Upgrade to 2.8? No way   [GGreen6859@aol.com]
  #6 Re: [UFT-L] Upgrade to 2.8? No way   [Bob Strock <bostrock@bright.net>]

Administrivia:
To unsubscribe from UFT-D, send a message to

     UFT-D-request@rootsweb.com

that contains in the body of the message the command
```

Digests show you the titles and then display the messages below.

Why Is Everyone Sending Me This?

Last year, while I was reading a message from one of the mailing lists to which I was subscribed, one person seemed to be responding to each message on the list. I felt sorry for this person, because she was growing increasingly frustrated in her responses. She didn't know the answers to the various questions, but most important, she didn't realize these messages were part of the mailing list. Finally, she e-mailed the list asking why she was receiving all these messages that she couldn't answer. I e-mailed her privately, explaining that the messages were part of the mailing list, and she was not expected to have the answers to or even respond to every message.

Because the mailing list messages do come directly to you in e-mail, it's easy to misunderstand what you are receiving. Probably the easiest way to determine if the message is to you personally or is something that was sent to the list, is to look at the message's "To:" field. If the message was sent to you personally, it will have your personal e-mail address. If the message has something like STANDERFER-L@rootsweb.com, then it is e-mail coming from the mailing list and does not necessarily require a personal response from you.

One way to help keep things clear as to what e-mail is for you personally and what is actually sent to the mailing list is to use your e-mail's filter

Heritage Hints

If you find that you need to cut back on your lists, first try going from mail mode to digest mode. This will cut down considerably on your actual e-mail. You can then scan the subject headings in the digest to see if any of the messages are of interest to you.

Heritage Hints

If you want to use a filter to corral your messages, you can select your e-mail program's "To:" field for sorting the mailing list messages. All messages from the mailing list will have the same address in the "To:" field.

Lineage Lingo

An **end-of-line ancestor** is the last individual of any of your lines that you can currently identify.

options to sort the mailing list messages into a separate folder. This way, when you go to read these e-mails, you will know that they are all from the list and do not need a personal response from you.

Remember that while you may have some input or helpful ideas to share with a mailing list, you are not expected to be able to help everyone. The point of a mailing list is to simply bring together folks with a common interest, whether it be for family interests, locality information, or information about a particular PC or genealogy program.

Sharing with Possible Online Cousins

Of course, usually the main point of joining a mailing list is to find additional information on your ancestors. We hope that we can find the names of the parents of our *end-of-line ancestor*. We hope that we can better flesh out these relatives' lives. From time to time, mailing lists will provide this type of information. But how should you correspond with someone on a mailing list who may be a cousin?

Similar to when you use newsgroups and bulletin boards, you should let others know what information you already have—especially the vital information on your research. You will want to include

➤ Names

➤ Dates

➤ Places

➤ Collateral names

➤ Your information researched

Of course, the dream is to have someone see your posting and contact you to say they have 10 generations of information for you. I just enjoy discussing the search with possible cousins. While I am thrilled if someone has information to share on generations about whom I do not know, I find that the more I've had to work to find the ancestor, the closer I feel to that person.

So, what should we do when we make personal contact with someone through a mailing list? You can continue your general research discussions via the mailing list, because you never know who else might have information to share. Remember that these mailing lists are intended for people to continue their discussions of researching a given individual or family.

However, some online communicators have a desire for a more personal bond, so these messages begin to include personal information about the message authors and their families. If the messages you receive or send begin to include personal information, you will want to take such discussions to private e-mail.

Heritage Hints

When receiving large amounts of data from a fellow researcher, don't immediately add it to your personal database. Keep the information separate until you have verified its validity. It's much easier to add the information later than it is to have to delete it.

The surname mailing lists are the ones where you are most likely to discover a cousin. After all, you will be communicating with others researching the same surname as you.

Even if you do not meet a cousin online, you can possibly find a fellow researcher with information on your family line. Often, as we research our different family lines, we make notes about and copy pages on other individuals with the same surname. We hope that the individuals will eventually fit into our family tree. However, if that information can be of help to another researcher, the information is then doubly valuable.

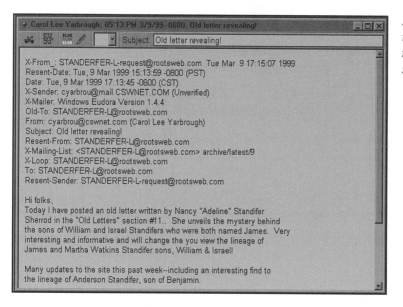

Mailing lists bring you into contact with fellow researchers who share the same interests you do.

You Got Anyone in Allegany County?

Another approach you should use in posting information to mailing lists is to focus your information exchange on the location rather than on the surname. Although our main goal is to get names for our family tree, posting questions on locality mailing lists can be very helpful.

Sometimes we get too focused on the surnames. But when you think about it, the bulk of our research is done using the records and resources of a given town, county, province, or country. To learn about the records of that locality, we should hear what others have learned and what research they've done in those areas.

Cousin Counsel

Keep in mind that just because you and a fellow researcher share the same surname, that doesn't ensure you are cousins. Right now, I've discovered three different SMITH lines that do not appear to be related to each other.

Although you will still include the names and dates for the ancestors for whom you are searching, when you post to a locality mailing list, your message should focus more on the locality. You will want to ask about records that might help you in your research.

For instance, if you don't already know, you will want to find out what vital records are available at that location. You can ask other people who are familiar with the location about the holdings of libraries or archives. By reading the messages of a mailing list, you may learn how to access the online searchable database of a library or archive.

Genie Goodies

Approaching your research from the locality will often help you break through the brick wall. To a large degree, this approach helps you to expand your tunnel vision, as you are no longer specifically concentrating on a given surname. Generally, the locality mailing lists have a larger number of participants than some of the surname mailing lists.

Locality-specific mailing lists can teach you about little known resources for that area. These locality-specific resources are the types of records and information that don't warrant space in the larger, general, genealogically-oriented, how-to volumes.

Locality mailing lists offer the major benefit of connecting you directly with the people who live in that area. Local people are often willing to do simple lookups for you in their local records. Usually all the local people will ask in return is to offset any direct costs they may have, like photocopy or parking lot expenses. Oftentimes, many locals won't even ask reimbursement for those expenses.

You have two ways in which to ask your questions on the locality mailing lists. You can stick to the standard questions of names, dates, and places. This query is the same one that you would use for a surname mailing list. However, you can also phrase your question or comments to ask about the specific records for the locality. So, instead of phrasing your message to include significant information regarding your ancestor, you should put more emphasis on either the types of records locally available, or the location itself. If I were new to researching Moultrie County, Illinois, I might visit the mailing list for Moultrie County to ask when that county's vital records begin. Or, I might ask about what records for Moultrie County have been microfilmed and where they are available.

Heritage Hints

Most of the time, fellow genealogists help you because they have been helped previously. When someone helps you, that person is hoping that you will help someone else later.

Help—My Software Ate My Database

Another area in which mailing lists are helpful is in regard to the genealogy software you use. Although most genealogy programs offer some form of technical support, sometimes you want to talk with others who use the program. Often with genealogy software, getting help from fellow genealogists is more helpful than any advice technical support can offer. After all, these people understand what you are trying to do with the software.

When you ask a question on one of the PC software mailing lists, most likely each answer will approach your problem from a different perspective. Additionally, all the answers will give you something to think about. Someone may even have brought up something you didn't consider. Another may have tried what you want to do and have some words of advice to help save you from despair.

Just like all the mailing lists, the ones designed for the specific genealogy software programs will bring you into contact with others with similar interests.

When posting questions on the computer program-specific mailing lists, it is a good idea to search any available archives first. Many times the question you need to ask has already been asked and answered many times before. Those subscribed to the mailing list won't usually point this out, but the best answer may be tucked away in the archive.

Cousin Counsel

In your frustration, which is often the result of fearing you have lost all your valuable data, don't type your note for help in haste. If you do not make yourself clear, people will not be able to help you.

Those reading the mailing lists will be more than happy to help you, but it is possible that the person who has the best answer to your question has just logged off for a two-week family vacation.

Jumping in with Both Feet

Okay, so just where do you find all these great mailing lists? And what do you do if you don't find a mailing list for your own surname, locality, or other genealogy interest?

Finding the Lists

First, finding the lists is kind of easy. There are a few places to check:

➤ RootsWeb.com, Inc. (www.rootsweb.com)

➤ John Fuller's Internet Resources (members.aol.com/ johnf14246/gen_mail.html)

➤ ONElist (www.onelist.com/)

➤ Listserv.Northwest.com General List Page (listserv.northwest.com/~haight/ generalpage.shtml)

RootsWeb.com, Inc. is actually a server of mailing lists. This service offers more than 6,000 genealogical lists, all in one place. You can subscribe to one or more of these lists. If you want to request a list, though, only contributors to RootsWeb can do so. RootsWeb works on contributions, much like public radio.

John Fuller's Page works hard to compile a list of all the known genealogy mailing lists. And his list is set up to include the steps for subscribing.

ONElist is another server that offers mailing lists on many different subjects, including the chance for you to create mailing lists for genealogical purposes. This service offers its mailing list for free.

Listserv.Northwest.com's General List Page has links to pages for states, countries, counties, and surnames. From these pages, you can locate mailing lists of interest to you.

Cousin Counsel

When you ask for help or guidance on a mailing list devoted to a given genealogy program, you will want to be sure to include the version number of your program. Different versions have different capabilities.

Heritage Hints

Another place that includes a listing of some mailing lists is Cyndi's List (www.cyndislist.com).

Heritage Hints

RootsWeb.com, Inc., is a major supporter of the free flow of genealogical information. They house some 6,000 mailing lists devoted to different aspects of genealogy. Contributors, those who have given a donation of funds to RootsWeb.com, get additional perks, including being able to request the creation of mailing lists.

Creating New Lists

Once in a while, you might not be able to find a mailing list that fits one of your interests. This problem occurs more commonly with some less common surnames. Earlier this year, I set up a mailing list for my STANDERFER line. This is my maiden name and one that I spend a lot of time researching. And, as I mentioned elsewhere, my mailing list has gathered a major crowd of researchers—about six of us. Even with six participants, I requested the mailing list for the name.

What does it mean to request a mailing list? And what happens after it is created?

Genie Goodies

Mailing lists are housed on powerful computers, known as servers. These are generally not a personal computer such as you and I have in our home. When you want to have a new mailing list created, you generally need to contact the owners of the server where your mailing list will be housed. You can usually request the name of the mailing list, but the creation of the list is done by the owners of the server. They then contact you with information about your list, including some directions on maintaining the list.

I requested mine from RootsWeb, and if you are a contributor, you simply submit a request. RootsWeb has a form to submit a mailing list request. Once the list is created, RootsWeb lets you know. You are now a list owner.

Being a list owner for a surname mailing list doesn't involve much work. Generally, most of your work will revolve around helping the PC novices work with the Internet. You will find that you can still devote plenty of your time to researching your family.

Lineage Lingo

A **list owner** is responsible for keeping control of the mailing list. You sometimes have to subscribe or unsubscribe people. And sometimes you have to play "topic witch" to keep things on track.

The Least You Need to Know

➤ When you subscribe to a mailing list, it automatically arrives in your e-mail.

➤ You don't need to respond to all messages you get from a mailing list.

➤ You can find mailing lists for all aspects of genealogical research.

➤ You have many different ways to find mailing lists, ranging from directories to the list servers themselves.

Chapter 12

Hunting Down Those Family Pages

> ## In This Chapter
>
> ➤ How can ya' find 'em?
>
> ➤ Is genealogy hunting like searching for a needle in a haystack?
>
> ➤ Can you use different tricks for different types of searches?
>
> ➤ How can you fine-tune your family-specific research methods?
>
> ➤ What about genealogy-only searches?

Finding family Web pages online can be like opening a buried chest and discovering the family treasure. Family Web pages come in all shapes and sizes, just like family members. Family history Web pages can include many different points of interest for us as researchers, including

➤ Family lineages

➤ Family stories

➤ Family pictures

➤ Pictures of family houses

➤ Sometimes, even pictures of tombstones

Finding Families

Of course, the first hurdle in ultimately enjoying family Web pages is in locating them. If you think about it, the Internet is somewhat like a large library. Sometimes, we can't easily find what we want. Other times, we know what we want, but we don't know the best way to find it. Yet still other times, we have only a concept of what we are hoping to find. Because of the Internet's vastness, you can easily become frustrated when you decide to search the Internet for genealogical pages. Usually, we surf online for surnames, but unfortunately, most Web pages have some sort of a name associated with them, such as the name of a president of a company, or the name of the webmaster. And these pages are not usually the ones we are looking for.

Heritage Hints

Want to know what the default Boolean search is for any search engine? A friend of mine has the perfect way to check on this. In the search field, type in **pizza genealogy** and see how many hits you receive. If it finds many, then the default search is OR.

Heritage Hints

When you know a lot about a given family, it is tempting to supply a search engine with all that you know. However, this often results in omitting the very person or information you were seeking. Start small, you can always add to the search if necessary.

A Needle in a Haystack?

As we have already discussed, when you search on the Internet, you sometimes have to do a little more than just plug in the word *genealogy*. After all, if you enter the word *genealogy* into a search engine, the search engine can easily return over one million pages as possible results. Doing searches on words like SMITH also results in the search engine responding with more pages than you could ever imagine. So, how do you find that needle of a surname in the haystack of the Internet?

How do we go about finding the right pages to go with the surname for which we are looking? It is all in how you work with the search engines. And as we discussed in earlier chapters, different search engines require different search techniques. However, you can learn some standard search techniques to take you from site to site. In fact, you can apply some of these search techniques to your general research in indexes at the library or archive, as well. Here are some techniques to try:

➤ Include places when you use a search engine

➤ Search for some given names

➤ Combine surnames

➤ Search first for the less common surnames

Search Engines for Genealogists

A good way to begin searching for family history Web pages is to start with those genealogically specific search sites. By these sites' very nature, they eliminate any sites that do not contain genealogy information. Therefore, when you enter a surname into a genealogically specific search engine, even a common surname, you have narrowed the search from, for example, 31 million pages to a more manageable 1 million pages or less.

In addition to the search engines I discussed in Chapter 9, another good genealogy-only search engine is I Found It! (www.gensource.com/ifoundit/index.htm). This is a directory of genealogy sites, with a search engine in the directory.

Genie Goodies

With the I Found It! site, the surname or other word or phrase that you enter is compared to the information about the site that the owner of the site has included. Although PC programs often compile many of the available directories, the I Found It! site allows the Web page owners to register their sites.

With the I Found It! Site, you can search personal family sites only, or search all of the site's categories. Searching this site for the surname SMITH revealed 186 sites, categorized as follows:

➤ 163 personal family history sites

➤ One surname study

➤ One associations and societies site

➤ One archives records on online cemeteries site

➤ One archives records on online church, marriage, and Bible records site

➤ Three locality-specific sites

➤ One locality-specific site: US GenWeb site

➤ One online resources: how-to guide site

➤ Two online resources: searchable database sites

➤ Two products and services sites

➤ One products and services site: magazines and newsletters

Lineage Lingo

A **genealogically specific search engine** is one that has searched out and catalogued only those sites that appear to be devoted to genealogy.

➤ One products and services site: professional researchers

➤ Five surname sites

➤ Three miscellaneous genealogy topics

Now, obviously, not all of these will be family history pages. The nice part about this site is that you have a better idea of what to expect, to a certain degree. For instance, with the previous example list, if you were to select the *Products and Services: Magazines and Newsletters* entry, the site would show you a link to "Genealogy and Local History in London," which is a journal on genealogy and local history of greater London that contains extracts and transcripts. So, the information may be useful to you, but the Web page is not actually a family history Web page.

I Found It! is a directory, which means it just compiles a list of links. However, the site relies on people submitting information to be included in the directory. The bonus here is that when you do your search, this search engine compares your topic to what the owners of the various Web sites say about their sites. The downside to this setup is that what the owner includes may not be all-encompassing. So the site may have information of use to you, but you wouldn't find it from your search. In all fairness, though, this problem can also happen with other search engines. So, what else can you do? This problem is one of the biggest reasons that we should always rely on multiple search engines. The metasearch engines can help you to do multiple searches with a single button click. However, most of these engines don't include any genealogically specific directories.

Cousin Counsel

Don't ignore sites just because they do not appear to be sites devoted to the history of a specific family. If you do this, you will overlook useful information about records, localities, and methodology.

Genie Goodies

Directories of Web sites and search engines are extremely useful tools. However, just because you don't find your surname when using one of them does not mean that a site doesn't exist. Directories rely heavily on the compiler of the site to organize the many Web sites into some system, whether it be strictly alphabetical or under subjects. Search engines may search the entire site (the main page and all its sub-pages) or it may limit its search to special coding found only on the main page. This means the search engine has the potential to overlook a site that could be useful to you.

Another useful directory for those looking for family history pages is Family Tree Maker's Internet FamilyFinder (www.familytreemaker.com/ifftop.html). This search engine's benefit is twofold. First, its *spider* will only include information on genealogy sites. Second, the spider goes deeper than most other search engines to include all the pages contained in the site, not just the first couple of paragraphs. This setup means that you have a better chance of finding a page with a surname of interest to you—even if the information is not on the first page of the site.

Lineage Lingo

A **spider** is an automated, computerized search tool that reads Web page information to categorize the information into a searchable database.

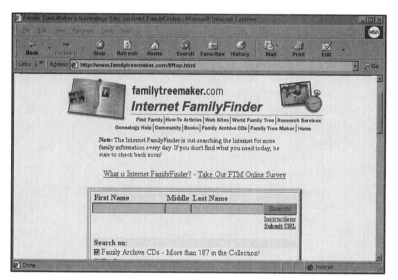

Family Tree Maker's Internet FamilyFinder searches all the pages of a site.

Looking for STANDERFERs Instead of SMITHs

I must confess that when it comes to working with any indexes, whether they are online or in the back of a book, I am a little impatient. My impatience comes from the number of book pages or the number of hits I get online when I search a common surname. I usually do not have enough time to devote to checking out all the pages of the book or to visiting the 2000 Web pages that were found with the Internet search. Right now, I have two BAILEY lines, two DAVIS lines, two JOHNSON lines, and three SMITH lines hanging on my family tree; and I descend three times from the immigrant WEBSTER ancestor. So, when I hit the indexes, sometimes my impatience gets the best of me.

But you can get around this problem if your SMITHs and DAVIS folks were kind to you and married someone with a surname like TOOTHAKER or SICKAFUS. And yes, those are also names on my family tree. One of the first tricks to narrowing a search is to type in the less common surnames that connect to your family tree.

151

For every item of good there has to be an item of bad, right? Well, the downside to searching on the uncommon surnames is that sometimes you can overlook information that is readily available. The Web page creator didn't know the name of the spouse (in single-family units with more than one marriage, or step-families) that you know is hooked to ancestors on that Web site. Remember that just because you know something about a given ancestor does not mean that everyone else knows it. You may know that John SMITH's second wife was Ursula TOOTHAKER. Unfortunately the compiler of a family history site devoted to John SMITH doesn't know that yet. If you search on TOOTHAKER, you will not discover their site about John SMITH.

Perhaps you wonder how this situation could be plausible? For many years I didn't think about first or second spouses in single-family units where there was more than one marriage. Then, I experienced a problem when I was researching my HERENDEEN surname. The name is uncommon, but I was having a difficult time finding information on it. To add to my "fun," this occurred before the advent of the Internet, though I was online at the time. Through a friend, I discovered someone researching this surname, and contacted her. The woman had extensive information on the HERENDEEN families. She kindly searched through her information, and when I compared her research with mine, I was certain that my Nathan belonged to a particular branch from New York. The problem was that the woman with the HERENDEEN information had only the name of a second wife and no names of any children. On the other hand, I had a list of children and the name of a first wife. Making a connection between her information and mine took some effort and sheer luck.

So, if you find nothing on your ancestors by using the uncommon name angle, you may have to bite the bullet and go on searching on the common SMITH surname. When you are researching extremely common names like SMITH, you'll first want to work with the genealogically specific sites, and be sure to combine given names with the surnames when you search.

Heritage Hints

In general, when searching not necessarily for family history pages only, and you don't have uncommon surnames, try searching on neighbors' names. If one of the neighbors has an unusual name, try plugging that one in to see what you come up with.

Cousin Counsel

Assuming anything in genealogy is generally going to cause you trouble. However, don't assume that everyone knows everything you do about any individual on your family tree. If a search using other surnames comes up empty-handed, see if a sibling's name is less common. Perhaps John SMITH has a sister named Temperance or Philadelphia that you can search for.

Genie Goodies

Boolean searches really can help you with your research. When a search engine defaults to an OR option, if you put Philadelphia SMITH in the search engine, you are telling it to look for ALL pages that contain either the word *Phildelphia* OR the word *SMITH*. This is not the same as an AND search. With an AND search, you are telling the search engine to show you only those pages that include both the word *Philadelphia* AND the word *SMITH*. The difference in hits between the two searches is dramatic.

Remember to pay attention to the search engine's default settings. Those old Boolean search settings greatly affect your search results. If the searcher's Boolean default option is OR, then you can include as many terms as you like in your search (surname, given name, and so on) limiting your search by stringing lots of terms together as you would with search engines that do not have OR as their default Boolean search option. With those defaults, you have to physically type in the AND Boolean search term. Then the search engine finds only those Web pages that contain both terms.

When you are searching common surnames, another way to often limit your searches is by including place names. Some of our ancestors' home locations are unique. Even when you are researching something like Allegany, the location has different spellings for the different localities. So by using the location and the surname, you have a better chance of narrowing down the number of hits on your search.

Much of my paternal lineage spent at least a little time in Moultrie County, Illinois. Usually, when I combine Moultrie with the surname, I can pare down the list of hits dramatically. And, even if I don't actually find one of my immediate ancestors, I often find tidbits of use to me with siblings, collateral lines, or just in regard to the county itself.

Cousin Counsel

When using the Family Tree Maker Internet FamilyFinder site, you will only be able to search either a surname, or a given name and surname. At press time, this site did not offer a way to refine the search other than to exclude certain items that their search engine includes, some of which are not on the Internet.

Fine-Tuning Your Family–Specific Research Methods

So, what steps would I take when trying to search for a family?

1. Search for an unusual surname, like Standerfer.

2. Search for the full name, like Thoulough Ayer.

3. Search for the location and surname, for example, Moultrie AND Davis.

Notice that when I used more than one search term, I put the uncommon term first. This way, the search engine has to find the uncommon word first, and then from those sites the searcher finds, it then narrows the list selected by the first term with the second term.

Heritage Hints

Don't limit your searches to a single search engine. While I encourage you to get really familiar with a given search engine, it is sometimes useful to conduct your searches in different search engines. The method in which they display the results generally guarantees that the list of hits will vary in some way from search engine to search engine.

Genie Goodies

Remember that computers are very literal. The computer comes to the first word in the search and goes off to search for sites that fit that word. Once it finds those, it looks at the next word, which could be OR or AND and then it knows that based on the next word it will either add additional sites or possibly remove some it already has. By putting an uncommon word as the first word the computer gets to, you limit the total number of sites the search engine is processing. This usually speeds up a search.

Getting Through the Maze

So we've now begun to do some searches. Sometimes the results can be confusing in themselves. Regardless of what search engine you use, you will be presented with a list of possible sites that it has determined fit your search terms. Some of the search engines have begun to put a percentage rating with each site they list from a search. All this tells you is that the Web search engine is 72 percent or 89 percent sure the site it has listed will be of interest to you. The percentage results are based on probability that the terms found are of interest to you, and how many times the terms were found on the given Web page. The figure below shows a HotBot search engine that lists probability ratings.

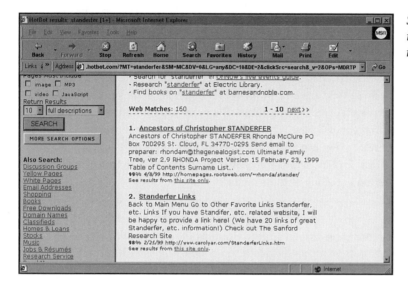

Some search engines include a probability rating.

But don't always assume that if a Web site has a lower percentage, this ensures that you are less likely to find the family information you want. I have done searches on my STANDERFER surname, and my own STANDERFER Web page has been rated by some search engines as having only a 79 percent accuracy rating.

Reality and Reliability Check

We now know some tricks to use in finding specific family history pages that might be of use in our research. But what can you expect from these pages? You should realize that the information included in any family history page is only as accurate as the researcher who put the information together in the first place. Family history Web pages are secondary sources, at best. They should be evaluated like any other secondary source, and as researchers, we need to strive to verify the accuracy of these private family Web site pages.

Heritage Hints

Search engines don't find everything. Sometimes, you will need to visit specific sites that have their own search capabilities if you want to locate your family information. For instance, if you have Eastern European families, you would want to search at the Federation of East European Family History Societies site (FEEFHS) for your Polish family.

> ## Genie Goodies
>
> Genealogists come in all shapes and sizes. You will find Web sites created by professional researchers. You will also see sites created by novices. The more you research the better you become. And it may be that you will have to reevaluate your own original research. Even the most experienced of researchers can find themselves back at the novice level when they begin researching a new locality, as there may be new record types to learn about and differences in the registration and filing of those records.

Over the last 16 years, I have been forced to reevaluate some of my own research. Also, I know many other researchers who have discovered that a line they had included in their family really wasn't theirs. We shouldn't feel shame in recognizing that we made mistakes in our research. Since we weren't there personally, we must rely on the interpretation of records at our disposal.

In many ways, my first trip to Salt Lake City was a learning experience. I got the chance to meet several people I had been conversing with online. I got to learn how to do research in this magnificent library. And I learned that everyone, even longtime researchers, can make a mistake.

> ### Lineage Lingo
>
> **Interpretation of records** refers to the inferences and assumptions we make based on the records currently available.

In one case, a friend of mine, Clare, discovered a great deal of data on a family line during her last hour at the library. This would be her only chance for at least a year to get copies of this information. Clare enlisted the aid of a number of us to create a production line of sorts. One of us fed the copy machine coin after coin. Another fed the change machine dollar after dollar. Yet another worked on the copied pages, trimming off excess paper, and Clare flipped pages as she copied the information.

We all had a good chuckle over our efficiency, and, yes, Clare did make it to the airport in time. However, about a month later Clare e-mailed us and told us she had a "genealogy for sale." All that hard work was for naught because the family in all those photocopies was not hers. Of course, to this day, we still like to remind her of it.

Just as we have learned of errors in published genealogies, researchers sometimes similarly make mistakes that no one discovers until after the Web pages appear on the

Internet. Unfortunately, in this case, by the time someone discovers the mistake, no one knows how many other researchers have copied those errors into their own databases.

Genealogists debate whether to include source citations in genealogically oriented Web pages. I confess a preference for always citing my sources. Also, whenever possible, I include them in my online pages. Some genealogists tell you that including sources gives away all your information, and that those visitors to your site will just take the information and run, never contacting you.

I suppose this accusation is true to some degree. But I believe that those Web site visitors who do take my information and run would likely do the same even if I didn't have the sources listed on my Web site. Instead of giving away all my information, I instead elect only to put a couple of generations at a time on my Web site, so that those who discover my Web pages will contact me to see what else I have to offer.

This may sound like I do not like to share. I am more than happy to share with other researchers. However, the key to this concept is *sharing*—give and take. So by limiting the number of generations I offer on my Web page at one time, I hope to hear from other researchers searching the same family.

Cousin Counsel

It is important to keep in mind that there are copyright laws to protect the works of others. Any compiled sources or published volumes, even manuscripts, may be covered by the current copyright laws.

Heritage Hints

Keeping down the proliferation of error-filed material is one reason that you must verify any information you find online, or in any secondary source, before you add it to your own database or publish it on the Web.

All Family Sites Are Not Created Equal

As you will quickly discover, the look, feel, and amount of information you find in each family history page you visit will vary. Much of this variance is directly related to which of the many available programs the creators used to build their Web pages. And, as you can probably expect, each Web page-creating program has different capabilities.

Before you buy Web page-creating software, first consider genealogy programs that have built-in Web page capabilities:

➤ Ancestral Question (www.ancquest.com/)

➤ Family Origins (www.parsonstech.com/software/fowin7.html)

➤ Family Tree Creator (www.familytreecreator.com/)

➤ Family Tree Maker (www.familytreemaker.com/)

Lineage Lingo

GEDCOM stands for **GENealogical Data COMmunication.** GEDCOM allows you to share most of your information with other genealogy programs without having to type it all in again. And now you can use this file type to create a Web page.

➤ Legacy (www.legacyfamilytree.com/)

➤ The Master Genealogist (www.whollygenes.com/)

➤ Ultimate Family Tree (www.uftree.com/)

➤ Win-Family (www.jamodat.dk/)

However, what do you do if your genealogy program doesn't have Web capabilities already built in? Before you throw your hands up in defeat and assume you must go out and purchase a Web page-creating program, I am going to let you in on a little secret. Several programs have been developed that allow you to use a *GEDCOM* file of your data to create Web pages. Also, most of the current genealogy programs can create GEDCOM files.

Genie Goodies

The domain of a URL starts after the slash marks (*//*) and ends with a two- or three-letter extension. The extensions can tell you from what country the Web page comes. Extensions such as **.com**, **.edu**, and **.net** tell you that the Web site's server is in the United States. Foreign extensions are two characters and represent the country: **uk** for the United Kingdom, **au** for Australia, **dk** for Denmark, and so on.

Not surprisingly, many of these programs include GED or GEDCOM in their name. Many are shareware programs, so you can have a chance to try the software before you buy it. The following list features programs that create GEDCOM files, along with the URLs that pertain to each of the programs:

➤ GED Browser (www.misbach.org/)

➤ GED2HTM (table.jps.net/~johns1/#gedpaf)

➤ GED2HTML (www.gendex.com/ged2html/)

➤ GED2Web (www.oramwt.demon.co.uk/GED2WEB/ged2Web.htm)

➤ GED2WWW (pw2.netcom.com/~lhoward/ged2www.html)

➤ GEDHTREE (www.users.uswest.net/~gwel/gedhtree/htm)

➤ GEDPage (www.frontiernet.net/~rjacob/gedpage.htm)

➤ HTMLGenie (www.geneaware.com/software/index.html)

➤ Indexed GEDCOm Method (www.rootsWeb.com/~gumby/igm.html)

➤ uFTi (www.ufti.demon.co.uk/homepage.htm)

➤ WebGED Progenitor (www.access.digex.net/~giammot/Webged/)

Different programs use the GEDCOM data file to create different types of Web pages. Some of these programs will create a Web page that resembles a pedigree chart. The following figure shows a Web page-displayed pedigree chart.

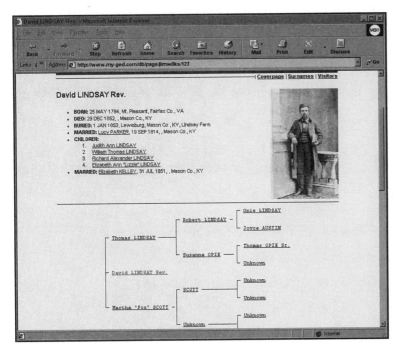

Some genealogical Web page generators display a pedigree chart.

Other types of programs create a journal-style or narrative-style report, allowing you to include more information and family stories about the people in your family tree. The following figure shows Web-based narrative-style pages that include family stories.

One final item to consider is whether the program features a graphics capability. Some will and some won't. Checking out the program's source citations are important, as we have already discussed.

Finding an online family history page is very much like locating a family history book at your library. Naturally, you will be excited about the possibilities of new information. You hope for new names. You become eager to add this information to your database. Adding the data is fine, so long as you include an extra step for checking the accuracy of the new data. Please take that extra step in confirming the accuracy of secondary sources, so that any Web page you may create will be as accurate as possible.

Narrative-style pages allow you to include family stories.

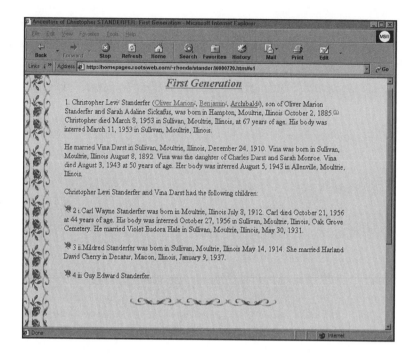

The Least You Need to Know

➤ Family Web pages hold your family's treasure.

➤ Don't limit your searches to a single search engine.

➤ Be creative with the terms you use in searching for family-specific Web pages.

➤ Individual family Web pages have a variety of looks, feels, and styles.

➤ Many, many programs are available to help you design, create, update, and post personal family Web pages.

Chapter 13

Query: I'm Looking for SMITHs

In This Chapter

➤ How your queries introduce you to the online genealogists' community

➤ Although we want everything now, we can't ask for it that way

➤ Looking for the psychic genealogist's hot line

➤ Reaping what you sow from the online experience

In the online world, the queries we post on bulletin boards, newsgroups, and mailing lists are very often our introduction to the rest of the genealogy community. And yet, somehow most of us do not make a very good first impression with these messages. The problem stems from novices not knowing what to expect. And considering that most genealogical novices are also new to the online world, this situation is totally predictable.

Never one to do things the easy way, I can still vividly remember my first online experience. Having discovered an ad in a genealogy magazine for a commercial online service, I signed on and headed for the chat room. I had no idea what to expect. As I found myself linked to a chat with about 10 other people, I began to question my good sense. From this experience, I can still remember asking my husband if the comment I had just read was directed to me. Oh my, I was as green as you can be.

But those chat room participants were very friendly and quite understanding about my plight. Although that experience was more than 11 years ago, I still remember my insecurity and being afraid I would do something wrong. I can appreciate the uncertainty and fear that Internet newcomers experience.

Genie Goodies

Many who are now beginning to use the Internet have actually been researching their family trees for many years. They may have already placed many queries in genealogical periodicals, which usually have a limit to the number of words that a query can have. So those familiar with published periodicals bring this mind-set online with them, and they limit the words in their queries. Of course, in the online world, we have more freedom for sharing what we currently know. And although you shouldn't post pages and pages, you are not limited to, say, 50 words when you post an online query.

So, let's look at some of the ways that genealogists sabotage their requests for help without even knowing it. I hope that after reading about some of the common mistakes, you will feel a little more comfortable when you post your first query.

Send Me Everything You've Got

Every time I read messages, I see one like the one you see in the following figure. People often post electronic messages that ask for others to send them everything they have on a family line.

Genie Goodies

Another reason you may never gain access to some records that others have been using for many years is record destruction. Fires and natural disasters may be the culprit, or the records may just be disintegrating from age. This is another reason to get a copy of the records when you see them originally, as you cannot guarantee you will see them again. If you cannot make a photocopy, at least transcribe the record.

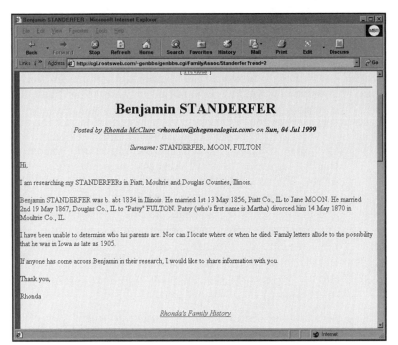

Genealogists are a very sharing group in general. We all realize that it takes the contributions of other genealogists to help us with our research. We realize that they have had access to records we may not get to see for 10 or 20 years, or perhaps never. Sometimes, the delay is because we will have to wait until our kids grow up before we can hang out for extended periods of time in county courthouses. Or, we just may not be able to afford to take the trip necessary to view the records we need. After all, seldom do we find ourselves living in the area where all our ancestors lived. And for those of us in the United States, eventually we have to go to another country to continue the search.

Sometimes, the other researcher may have approached the problem from a different angle. Some people are researching the descendants of a couple, rather than tracing the ancestors in the same manner we are. Therefore, with such an approach, they are accessing records at different times than us, and they have a different view of the family than we do.

By asking for help online, we are hoping to find a friendly genealogist willing to share some of what she has learned. This is the point: We are asking her to give us something that she has worked very hard to gather for herself.

Lineage Lingo

Ancestors are the people from whom you descend, your parents, grandparents, and great-grandparents. **Descendants** are those who descend from someone. You are the descendant of your grandparents.

If I ask to borrow a dollar, my friend is likely to loan it to me. If I ask to borrow 100 dollars, my friend is much less likely to loan me the money.

If I ask a genealogist for a copy of a death certificate or a couple of pages from a book, in most instances, the genealogist will send me the copies I requested. If I just blithely ask that genealogist to send me everything she has on a particular family line, I am sure you can guess that she is going to be less likely to do that.

Heritage Hints

Whenever you are asking for help through bulletin boards, newsgroups, or mailing lists, you will want to be sure to include words like *please* and *thank you*. Remember that you are asking people to give you help and information. We would say thank you if we saw them in person, so we should do the same through online messages. Remember to send the thank you privately.

Of course, the reason that I am researching my family tree is that I love the hunt. Yep, you now know my secret—I am a frustrated private investigator. I have the most fun when I am on the trail of an elusive ancestor, and because they are all dead, no one is shooting at me, as a private investigator might experience. So, while I do rely on help and copies from other genealogists, I don't think I would ever want someone to give me everything she has on a family line, because then I wouldn't have near as much fun with my hunt.

Another variation on the "give me everything" posts is to ask for everything to be sent by e-mail. When you make this request, you are much less likely to get any response whatsoever. Why? Because everyone assumes that someone else will respond to you. Not only do you not get any information; you don't even get acknowledged in some cases.

You don't want to give the impression that you aren't willing to work together.

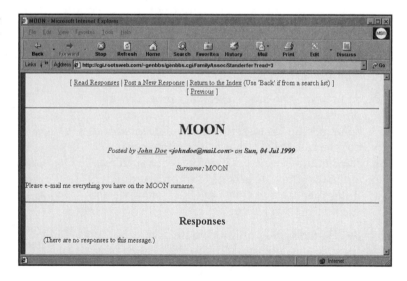

In the preceding figure, you can see the ultimate mistake resulting from this type of request. By qualifying your request with comments about being too busy to return to check for answers, you give people an indication that you may not share vital information you have that they may need.

Usually, people who post these types of messages don't realize the impression they are giving to those who read the boards.

Why Are You Asking Me This?

Over the years, I have moderated a number of online areas that offer bulletin boards and other message areas to genealogists. A moderator's job can range from just watching over things, to trying to keep the peace between participants, to recommending research options.

When I had to make suggestions, very often I realized that the original message poster had not supplied me with enough information. As a result, I was forced to ask them certain questions. Of course, the person who posted the message would come on and see that there was a response to his post. He was all excited because someone had answered him, but then he became frustrated when he realized my message asked him for additional information. His response was often something like, "Why are you asking me this?"

Perhaps the first thing I learned about genealogy is that each genealogist needs certain basic facts before anyone can offer help. The figure that follows shows an example of a less-than-complete message.

Without basic information, either your request is ignored, or the moderator is forced to ask questions to get you to provide the additional necessary details.

By supplying the pertinent data, you can avoid the crushing disappointment of seeing questions returned to you, instead of getting answers. You will want to include the following information:

➤ Full names of each person (don't forget maiden names for women)

➤ Dates of all events mentioned

➤ Full place names (many town names can be found in multiple states or countries)

➤ An overview of the records you have already used

➤ Your e-mail address

Should a moderator or someone else respond to you and ask questions, don't take offense. Asking for more information is a good thing. Take note, too, that someone is reading your message, and

Cousin Counsel

Avoid distinguishing individuals only by their relationship to you. I am 36, and if you are 60, your grandparent would have been born long before mine. In fact, with the 24-year gap between us, there is the potential for a 24-year difference in the birth of our grandparents. Record availability could be affected by this difference in years.

that person has taken the time to post a response. There is every indication that they will continue to interact with you to help with your research problem.

The give and take that goes on between you and the person asking you about your research also keeps the information flow current in the eyes of those reading the mailing list or bulletin board. The more often your surnames are seen, the more likely another researcher will take notice—and that person could just be the one with the family Bible, family letters, or diaries.

The more info you share, the better your chances of getting help.

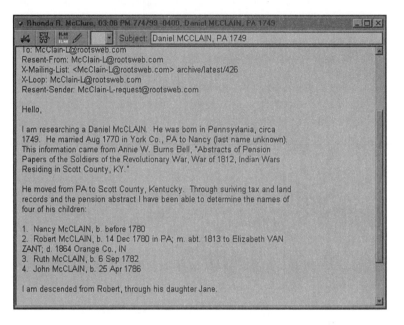

```
Rhonda R. McClure, 03:08 PM 7/4/99 -0400, Daniel MCCLAIN, PA 1749          _ □ ×
                       Subject: Daniel MCCLAIN, PA 1749
To: McClain-L@rootsweb.com
Resent-From: McClain-L@rootsweb.com
X-Mailing-List: <McClain-L@rootsweb.com> archive/latest/426
X-Loop: McClain-L@rootsweb.com
Resent-Sender: McClain-L-request@rootsweb.com

Hello,

I am researching a Daniel McCLAIN.  He was born in Pennsyvlania, circa
1749.  He married Aug 1770 in York Co., PA to Nancy (last name unknown).
This information came from Annie W. Burns Bell, "Abstracts of Pension
Papers of the Soldiers of the Revolutionary War, War of 1812, Indian Wars
Residing in Scott County, KY."

He moved from PA to Scott County, Kentucky.  Through suriving tax and land
records and the pension abstract I have been able to determine the names of
four of his children:

1.  Nancy McCLAIN, b. before 1780
2.  Robert McCLAIN, b. 14 Dec 1780 in PA; m. abt. 1813 to Elizabeth VAN
ZANT; d. 1864 Orange Co., IN
3.  Ruth McCLAIN, b. 6 Sep 1782
4.  John McCLAIN, b. 25 Apr 1786

I am descended from Robert, through his daughter Jane.
```

Heritage Hints

Family Bibles, letters, and diaries may end up in the strangest places, including garage sales. If you like to rummage at garage sales, keep a lookout for such treasures. Help save them from obscurity by picking them up. You can then mention them online and possibly find a relative to give them to.

Even if you included all the information that I suggested, other researchers may still ask questions. People reading your messages will have different knowledge and levels of experience than you. They may ask if you have tried a certain record type. If you haven't, their suggestion is great, and this exchange now becomes a learning experience for you. If you have tried their suggestions, then those reading your response will have the chance to discover a little more about your research. In this case, you may become a learning experience for someone else who is reading the messages.

The questions another researcher asks may touch on any aspect of genealogy, including:

➤ Certain record types that might help that you did not mention

➤ Additional clarification about events you already know

➤ Additional clarification about your family

➤ Clarification about the information that you posted

➤ Clarification about your knowledge of certain records

When you think about it, the ability to ask you questions about your research is a blessing. Back when we relied only on regular letters, when someone asked questions back and forth, the time interval between the asking and the answering was much longer. Today, we have this wonderful electronic ability to clarify a person's research with almost no delay, and, therefore, be of more help. All this activity occurs within the space of a day rather than a couple of weeks.

Once in a while, the message that someone posts makes no sense whatsoever. That's when we have to call in the "big guns."

Heritage Hints

Don't ever be afraid to ask questions yourself. If someone suggests a record type with which you are not familiar, or uses an acronym that you don't know, ask. With genealogy, the only stupid question is the unasked one.

Psychic Genealogist Needed

I admit that I get more mail than many genealogists, partly because most of what I do is work online. However, even when I pass through other topic areas, I have often stumbled on some messages that unfortunately made no sense whatsoever. The following figure shows an example of one of these messages.

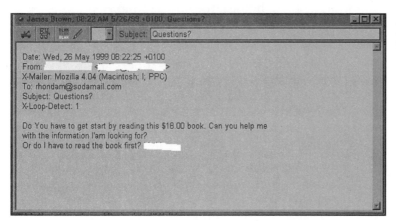

In order to get help online, your message needs to be understandable.

From the sample message, I unfortunately have no idea what the individual is asking. At the time the author wrote the message, he definitely had something important to write, but because I haven't honed my psychic skills, I can't determine what that topic was. I did contact the message sender to see what he was talking about, but in most cases, people who see these undecipherable messages just move on to the next message, not giving it the time it takes to ponder what the author meant.

While I'm tempted to chuckle over these messages, I feel kind of bad for the message creator. Because of lack of information or understanding, that person may never get any help researching his family tree.

With the Internet, people are sharing and posting messages and queries from all over the world. Oftentimes, a language barrier can be the problem with a message that makes no sense. To determine the country of origin of any message, check the e-mail address. Remember that if the domain ends in a two-character extension, it is very possible that the person is from a foreign country.

Frequently the problem arises from a lack of communication skills. People are so used to talking on a phone or face to face that they have very little skill with the written word. Most of us no longer write lengthy letters to cousins and grandparents. Nowadays, we simply call them on the phone.

Cousin Counsel

While you may find it easier not to use the Shift key to add uppercase letters or punctuation to your e-mail messages, the lack of these elements makes your messages much harder to read. Be sure to include capital letters where appropriate, and use complete sentences.

Heritage Hints

For genealogists, a good place to look for help is the Computer Interest Group of your local genealogy society. Through guest speakers and demonstrations, you can learn a lot.

But when you find yourself on the Internet, you quickly discover that the written word is everything. You can have great difficulty making yourself understood in this environment, if you are not comfortable with the written word.

Let's not forget that "mean machine"—the PC. For many genealogists, a child or grandchild has set up the PC for them. In some cases genealogists have even had to rely on the local neighborhood teen to come and help. This unfortunately means that, in these cases, the genealogist, himself, has no idea what PCs can do, short of what someone has told him.

If you are one of these unknowledgeable PC users, don't be ashamed. However, if you want to enjoy your online time and make it productive, you will want to learn about your PC and become its master. You can learn more about your PC by taking adult education classes, reading some great PC books, or just by asking questions.

Of course, to ask questions that get answers, your online messages need to make sense. Here are a few guidelines to help you, so your message won't need a psychic genealogist's intervention;

➤ Don't start your message in the subject field.

➤ Don't think about writing online. To minimize stress, think that you are writing to a dear friend.

➤ Remember that following standard rules of grammar and punctuation helps everyone who reads your message.

➤ Always reread your message before you send it. If it doesn't make sense to you, it won't make sense to anyone else.

➤ Never assume anything. Always spell out what you are thinking when you are writing the message.

➤ If you are responding to a message, you should quote the part to which you are responding.

Genie Goodies

E-mail software comes with lots of goodies, even the freebie types like the ones built into Netscape Navigator and Microsoft Internet Explorer. One option is the ability to quote the message you are responding to within the body of your reply. When you click on the Reply button, the original message appears in the new window you use to create your answer. Just remember to pare down the quoted material to only the part to which you are responding. To cut the unneeded text, use your mouse to highlight the unwanted text and then press your Delete or Backspace key.

You Reap What You Sow

I hope that you now have a better handle on how to write effective queries online. We looked at important aspects of what you should include in your messages and some of what you can expect in terms of responses from others. We also looked at flames, or online arguments, earlier in the book. So, what's next? That age-old saying—"You reap what you sow"—holds much truth in the world of online communication.

Online messages are a two-dimensional medium in which you cannot read emotions, thoughts, or inferences. Therefore, when we are writing for online purposes, we need to be concise. If we aren't concise, that's when the trouble can start.

If I post a message that reads "I need help," no one is going to help me. If I respond with what seems at a distance to be an unappreciative message to someone's offer to help, I then open myself to online flames. If I flame back, I'd best put on my asbestos suit.

On the other hand, if I ask specific questions, and thank people in advance, I am very likely to get the information I requested. If I do my best to help others, then when I ask for help, I am more apt to receive it.

The Golden Rule is very much alive and prospering in online genealogy circles. "Do unto others as you would have them do unto you." You won't be disappointed. But remember, although you may follow the Golden Rule, don't forget to live also by the rules of good grammar, good punctuation, and good forethought so you are understood in the first place.

The Least You Need to Know

➤ You are often evaluated by your queries.

➤ Don't ask for everything, including the kitchen sink.

➤ Let other researchers realize you are willing to share.

➤ Don't be afraid to ask questions.

➤ Don't be offended when others ask questions about your message.

➤ Make sure that your messages are readable and understandable.

Part 4

Diggin' Up Bones—
Online Style

Although you will still find it very important to work with records located in various libraries and courthouses, more and more, these types of records are beginning to appear online. Finding the online versions of these important records and evaluating them is the core of genealogical research whether it is online or offline.

In Part 4, I begin to show you what types of electronic records are currently appearing on the Internet, both through official sites run by state and county organizations, as well as informal ones created and maintained by private researchers and individuals. Increasingly, genealogists are looking first at the available online resources before they plan their next trips to libraries and courthouses. And once you get the hang of using the Internet and successfully finding important information electronically, you, too, will be "digging up your genealogical bones" online first.

Resources for Vital Records

We've spent some time looking at the ways you can communicate online. But now we're ready for the really fun part—searching the Web for all those great Web pages where we know we'll find great genealogy stuff. In addition to discussing family history Web pages put up by our fellow researchers and geared toward specific family research, we will discuss sites devoted just to data. And we genealogists are happiest when we get the chance to get lost in raw data.

Now obviously, not all of the Internet's one million genealogy pages are family history pages. As we will discuss in this chapter, many of the Web pages have juicy information just waiting for us to stumble upon it.

When you first begin researching your family history, you begin with yourself and you talk with other living family members. Once you complete interviewing your relatives, then you can start researching vital records. Once online, we have looked again at starting with ourselves and talking with others. Now we are going to begin to see what the Internet has to offer us with respect to vital records. In this chapter, we'll learn about other records of use to genealogists.

Births, Marriages, and Deaths

Vital records are the birth, marriage, and death records generated by civil authorities. In the United States, we call these documents vital records, but in many other countries, genealogists refer to these records as *civil registration*. Knowing this change in terminology is important if you begin to research ancestors in England or Germany. Because online search engines are very specific, you would need to use the term "civil registration" when you are searching for births, marriages, and deaths in countries like England, Scotland, Germany, and Norway.

Cousin Counsel

While vital records are traditionally viewed as a primary source, when you locate them online, they may now be secondary sources. Unless the Web page features actual certificates that someone has scanned into electronic form to make them viewable online, someone had to type in the information, which opens the data to possible mistakes. Because of this reason, these sources are now considered secondary sources.

While you cannot currently view scanned images of vital records online, you can access many useful pages that can help you learn what the vital records cover, and where they are located. You can also find information for ordering the records so you can look at them at a location convenient to you.

For a genealogist, knowing where to locate the necessary vital records is essential. It is not always as simple as contacting the state vital statistics office. In many cases, you have to access vital records in other repositories, like

➤ State archives

➤ Historical societies

➤ County courthouses

Genie Goodies

In the United States, each state began to keep vital records on a state level at different times, although most of the states began keeping them in the 1900s. However, many times you will find the counties and, in the case of New England, the towns began to record vital records much sooner. However, you won't find those earlier records at the state vital statistics office.

And with the how-to sites available online, you can visit one of the sites to find out what you can and cannot request from the state vital records office. You can find more about these by seeing Appendix A, which gives you URLs to the state resources.

Finding Vital Records at the State Level

The Internet has several valuable sites from which you can get much-needed information about ordering vital records from the states. You can find these sites according to the following list:

➤ Write for Vital Records (www.cdc.gov/nchswww/howto/w2w/w2welcom.htm)

➤ VitalCheck Network (www.vitalchek.com/index.html)

➤ Vital Records Information (vitalrec.com/)

Each of these sites offers you a little different information.

The Where to Write for Vital Records site is now housed on the National Center for Health Statistics site. The information found at this site is strictly about the records housed at the state level.

For each state, the site offers details on

➤ The certificates you can get

➤ The cost of the copies

➤ The address to which you need to write

➤ Remarks about record availability

➤ In some cases, a link to the state's department of public health or other appropriate online site

The VitalCheck Web site offers information on the states and some of the counties. For each state, the site has a form showing county, city, vital record provider, and vital records available. The vital record provider is a link to an additional page. This page includes:

Lineage Lingo

Civil registration is another name for the records of births, marriage, and death generated by civil authorities.

Heritage Hints

State vital records offices are often bound by laws that limit the accessibility of the records. Many states have a law protecting the records for 50–75 years for privacy reasons.

Cousin Counsel

While a Web site about the state vital records office may supply a phone number, you will want to be careful when calling them. For time-sensitive requests, most state vital records offices will process requests over the phone; however, they will also charge additional fees and require payment by credit card.

➤ The mailing address, phone numbers, and sometimes Web page URLs for the repository with the records

➤ A form that shows the record type, ordering methods, records description, and costs

Depending on what link you select from these Web pages, you may get a form that you can print out and mail, or instructions on how to order by phone or fax. And once in a while, you will find the capability of ordering records online, such as Illinois offers. Currently, not many of the states offer this option. The second following figure shows a form for online records ordering.

By far, the most comprehensive site for vital records is Vital Records Information—United States. This site gives you information and addresses for the state vital records offices and additional information, which may include

➤ The address, phone number, and Web link to the state archives

➤ Links to vital record order forms that you can print

➤ Links to addresses and phone numbers for the county courthouses

➤ Related links for various counties

Heritage Hints

Unfortunately, the Vital Records Information site is very limited in information on record availability for the counties. You will either need to call the counties directly, or check a book like Ancestry's *Red Book, American State, County & Town Sources* for the records' inclusive dates.

Where to Write for Vital Records is a great first step.

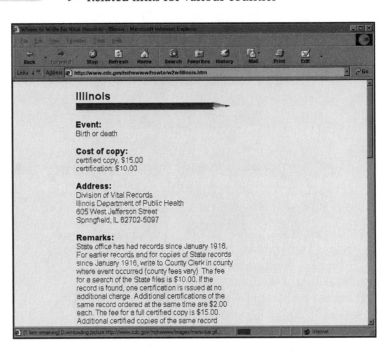

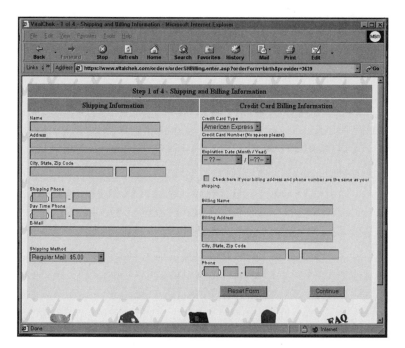

Some vital records reposi-tories are beginning to offer online ordering of vital records.

Finding Vital Records at the County Level

If you are looking for pre–twentieth-century vital records, you will usually need to find that information at the county level. Perhaps the best place for you to begin searching for this type of information in the United States is at the USGenWeb Project (www.usgenWeb.org/).

Although the information may not be posted on the county GenWeb page, you can ask others on that site what vital records are available. These researchers will know what is available on microfilm, as well as how to access the microfilms.

Transcription projects of county vital records are very prevalent on the Internet. Usually, the available information covers pockets of time ranging from 20–80 years. Each county-related site differs in feel, organization, and content. The people who are designing these sites are usually avid genealogists, but like you, they may be relatively new to the Internet.

Lineage Lingo

USGenWeb is a project supported by volunteers. There are volunteers who manage state sites and then under them are county coordinators. These county coordinators maintain Web sites with information of all kinds that is pertinent to the county in question.

Using those same search engines that we discussed in earlier chapters, you can locate county pages with vital records. You can also find some of these pages by selecting the appropriate state page at Cyndi's List (www.cyndislist.com). At Cyndi's site, you can see what links she has for your county in question.

Lineage Lingo

Transcription is the copying of a record's information, word for word.

Often, the records most genealogists seek at such sites are usually marriage or death records. And the bulk of such transcription projects appear to be from the 1800s. Depending on the Web site designer's skills, the site may have only simple text pages listing the important names, dates, and places. Other times, some sites may provide ways to do simple searches for the names, either the surname, or including the given name as well.

Vital records sites can hold the key to your ancestors.

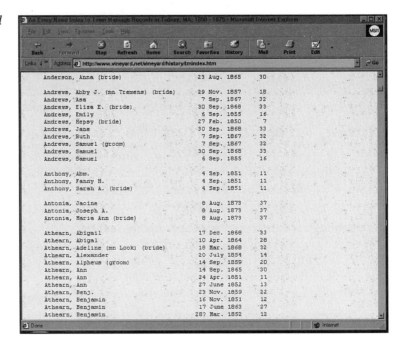

Indexes

By far, when it comes to vital records online, you will most often find indexes of some sort. Although what you find may only be indexes, they can help you to

➤ Narrow down your search

➤ Get identifying information so that you can more easily order vital records

➤ Eliminate certain localities

Genealogists love indexes. Think about it: With indexes, you don't have to go page by page through some 400 or 500 illegibly written documents. If you have to go through records page by page, the ancestor for whom you are looking won't be found until you get to the last page. Oh, and don't think that you can fool the system by starting at the end of the research documents. When you start at the end of a research document, you won't find your ancestor until you go back clear through to the beginning. It's some kind of psychic thing where our ancestors don't appear until they feel we have put enough effort into the hunt.

So, we love indexes. And online indexes are great, because we can access them anytime we want. Of course, we always stress that such searches are an absolute necessity. These online searches rate right up there with eating, and are usually higher in priority than sleeping.

Heritage Hints

When you are working with search engines built into Web pages, like those devoted to some vital records transcriptions, you will want to keep your search simple. Remember, in this instance, less is best. If your search results are too large even if you just use the surname, you can always do your search again and add the given name to limit the number of results.

Genie Goodies

Usually indexes are arranged alphabetically. When we search the index, we don't always remember to search them for all spellings of the surnames we are checking for. It is important to be sure to look for all variant spellings when working with any indexes. However, not all indexes are created equal. To test an index, open the book to a page and pick some names out of the text and footnotes, then see if they are included in the index. If they are, then the index is one of the more thorough ones. If you don't find them, then you will need to make a note on your research log that the index is limited.

At the very least, vital records' indexes will supply you with

➤ The name of the person, or persons in the case of a marriage

➤ The date of the event

➤ The locality of the event (county and sometimes town)

➤ Some identifying information (record number, page number)

Indexes of State Records

Not surprisingly, the state level doesn't offer too many indexes to records. However, I did find a few:

➤ Colorado Marriages and Divorces Search (www.quickinfo.net/madi/comadi.html)—offers a searchable index of marriages (1975–97) and divorces (1975–98) for the entire state of Colorado.

➤ Kentucky Vital Records Index (ukcc.uky.edu/~vitalrec/)—includes searchable indexes for deaths (1911–86, 1987–92), marriages (1973–93), and divorces (1973–93).

➤ Marriage History Search Form (thor.ddp.state.me.us/archives/plsql/archdev.Marriage_Archive.search_form)—allows you to search for marriages in Maine for the years 1892–1996.

➤ Ohio Death Certificate Index (dps.ohiohistory.org/dindex/search.cfm)—includes a searchable database of Ohio deaths for the years 1913–37.

➤ Western State Marriage Record Index (abish.ricks.edu/fhc/gbsearch.asp)—includes marriages for the states of Arizona, Idaho, Nevada, Oregon, and Utah for the years 1850–1951.

The Western States Marriage Record Index, shown in the following figure, gives you everything you need to get a copy of a marriage record.

The Western States Marriage Record Index gives you everything you need to get a copy of a marriage record.

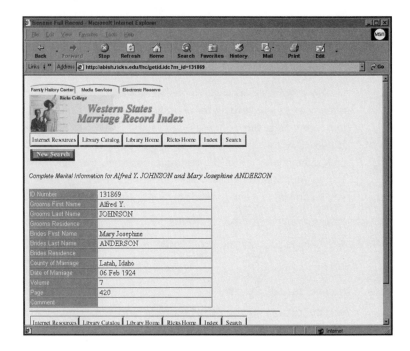

Indexes of County Records

Finding indexes of records online is similar to searching for your family Web pages. When looking for records, you're going to have to think about what you are looking for before you begin your search. Again, keep in mind that most of the vital records you will be able to find will be marriage and death records.

Select your favorite search engine and then begin entering terms for searches. You will want to include the following as possible search terms:

➤ County name

➤ Record type (marriage or death)

➤ Possibly the state's name

If you include the state's name, you will help eliminate any sites with the same county name that may be located in other states.

In addition to using search engines, you can also check out the appropriate county page from the USGenWeb site, as well as the state page on Cyndi's List, to look for additionally available indexes to town and county records.

Obituaries

Obituaries can hold a wealth of information for you about the family of the deceased individual. While obituaries are not technically vital records, they are often a great substitute when you cannot find a death record on a particular relative. And obituary information can provide you with additional birth and marriage records. In the past, locating obituaries often required visiting the local town in which your ancestor died. Once you were at the ancestor's town, you would have to thumb through the local newspapers. As an alternative, you can also write letters to the town newspaper or local library.

However, if you search for obituaries online, you just might find the very one you need. Putting obituaries online seems to be one of the most popular projects for people adding data to the online genealogical information pool.

Cousin Counsel

It can't be stressed enough. Don't stop at the index. Even if the index appears to supply you with all the information you feel you need, don't just use that as your source. When working with vital records, always request a copy of the original record.

Cousin Counsel

When you search for county records, use only the county name. To search records on Moultrie County, Illinois, I would use the search word *Moultrie.* Not all sites will include the word *county,* and if I include the word *county* in my search, I could eliminate sites of use to me.

Obituaries are likely to tell you

➤ The deceased's name

➤ The deceased's age at the time of death

➤ The deceased's birth information

➤ The deceased's parents' names

➤ The deceased's name of spouse(s) and children (including married names for daughters)

➤ The deceased's place of residence

➤ The deceased's occupation

Heritage Hints

At the present time, a large percentage of the obituaries that are available are current—deaths from within the last five years or so. However, transcription projects are beginning to bring older obituaries online.

Many of the GenWeb county pages include some obituaries. The site also encourages you to submit any obituaries you have for your family. If you want to submit an obituary, you will want to submit your information to the appropriate county's coordinator. Of some of the obituaries on the GenWeb pages, one of the aspects I like is when the county coordinator has included the name and e-mail address of the person who submitted the obituary. With this information, I can contact the submitter to see if we have a possible connection. If nothing else, that person may be able to supply me with some additional data about my ancestor.

A few sites that have compiled links specifically on obituaries are:

➤ Free Obituaries Online (www.king.igs.net/ ~bdmlhm/obit_links.html)

WWW3.SYMPATICO.CA/BKIN ObIT_L .ht ?

➤ The Obituary Links Page (www.geocities.com/ Heartland/Bluffs/7748/obit/obituary.htm)

➤ Obituary Links (www.familyworkings.com/links/ obits.htm)

Heritage Hints

A great place to start your online search for obituaries is Cyndi's List, in her Obituaries section (www.cyndislist.com/obits.htm). However, just because you don't find something listed at this Web site doesn't mean you won't find it somewhere else on the Internet. You will just have to be more creative in your searching.

Keep in mind that when you are looking for obituary sites, many of them may be too current for your interest. Some of the newspapers have begun to place their obituaries online, but these listings will be for individuals who have most recently died. Most online newspaper obituaries will generally include obituaries for only the last two to three years. The following figure shows *The Houston Morning Star* death notices for the years 1839–44.

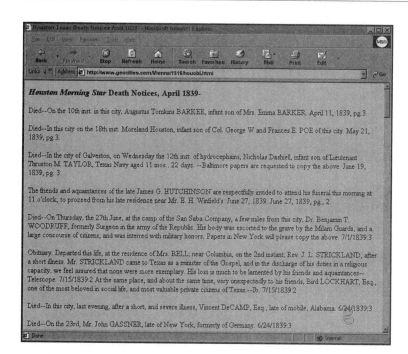

Houston Texas Death Notices April 1839 - Microsoft Internet Explorer

File Edit View Favorites Tools Help

Back   Forward   Stop   Refresh   Home   Search   Favorites   History   Mail   Print   Edit

Links Address http://www.geocities.com/Vienna/1516/houobi.html   Go

***Houston Morning Star* Death Notices, April 1839-**

Died--On the 10th inst. in this city, Augustus Tomkins BARKER, infant son of Mrs. Emma BARKER. April 11, 1839, pg. 3.

Died--In this city on the 18th inst. Moreland Houston, infant son of Col. George W and Frances E. POE of this city. May 21, 1839, pg. 3.

Died--In the city of Galveston, on Wednesday the 12th inst. of hydrocephalus, Nicholas Dashiell, infant son of Lieutenant Thruston M. TAYLOR, Texas Navy aged 11 mos., 22 days. --Baltimore papers are requested to copy the above. June 19, 1839, pg. 3.

The friends and acquaintances of the late James G. HUTCHINSON are respectfully invited to attend his funeral this morning at 11 o'clock, to proceed from his late residence near Mr. E. H. Winfield's. June 27, 1839. June 27, 1839, pg., 2.

Died--On Thursday, the 27th June, at the camp of the San Saba Company, a few miles from this city, Dr. Benjamin T. WOODRUFF, formerly Surgeon in the army of the Republic. His body was escorted to the grave by the Milam Guards, and a large concourse of citizens, and was interred with military honors. Papers in New York will please copy the above. 7/1/1839:3

Obituary. Departed this life, at the residence of Mrs. BELL, near Columbia, on the 2nd instant, Rev. J. L. STRICKLAND, after a short illness. Mr. STRICKLAND came to Texas as a minister of the Gospel, and in the discharge of his duties in a religious capacity, we feel assured that none were more exemplary. His loss is much to be lamented by his friends and acquaintances-- Telescope. 7/15/1839:2 At the same place, and about the same time, very unexpectedly to his friends, Bird LOCKHART, Esq., one of the most beloved in social life, and most valuable private citizens of Texas.--Ib. 7/15/1839:2

Died--In this city, last evening, after a short, and severe illness, Vincent DeCAMP, Esq., late of mobile, Alabama. 6/24/1839:3

Died--On the 23rd, Mr. John GASSNER, late of New York, formerly of Germany. 6/24/1839:3

Done   Internet

The Houston Morning Star *death notices cover the years 1839–1844.*

To find information on older obituaries, you will want to visit county society Web pages. Often these sites have transcriptions of older obituaries for sale. Some of these Web sites may even have a lookup service available so you can hire them to do the research for you. If you choose this option, remember to give the lookup service as many details as possible, so you won't be disappointed by receiving the wrong obituary.

Genie Goodies

A wonderful ongoing project is the Obituary Daily Times (www.rootsWeb.com/~obituary/). At press time, the Web site had a little more than three million entries in its searchable database. You can elect to receive a mailing list with 1,500–2,000 entries that the Web site sends out daily. At the same site where you can search the database, you can also click on links to select listings of online obituaries in Canada and the United States. This Web site has the added bonus of highlighting those entries that are being indexed. You can also find out what newspapers the project volunteers are currently indexing, because the project supplies only a short list of newspapers worldwide.

Some sites that include older obituaries are

➤ Ancestor Obituaries of Coshocton covers dates from mid-1800s on up (www.pe.net/~sharyn/obits.html)

➤ *Houston Morning Star* Death Notices as found on Marilyn Hoye's Home Page (www.geocities.com/Vienna/1516/index.html)

➤ OKBits 1883–1998 (www.rootsWeb.com/~okbits/howto.html)

➤ Texas Telegraph 1841–1850 as found on Marilyn Hoye's Home Page (www.geocities.com/Vienna/1516/index.html)

Don't be discouraged if the obituaries you need are not yet online. Each week, a new Web site springs up. Of course, you can always help out by volunteering to type up some of the necessary transcriptions. This is a wonderful way to become part of the genealogical online community.

Volunteer Projects

Volunteers are the backbone of the creation of most of the genealogical information you are going to discover on the Internet. Fellow genealogists with an urge to share data spend tireless hours typing information into their PCs, so then someone—maybe even them—can create Web sites to provide the information to the Internet.

Genie Goodies

Volunteers have been the backbone of genealogy since the beginning. Many of the resources we rely on every day, especially indexes of published genealogies and transcriptions of cemetery and other records, were done by volunteers. The DAR chapters around the country have devoted countless hours to gathering and disseminating information for use by genealogists.

Usually, a genealogist with an interest in a particular area will index, abstract, or transcribe Web pages that list vital records and obituaries for that area. We all owe these sharing individuals a big thanks because they have taken their time to make this important information available to others, rather than simply take the information for themselves and run.

Some time ago, I got involved in coding pages for the Internet. Few of us really understand what this process entails. You are working with raw data such as you find in original vital records and obituaries. The process is like creating a book from a blank piece of paper. Not only must you worry about the transcription of the data, but you must also keep in mind the format of the finished product.

Some of the Web sites that contain an index or transcriptions may cover only a short time span. However, when volunteers do the work, the transformation of the data into Web form moves more slowly. Some Web sites may show only the records for two years of deaths, but that Web site may contain the very clue you need.

Whenever you discover information from a records page that has been posted to the Web by a fellow researcher, take a moment to send that person an e-mail. Thank him for making your search a little easier. A thank-you can go a long way in the online world, primarily because it isn't offered nearly often enough.

Earlier in this chapter when we discussed obituaries, I mentioned a volunteer project—that of the *Obituary Daily Times*. This project's coordinators are always looking for people willing to help extract obituaries from local papers. The people involved in this project would welcome your involvement.

Although your local genealogical society is not an online source, it is another great place to find out how you might volunteer for the greater genealogical cause. Many of these societies are beginning to put their information on their own Web sites. These small societies no doubt have some ongoing projects for which they could use new volunteers.

By helping your local society, you may find valuable information on your own ancestors. But even if you don't, I guarantee you will have a feeling of satisfaction. You'll know that you helped add to the amount of data on the Internet for other genealogists.

Heritage Hints

You can always check with the USGenWeb or WorldGenWeb coordinators for your county, state, province, or county to see what volunteer projects they are currently working on. Each one of these volunteer projects always benefits from another set of hands.

I know you were expecting me to list a number of great ongoing projects, and in other chapters as we look at other record types and resources, I will mention some of those projects. But everyone who does any family history research needs to know that we—the genealogical community—need help to get all the available vital data transformed into Web-accessible form. Because the Internet links us all country-wide and world-wide with such ease, volunteering is easier than ever before. We can put the great wealth of raw data into a form that we can all share, if we all put in a little effort.

The Least You Need to Know

➤ You can use the Internet and the World Wide Web to find where you can access vital records.

➤ The Internet currently features a few searchable databases of vital records.

➤ In the online world, there is no such thing as a "little site," because even the smallest Web site can give you the information you need.

➤ Don't assume that someone else will take the time and initiative to put critical information in a form for Web site use.

➤ To truly become part of the online genealogical community, you need to make your information accessible via the Web, and you need to volunteer to help put vital information into a form usable by Web sites.

Chapter 15

Mastering Other Genealogical Resources

In This Chapter

➤ Finding census information around the world

➤ Digging deep for land records

➤ Searching cemeteries without bugs and snakes

➤ Uniting volunteers on the Web

As genealogists, we do not rely solely on vital records. If we did, our task would certainly be daunting, because vital records do not go back more than 150 years or so for some areas. Instead, genealogists use other records to aid us in our research. Some of those records include

➤ Census records

➤ Land records

➤ Cemetery records

➤ Compiled records

Fortunately for us, many of these records are being transcribed, scanned, or otherwise converted to formats that we can view and read on the Internet.

Census Online

Once you have some names, dates, and places, you should turn to checking the census records. Whenever I begin to work on a new family line, I often head to the two census years surrounding the time period that I have established for that ancestor.

Lineage Lingo

A **census** is a count taken by the government of the people living in a civil division for a given year. In the United States, we take most censuses in 10-year periods.

Heritage Hints

Even if a particular country did not begin to record census counts until after your ancestor left the area, don't overlook them. There are always relatives that remained behind. Sometimes branching out to these relatives is the only way to push a line further back.

Lineage Lingo

Soundex is an index based on the phonics of a surname rather than exact spelling. The soundex code is a four-digit code that takes the first letter of the surname followed by three numbers based on the next letters in the surname. The index comprises an entire state and will show you the entry information to locate your ancestor in the actual census.

Most countries have taken census records over the years. Learning whether the census results have survived and are now available requires a little sleuthing on your part. However, the Internet has some useful sites to point you in the right direction. Also, don't forget to check at your local Family History Center to order microfilmed copies of many of these census records.

The census records genealogists find most useful are the ones that list everyone in the household and include each person's age and birth place. Depending on what country's census records you are using, these may include other important information regarding occupations, immigration, naturalization, and military service. You can get many pieces to the puzzle of who your ancestor was from these types of census records.

Although many countries have census records, in this chapter, we'll concentrate on what is available for the following countries:

➤ United States
➤ Canada
➤ England
➤ Scotland
➤ Ireland
➤ Norway

U.S. Census Information

The United States has been recording federal censuses every 10 years since 1790. From 1790 through 1840, the census records included the name of the head of the household only. Everyone else was tallied under gender and age. The 1850 census was the first to include the names of everyone in the household. Not until 1880 did the census information record the relationships of everyone in the house to the head of the household.

The most recent census to be released in the United States is the 1920 census. This is due to the 72-year privacy act that keeps these records sealed for 72 years after it is originally taken. The 1930 census will be released in the year 2002.

Researchers have been developing indexes to the various census records for many years. About 10 years ago, we had indexes to census records from 1790–1850. Today, we have census indexes for many states through 1870. The 1880 and 1910 censuses are partially soundexed. The 1900 and 1920 censuses are completely soundexed.

The following chart includes the letters that are associated with the various codes for soundex.

Code	Letters
1	B, P, E, V
2	C, S, K, G, J, Q, X, Z
3	D, T
4	L
5	M, N
6	R
The following letters are ignored	A, E, H, I, O, U, W, Y

ROBERTSON SOUNDEX =
R163

If all this soundex stuff sounds Greek to you, not to worry. Your genealogy program may have a soundex creator built into it. And if not, some Internet sites let you plug in the surname and get the appropriate code.

➤ The National Archives Soundex Machine (www.nara.gov/genealogy/soundex/soundex.html)

➤ Surname to Soundex Code (searches.rootsWeb.com/cgi-bin/Genea/soundex.sh)

➤ Yet Another Soundex Converter (YASC) (rashoman.tjp.washington.edu/forms.soundex.formCGI.fcgi)

Genie Goodies

Indexing of the census through the soundex cards can be traced back to a Works Project Administration (WPA) project, after the Depression. In an effort to generate revenue for the failing U.S. economy of the 1930s, many such projects were created. The benefit of the soundex is that when searching the census that is soundexed, you have an index to the state for the given year. Also, because the soundex cards contain so much information, you can read through those cards and narrow your search for a family down to just a few at most.

The first step in locating an ancestor in the census is to see if there is a census index available. Indexes to the census, excluding the soundexes, have been published for many years in book format, and then on fiche and finally on CD. Now these indexes are beginning to make their appearance online.

Cousin Counsel

While soundex codes are intended to keep like sounding names under a single soundex code, this coding system works best with Anglo-Saxon surnames. Eastern European surnames sometimes have different soundex codes, depending on how you spell the name. You will want to keep this important difference in mind.

Those who order a subscription on Ancestry's database site (www.ancestry.com) have access to some of these indexes online.

One of the most interesting aspects of modern technology that we have at our fingertips is the ability to make the actual images of the census available online and on CD. This new technology allows you to view a scanned, and often enhanced, image of the page. For genealogists this is a good chance to discern previously difficult-to-read names on faded or blacked-out sections of the page. Some of the companies that are now doing this are contained in the following list. The following figure shows an example of an actual census page online. This capability illustrates today's technological power:

➤ Heritage Quest (www.heritagequest.com)
➤ Broderbund (www.genealogylibrary.com)

The chance to view an actual census page online shows the power of today's technology.

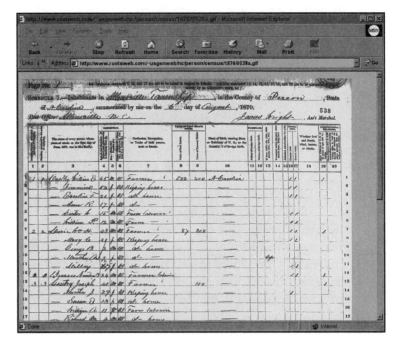

Genie Goodies

Although we are experiencing new technological advances, the implementation of these advances is not yet complete. However, you may be able to find transcriptions of the census data you need online. One active project dealing with U.S. census records is the USGenWeb Census Project (www.usgenweb.org/census/). With this project, researchers are transcribing the census records to make the transcriptions available for anyone to view online.

Canadian Census Information

Canada did not take an actual Canadian census until 1871. Although some provinces have censuses for 1851 and 1861, Canada did not do its first countrywide census until 1871. Currently, for Canada there are census records available for the years 1851, 1861, 1871, 1881, 1891, and 1901. Canada's 1901 census was not released to the public until 1993. Such limitations are intended to protect the privacy of living persons who may appear in the census.

Although Canadian census images are not available, the Internet offers some useful sites for the following provinces:

Heritage Hints

The Family History Library has microfilmed copies of the Canadian census for the years 1871, 1881, 1891, and 1901. This means you can borrow the films you may need from your local Family History Center. However, unlike the US census records, very few of these records are indexed.

➤ Alberta—index to the 1891 Dominion Census Lethbridge Sub-District (mypage.direct.ca/d/dobee/lethmain.html)

➤ British Columbia—Nominal Census Homepage with searchable database to the 1881 and 1891 Yale District (royal.okanagan.bc.ca/census/index.html)

➤ Nova Scotia—extracts from the 1901 Lunenburg County census (www.rootsWeb.com/~canns/lunenburg/1901census.html)

➤ Prince Edward Island—index to the 1891 Census (www.edu.pe.ca/paro/1891/index.asp)

➤ Quebec—French-Canadian Heads of Households in the 1871 Census for cities beginning with A–C, D–I, L–M (www.oz.net/~johnbang/genealogy/)

Finally, genealogists can get information and microfilm numbers (for both the Canadian National Archives and the Family History Library) for the 1901 Canadian census from the site at www.tbaytel.net/bmartin/census.htm.

England and Scotland Census Information

At the present time, the most recent available British census is for 1891, which was released in 1992. England has a 100-year restriction on releasing its census records.

For English ancestry researchers, an interesting census site is Strays by County Census Indexes (207.176.42.192/county/), which lists those individuals living in counties other than the counties of their births. Eventually, this site will include such *strays* for all of England, Scotland, and Wales.

You can also find census information at the Genuki Web site (www.genuki.org.uk/big/eng/census.html).

Cousin Counsel

The 1841 British census does not give accurate ages. The ages were rounded up to the next five years. So, whenever possible, you need to search a later census to get additional information on the family.

Ireland Census Information

Although Ireland has taken a census every 10 years since 1821, the country has few records to show. Those censuses taken in 1821–51 were almost completely destroyed by a fire in the Public Record Office in 1922. The 1861 and 1871 censuses were completely destroyed by a governmental order. Because ordinarily Ireland restricts its census for 100 years, the country has waived this rule for the 1901 and 1911 census records, which are already available.

County Antrim has an online searchable index for the 1851 census (www.genealogy.org/~liam/sea2.html). You can also learn more about the Irish census at the Web site Irish Ancestors; Census (www.ireland.com/ancestor/browser/records/census/index.htm).

Heritage Hints

The Public Record Office of Northern Ireland has a few census records for Northern Ireland. However, the National Archives in Dublin has all census records for Northern Ireland.

Norway Census Information

Norway took its first census by inhabitants' names in 1801. The country didn't take the next one until 1865. The 1801 Norwegian census is available online at the Web site Sources from Bergen, Norway (www.uib.no/hi/1801page.html). To read more about the Norwegian census, you will want to see Michael Drake's Getting Into the Norwegian Census, which you can find at www.isv.uit.no/seksjon/rhd/nhdc/michael02.htm.

Land Records

If you have ever looked at the deed to your house, you are probably wondering what the big deal is about land records. These days, land records are very specific with the land descriptions, but there was a time when the descriptions might have included more than a legal description of the land.

You may find any number of clues to your ancestors through the information included in land records, including these tidbits:

➤ The record may mention the wife's name, if she signed her release of dower.

➤ If the land was the first piece of property in a new area for your ancestor, the record may list where he came from.

➤ If the land was measured using metes and bounds, the description will most likely include the names of the surrounding land owners.

➤ If the land was being divided among heirs, you may find the locations of children who had moved away.

Land records come in all shapes and sizes. Each record you come upon will differ just a bit in information and organization. Some of them will be completely handwritten, while others will have a fill-in-the-blank form, with a large blank section for the description of the land.

You will find that many of the local county land records (and for parts of New England, especially the towns) have been microfilmed and are available through your local Family History Center. However, more and more indexes, and in some cases scanned images, are becoming available on the Internet. We will be able to enjoy a wonderful experience, as we search these sites for our ancestors. Even if the new information consists of just an index, and we need to order the actual land records, we will still be able to accomplish much online.

Lineage Lingo

When a woman signed a **release of dower,** she was relinquishing her one-third right to the property. Women were entitled to one-third of their husband's property at the husband's death. But if the husband wanted to sell his land, his wife had to give her consent. I have never seen a woman not agree to the release of dower.

Cousin Counsel

Don't bypass the land records. Many people skip these valuable records assuming that they don't have family relationships in them. However, I have seen children identified in the land records, as well as other relationships to neighbors. In addition, land records can help you identify when a person came to a certain location and when they left.

Some of the sites, like the Library of Virginia's, are excellent because they feature both an index and also scanned images. The following figure shows the Library of Virginia's scanned card image, which is useful to those researching Virginia ancestry.

Some of the searchable databases that are currently available on the Internet are

➤ Illinois Public Domain Land Sales offers a searchable database of the first sales of land in Illinois. Many of these are in the early 1800s. (gopher::://gopher.uic.edu/11/library/libdb/landsale)

➤ Land Office Records at the Indiana State Archives has computerized the tract books from the Ft. Wayne and LaPorte-Winamac land offices. (www.state.in.us/icpr/Webfile/land/land_off.html)

➤ Library of Virginia's Land Office Patents and Grants offers an index of surnames and then scanned images of the card index itself. (image.vtls.com/collections/LO.html)

The Library of Virginia's scanned card image is useful to those researching Virginia ancestry.

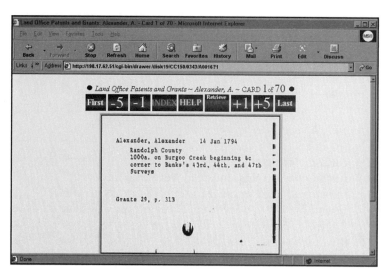

One of the most talked-about Web sites for land records is the Bureau of Land Management (www.glorecords.blm.gov/). The BLM site is home to a database of more than two million land title records for the states of

➤ Alabama	➤ Michigan
➤ Arkansas	➤ Minnesota
➤ Florida	➤ Mississippi
➤ Illinois	➤ Missouri
➤ Indiana	➤ Ohio
➤ Louisiana	➤ Wisconsin

When you first visit the BLM site, all they ask for is your zip code (for demographic purposes). You can then select the state you wish to search. The search form that appears allows you to search on a number of different aspects of the patent descrip-tion, including

➤ Document number

➤ Patentee last name

➤ Patentee first name

➤ Warrantee last name

➤ Warrantee first name

➤ County

➤ Legal land description

Once you have filled in the information you wish, there are a couple of buttons at the bottom of the form. The Genealogical Search Results button will display a list of possible patentees. You can then click on one of the names, and it will display the data for that entry, including all of the items listed in the previous list. This resource is a great one, but this site also gives you the ability to view the actual patents online, as shown in the following figure.

Heritage Hints

The searchable BLM database's records cover a time period from 1820 through 1908.

Cousin Counsel

To view the images, you need to be able to view TIFF images. If you don't have this capability, you can link from the BLM site to another site where you can download the TIFF viewer for your browser.

The icing on the cake is the ability to view the actual patents.

195

When you are working with the BLM site, you want to be sure to search for all spelling variants. The site does not assume anything when you search. It will display only those names for the information you supplied. Because you don't have to supply information for all the fields, you can locate all those of a given surname.

One of the searches I did recently was for my McCLAIN ancestors, specifically Robert McCLAIN. When I did my search for McCLAINs at the BLM site, I had to do searches on the surname spellings of: McCLAIN, McLAIN, and McLEAN before I found Robert. Of course, I now also have a number of additional names that may prove to connect to my family in one way or another.

When you view the Patent Description, you will want to pay attention to the Authority field. This field is where you will see how the land was purchased. For each of the patents that we can view online, there is a land entry case file. If the purchase was a cash entry sale, then all the file will show is a copy of the purchase receipt. However, if the authority is of military service or homestead, then you will definitely want to order the file. The file might include letters from neighbors, proof of military service, or other family records. All the information you need to order the file can be found in the Patent Description.

In many ways, land records are the forgotten cousins. People don't realize all the help they can be. You can find more information regarding land records at any one of the following sites:

Lineage Lingo

A **homestead** in land records was generally the 160 acres an individual could acquire from the United States under the Homestead Act of 1862.

➤ Land Records on the Internet (www.ultranet.com/~deeds/sites.htm)

➤ Linda Haas Davenport's Land Records: History of and How to Use Them (homepages.rootsWeb.com/~haas/landinfo.html)

Cemetery Records

One of the best things about researching cemetery records online is that you are not likely to fall into any freshly dug graves. I personally know someone who is quite happy to hear this.

I always look forward to checking out cemetery sites. Some of them offer not only transcriptions, but also images of the actual tombstones. This is particularly true for the tombstones of the famous and infamous.

Although we can now view some cemetery information online, sometimes you will still have to visit a cemetery. If you get such a chance, do not pass it up, because visiting an ancestor's final resting place has a unique aspect to it. Even when the ancestor is long since gone, and you know them only from your research, your visit to the grave site confirms the family connection.

Before you go to visit the cemetery, you may want to check out some of the Web sites on tombstone preservation and preparation. Over the years, we genealogists have taken a heavy toll on some of the tombstones with our use of harsh chemicals in our attempt to read faded inscriptions.

Here are a few sites to help get you going with your tombstone education.

➤ CGN Cemetery Do's & Don'ts (members.aol.com/ctgravenet/dosdonts.htm)

➤ How to Do Tombstone Rubbings (www.mindspring.com/~mooregen/ tombstone.htm)

➤ Finding the Hidden Treasures in Tombstone Rubbings (www.firstct.com/fc/ t_example.html)

Lineage Lingo

Inscriptions can be as simple as the individual's name and the year of death, or as elaborate as a poem or other tribute by the surviving spouse or relatives.

While not all cemeteries have had their tombstones transcribed and placed on the Internet, the Web has a great site to begin your search. The Index of United States Cemeteries (www.gac.edu/ ~kengelha/usframe.html) is seeking to list all the available online transcriptions by state and then by county. This undertaking is massive, and one that genealogists everywhere should check out.

What makes this particular site so great is that rather than recreating the wheel, Kimberly Engelhardt, the site's creator, is linking to available records. The following figure shows the Cemeteries of the United States Web page links to all known, available, transcribed cemetery sites.

Genie Goodies

The transcribing of cemetery records has long been one of the favorite projects of such organizations as the DAR. Many of the cemetery records found on microfilm through the Family History Library have been microfilmed from manuscripts created by various local DAR chapters.

The Cemeteries of the United States site links to all known available transcribed cemetery sites.

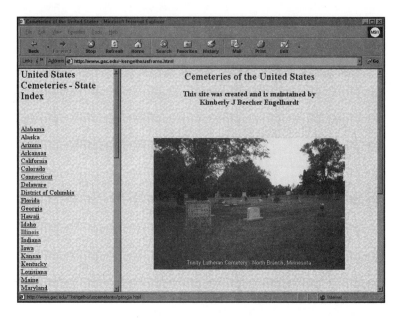

Finally, I can't leave this subject without mentioning a fascinating Web site. Although this site is not necessarily genealogical in nature, the City of the Silent (www.best.com/~gazissax/city.html) is a peaceful look at all the different aspects of cemeteries. This site has an excellent section that deals with the symbolism we find on many tombstones.

Heritage Hints

Sometimes it is necessary to locate the funeral home to try to get records on our ancestor. Now, rather than having to visit your local library or funeral home to search their national directory, you can make a stop on the Internet. Visit the FuneralNet site (www.funeralnet.com/) to search for addresses of currently operating funeral homes.

Cemeteries should be visited in person. But it is great to know that we can do our preparations online. Now we can spend all our visitation time enjoying the cemetery and the family we locate there.

USGenWeb and WorldGenWeb

As genealogists we rely heavily on the compiled works of others. Go to any genealogical library and you will find shelves and more shelves, all bursting forth with wonderful books. Almost makes me drool just thinking about it. For me there is nothing more relaxing than going to a library and getting lost in the search for an elusive ancestor.

Of course, many of the books we rely on in our local libraries were compiled by folks like you and me. The catch being that generally we had to live near each other. Now, with the Internet, we just need to have an interest in the records of a particular area to contribute to the information that is online.

The USGenWeb and WorldGenWeb projects were begun on the Internet. The goal of these projects is to make available online resources that can assist genealogists in their searches for their family heritage.

USGenWeb

The USGenWeb site (www.usgenweb.org/) began in June 1996. It blossomed out of the Kentucky Comprehensive Database Project, also known as the KyGenWeb Project. This project sought to provide a single online point for genealogists to find information on all the counties of Kentucky.

As happens with great ideas, others decided that there should be similar pages for all of the United States. From that idea, the USGenWeb Project was born.

Volunteers are the backbone of this project, with state and county coordinators. These coordinators' jobs are to design the Web sites for each state and county. The coordinators work very hard to make data available online for the rest of the genealogical world.

Most of the time when you are using the USGenWeb sites, it will be because you have headed directly to the page for the county you are researching in. However, the USGenWeb site has some great ongoing projects. Among them are

➤ Census transcriptions

➤ Tombstone transcriptions

➤ Archives of public domain records

➤ Lineage projects

➤ Kidz project with resources to help kids get started

Data on a county site can range from cemetery records to marriages to family lineage information. There are bulletin boards and other ways to communicate with fellow genealogists. And most county sites have lots of links to other great sites of interest.

Heritage Hints

When you look at the list of counties for a particular state, you may see a county that is crying out to be adopted. This means no one has volunteered as coordinator for that county. If it is a county of interest to you, you might want to find out more about being a coordinator. You don't need to live in the county to be the Web coordinator.

Cousin Counsel

Don't hesitate to volunteer with either the USGenWeb or the WorldGenWeb projects. Even if you do not know a lot about the Internet, you may have other knowledge that might be very beneficial to this group. We all so often assume that someone else will do the work, but in genealogy, we all need to share our knowledge, talents, and time.

WorldGenWeb Project

The WorldGenWeb Project (www.worldgenWeb.org) was created in 1996. Currently the world has been divided into 15 regions:

- ➤ AfricanGenWeb
- ➤ AsisGenWeb
- ➤ BalticSeaGenWeb
- ➤ CanadaGenWeb
- ➤ CaribbeanGenWeb
- ➤ CenEuroGenWeb
- ➤ CentralAmGenWeb
- ➤ EastEuropeGenWeb

- ➤ MediterraneanGenWeb
- ➤ MexicoGenWeb
- ➤ MidEastGenWeb
- ➤ PacificGenWeb
- ➤ SouthAmGenWeb
- ➤ UKGenWeb
- ➤ USGenWeb

Each of these regions is then further broken down by country, and then each country is broken down into provinces, states, or counties.

With bulletin boards and transcription projects of cemeteries and obituaries, these country pages will be of great benefit. If you are just launching out in researching a new country, be sure to start your adventure here.

The Least You Need to Know

- ➤ Transcriptions of records online are growing.
- ➤ Census records are great for finding family units.
- ➤ Searchable indexes of land records are beginning to pop up online.
- ➤ Transcribed tombstones can help you with your family tree.
- ➤ USGenWeb and WorldGenWeb sites are striving to bring records to online genealogists through volunteers.

Chapter 16

Off the Beaten Path

In This Chapter

➤ Using the National Archives records

➤ A NAIL of a different kind

➤ If Columbus had only known of these maps

➤ Where, oh where, has my little town gone?

We are always on the lookout for new and nifty resources to aid us in our research. After all, we spend a great deal of effort learning how to use vital records, census records, and even land records, although we may have previously considered land records to be a waste of time.

However, the National Archives is a wonderful repository for genealogists. Without it we wouldn't have access to the census records. But this resource has much more to offer than census records. And best of all is that some of the National Archives' holdings is making its way to the Internet.

Need Something from the National Archives?

The National Archives has long been a major repository for historical documents of the United States. In addition to the already discussed census records, this resource is responsible for the preservation and cataloging of a wide variety of records, including

➤ Passenger lists

➤ Naturalization records

➤ Military records

➤ Pension records

➤ Bounty land warrant records

➤ Records of African Americans

➤ Records of Native Americans

➤ Records of merchant seamen

➤ Records of civilian government employees

➤ Cartographic records

➤ Pictures and other historical documents

Of course, like all other records and resources that we use, we have to learn what records are available and what genealogical information you are most likely to get from them.

Genie Goodies

Genealogists live on books. There are many different books available on just about every aspect of genealogical research. So it should not be surprising to discover there are books about the National Archives. A standard for all genealogists should be the *Guide to Genealogical Research in the National Archives,* published by the National Archives Trust Fund Board in 1982. Armed with this volume, you have a jump-start to the records in the National Archives.

By the very nature of the National Archives holdings, you may be questioning what this organization could possibly put on the Internet. When genealogists want information from the National Archives, we know that we will need to use microfilms or request copies from them. In the past, if we needed to see what the Archives may have had on microfilm, we either had to have a copy of the catalog in our personal library, or we had to hope that our local genealogical library had the catalog, meaning that a researcher would have to wait to check the catalog until the next visit to the library. All this waiting was very frustrating.

Well, the patron saint of genealogists has been at work, and the National Archives has placed many of its catalogs online. Yes, you still need to order the microfilms, but you have a much better chance of getting the information you need, instead of having to go to your local library or Family History Center to find out what you want to order.

Genealogists rely heavily on the records of the National Archives, an example of which is shown in the following figure.

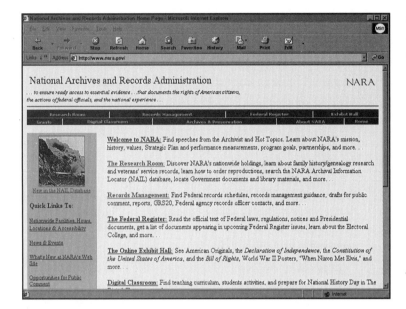

Genealogists rely heavily on the records found in the National Archives

Presently available, the National Archives Web site (www.nara.gov/) is a wonderful site for genealogists. You can find much information on the archives' holdings at this site. The National Archives has also put its various microfilm catalogs online (www.nara.gov/genealogy/#cats1). Here is a current list of the National Archives catalogs available:

➤ *Microfilm Resources for Research, A Comprehensive Catalog* (this catalog gives you insight into what record groups are available on microfilm)

➤ *Census Record catalogs* (includes catalogs for the 1790–1890 censuses, the 1900 census, the 1910 census, and the 1920 census)

➤ *Military Service Records, A Select Catalog of NARA Microfilm Publications* (includes service records, pension records, and other papers pertinent to wars from the American Revolution to World War I)

➤ *Immigrant and Passenger Arrivals, Select Catalog of NARA Microfilm Publications* (contains indexes to passenger lists from the early 1800s through 1957 for different ports)

➤ *Genealogical and Biographical Research* (a catchall of different resources useful to genealogists, including land records, bounty warrants, tax records, pardons, and more)

➤ *Federal Court Records, A Select Catalog of NARA Microfilm Publications* (includes films available on bankruptcy records, land grants, and other miscellaneous records)

➤ *American Indians* (includes lists of microfilms available on the researching of Native Americans, including census rolls, records of the Bureau of Indian Affairs, and enrollments)

➤ *Black Studies* (includes listings of records from the Freedmen's Bureau, military records, records from the Public Health Service, and more)

Heritage Hints

One of the bonuses to reading through the catalogs online is the capability of using your browser's **Find** feature (located in your browser's menu) to search the lengthy catalog pages for the state, county, town, or record of interest to you. The Find feature will only search the currently displayed pages, but this feature is a real timesaver.

In my family history research, I have often turned to a number of these catalogs. In fact, the census records alone are comprised of four catalogs. The Military Service Records catalog is almost an inch thick. Together, the catalogs take up about four inches on one of the shelves in my office. And now the National Archives have made these catalogs available for viewing and reading online for free.

In addition to being able to view the microfilm catalogs, you can now request the necessary order forms online for copies of some of the records available from the National Archives. Go to Order Forms for Military Service and Family History Records (www.nara.gov/research/ordering/ordrfrms.html) for information on how to get the necessary forms to request the type of record you wish. The following chart shows you the form number and type of records available.

Record Type	Form Number
Military service and pension records from the National Archives	NATF Form 80
Military service records from St. Louis, MO	Standard Form 180
Ship passenger arrival records	NATF Form 81
Census records	NATF Form 82
Eastern Cherokee land application records	NATF Form 83
Land entry files	NATF Form 84

Although you still have to have these forms mailed to you, you can at least send them an e-mail with your request. I received my forms within three weeks. This time span is much faster than when I used to write and request forms through snail mail.

Regardless of how you contact the National Archives, your message should include only the following:

1. Your name and postal address
2. The form number you want
3. The number of forms that you wish to request (they limit you to six forms per order)

If you wish to request these forms through e-mail, send your e-mail message to inquire@nara.gov. If you wish to mail your request, you can write them at National Archives and Records Administration, Attn: NWCTB, 700 Pennsylvania Avenue, NW, Washington, DC 20408-0001.

Cousin Counsel

While the National Archives can now handle e-mail requests for copies of the forms to be mailed to your home, please limit your e-mail request to a single form number.

I suspect you are probably wondering how the Internet is going to help you with these forms. After all, I have just told you that you have to request the forms to be snail mailed to you to get copies of military, census, passenger, and other records. We need to remember that the National Archives is practically swimming in paper, pictures, maps, recordings, and other nondigitized items. But record by record, the interesting and unique records are making their way out onto the Internet on NARA's latest Web site.

Hitting the NAIL on the Head

The National Archives has set upon a course to bring its holdings online in many different forms. And genealogists are having a great time checking out what is most currently available for us.

NAIL is the acronym for NARA Archival Information Locator. At present, the National Archives is calling this a "working prototype for a future online catalog of holdings in Washington, D.C., the regional archives, and the Presidential libraries."

NAIL is the National Archives card catalog, of sorts. It will include information on all types of holdings, including:

➤ Textual holdings
➤ Films and videos
➤ Sound recordings
➤ Still pictures
➤ Maps and charts

Lineage Lingo

Textual holdings can be letters, census pages, passenger lists, and homestead applications. Anything that has been written or typed on a piece of paper would be included in this group.

At press time, NAIL's holdings included more than 3,000 microfilm publications descriptions, more than 400,000 archival holdings descriptions, and about 124,000 digital copies. This is just a small portion of the actual resources housed in the National Archives.

Famous and Infamous at Your Fingertips

It is perhaps not too surprising that many of the currently available digitized records are for the more colorful citizens in the country's history. However, hidden in the NAIL's digitized copies are tons of photographs.

When you search NAIL, there are ways to narrow the number of hits found. However, don't always limit your searches to those records you can view online, as the descriptions of the records in their holdings are fascinating to read. Like most search engines, you type in keywords. You can then further narrow the search with

➤ Additional keywords

➤ Boolean operators

➤ Type of media

➤ NARA unit

➤ Whether digitized copies are available online

Once you have set your search criteria and asked NAIL to display the results, your real adventure begins. The following figure shows NAIL's search results chart, which is the on-ramp to the organization's holdings.

NAIL's search results chart is the on-ramp to their holdings.

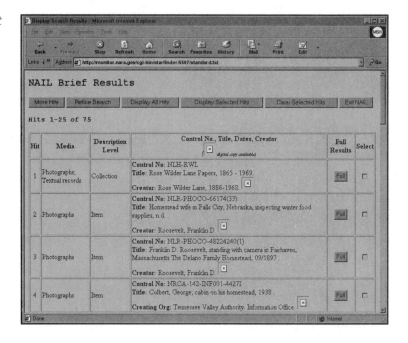

Viewing the "Full" description of one of the entries will tell you a great deal about the record, and it may have digitized images that you can view.

Each entry in NAIL includes the following information:

➤ A control number
➤ Media type
➤ A description level
➤ The collection code
➤ The title of the collection
➤ Dates (could be the time of the event or the life span of a person)
➤ Creating individual or organization
➤ Record types
➤ Scope and content
➤ General notes
➤ Finding aids
➤ Access
➤ Restrictions on use of data
➤ Contact or location

Heritage Hints

As with most search engines, you will want to play with different searches of surnames, record types, and locations. Because this is a national collection, localities and record types are likely to reveal more possible hits.

I can almost imagine you thinking, "Too much information." The reason for my preceding lengthy list is to show you how complete the listing is. Once you get familiar with this system, you can possibly search by many of these fields. This way, you can narrow down your search even further.

Genie Goodies

Photos abound in the NAIL digitized collection. There are photographs of farmers and homesteaders, and of ships and machinery. Looking through these images is like stepping back in time. And each of the photos will have details pertaining to the date and place it was taken.

Recently, I did a search on the keyword *homestead*. Although I had done a previous search on a name that revealed a homestead application, I wanted to see what other records NAIL had about homesteads. I'm glad I did this search. The photos included in the search list were amazing and included photographs from homesteads and pioneers of different time periods. I couldn't help thinking how fortunate anyone researching one of those people would be to discover these pictures.

One of the records I found when I did my homestead search was for the homestead application of Charles P. INGALLS. Many of you probably recognize this name. This is Charles INGALLS of *Little House on the Prairie* fame. Because I grew up watching the television show and reading the books, and then watched my own daughters read the books, I felt that discovering this application was like being able to touch history. The following figure shows how homestead applications can be a gold mine.

Genie Goodies

Homestead application files can supply you with significant information. In addition to the application, the file may include: certificates of publication of intent, final proof, testimonies of the claimant and two witnesses, and copies of naturalization papers (for those who were immigrants). With these records, you are likely to find names, ages, dates of residence, relationships, and proof of citizenship. You could find enough information to document two or three generations, once you get through extracting information from NAIL's pages.

Working with NAIL's holdings, you can discover a world of resources within a single source to libraries and archives around the country.

At the bottom of each Full Results Format, you will want to pay attention to the contact information. This is where you will find the original record(s). You might be able to write or telephone for copies. However, you might need to hire a professional researcher to actually go to the repository to get the copies for you. But most of your research battle has been won, because you know where the records are housed.

Many times, you can find records in one of the presidential libraries. At present there are libraries for 11 of the past presidents:

➤ George Bush (csdl.tamu.edu/bushlib)

➤ Jimmy Carter (carterlibrary.galileo.peachnet.edu/)

➤ Dwight D. Eisenhower (www.eisenhower.utexas.edu)

➤ Gerald R. Ford (www.ford.utexas.edu)

➤ Herbert Hoover (hoover.nara.gov)

➤ Lyndon B. Johnson (www.lbjlib.utexas.edu)

➤ John F. Kennedy (www.cs.umb.edu/jfklibrary/)

➤ Richard M. Nixon (sunsite.unc.edu/lia/president/nixon.html)

➤ Ronald Reagan (www.reagan.utexas.edu)

➤ Franklin D. Roosevelt (www.academic.marist.edu/fdr/)

➤ Harry S. Truman (www.trumanlibrary.org/)

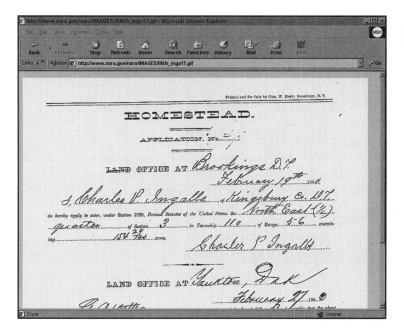

Homestead application files can be a gold mine.

Genie Goodies

In addition to the officially recognized presidential libraries, one other stands alone. The Rutherford B. Hayes Presidential Library (www.rbhayes.org/) is not a part of the national system of presidential libraries, although it was the first one created. Opened in 1916, this facility is the only one to honor a nineteenth-century president. Unlike the other presidential libraries, this one is funded by private funds, the Ohio Historical Society, and the Hayes Presidential Center. This funding excludes it from the federal presidential library system.

Few people understand what you can find in these libraries. And now with the results you can find in NAIL, as well as visiting the Web page for any given president's library, you can get an insight into what is housed in the collection.

However, even in surfing along and stumbling across the presidential libraries, I soon learned that there was one I was not aware of. I have since done a little more investigating and discovered that there are other libraries devoted to presidents and more on their way. For instance, The Illinois Historic Preservation Agency is working to open a Lincoln Presidential Library. And for those interested in the President of the U.S. Confederacy, there is also a Davis Presidential Library (beauvoir.org/).

Lineage Lingo

Presidential libraries are established to prevent the loss of papers when a president's term is finished. The records in the currently available libraries include more than 250 million pages of textual materials, 5 million photographs, 13.5 million feet of motion picture film, 68,000 hours of sound and video recordings, and 280,000 museum objects.

Reading Newspapers with Ink-Free Hands

While I can easily get lost in a newspaper story from the past, I confess that I do not like getting all that black ink all over my hands and clothes. For as long as I can remember, I have been one of those "newspaper-challenged" folks. So, I can now pleasurably indulge in newspaper reading without having to meet that challenge of folding the pages and keeping my fingers clean.

Although many online newspapers are current, many of them have sections devoted to local history and family sections. These sections may include stories of genealogical interest.

The best way to begin your search, unless you know the newspaper's name, is to check out one of these compiled sites:

Cousin Counsel

When searching for newspapers online, if you want those with genealogical information, you will not want to search on *newspaper* in a regular search engine. Such a search would reveal all the current newspapers that are online.

➤ The Ultimate Collection of News Links (pppp.net/links/news/)

➤ MEDIA-Link Newspapers (www.dds.nl/~kidon/papers.html)

➤ My Virtual Newspaper (www.refdesk.com/paper.html)

Mapping Your Course

Maps. We think of them as the ultimate manual dexterity test, as we stress over trying to get them refolded after trying to use them. And, regardless of the map, I usually get lost.

But, for genealogists, maps can paint a much better picture of the time in which your ancestor was living, regardless of the area. (I should add that I love looking at old maps.)

Today, our maps are full of highways and numbers for exit ramps. With all the satellites floating in space, we can now even use interactive maps to show us where we are and where we are going. Early maps, on the other hand, are works of art. They are beautifully designed, often with intricate pictures.

Sometimes, the maps we find will detail where everyone lived. With the right maps, I no longer need to guess how close to each other my ancestors, the HERENDEENs and my STANDERFERs, lived in town.

Maps can show you how the various boundaries between towns, counties, states, and countries have changed through the years. Many of the early states had disputes with neighboring states over where the separating boundary actually was located.

Counties also have changed dramatically. It is entirely possible for your ancestor to have lived all his life in the same house in the same town and to end with his life documented as having occurred in up to three different counties. Maps can show you how this happened.

Heritage Hints

When you are documenting places in your ancestors' lives, be sure to record the name as it was at that time. Also, don't list counties that weren't created at that time.

Probably the best book for seeing changes in the counties over the years from 1790–1920 is William Thorndale and William Dollarhide's *Map Guide to the U.S. Federal Censuses, 1790–1920,* published by Genealogical Publishing Company, 1988.

Online, we have some great sites for viewing historical maps and current maps, as well. Here is a good list to get you started.

➤ Rare Map Collection as found in the Hargrett Library of the University of Georgia (scarlett.libs.uga.edu/darchive/hargrett/maps/maps.html) offers researchers a collection of more than 160 digitized U.S. maps ranging from its first discovery to the present.

➤ The Perry-Castaneda Library Map Collection of the University of Texas (www.lib.utexas.edu/Libs/PCL/Map_collection/Map_collection.html) includes more than 700 digitized maps for just the United States. They also have maps from around the world. Their digitized collection is quite impressive.

Finally, if you don't have the census map book I mentioned, you may want to check out Historical County Lines (www.geocities.com/Heartland/2297/maps.htm). This Web site lets you see changes in the boundaries for the different states in the United States. The following figure shows how maps can give you some insight into the past.

Maps give you a peek into the past.

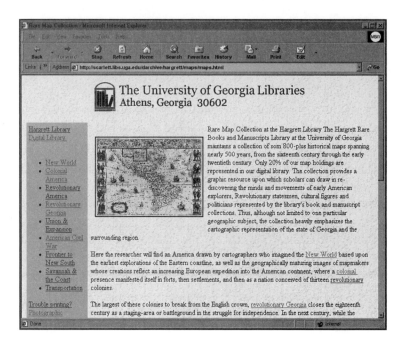

Genie Goodies

There are many different maps, each serving its own purpose. There are surveyors' maps, plat maps, and topographical maps, just to name a few. It is the plat maps that will show you the owners of land in a given town or county. Sometimes a plat map is the best way to see how the land that your ancestors owned interacted with others in the community.

Where Are They, Geographically?

One of my pet peeves is to receive family information that includes just the town and state, or the town and province. Without a county for reference, I must search for that county's name. And, as I previously mentioned, because county lines often change throughout the years, I then need to verify whether the county name I now have was the county name at the time of the family history event.

While larger cities aren't a problem, as any map or atlas is likely to show it, my ancestors didn't tend to live in those large cities. My ancestors were the farmers who felt compelled to move out into the vast expanses and build their own little communities.

Of course, because my relatives lived in rural environments, I don't suffer too much searching a census line-by-line. I guess I should be thankful about where my ancestors located, after all.

But, what can you do when you have a place name but can't locate it on any map? Gazetteers are the answer.

Genealogical publishers often reprint Gazetteers. Reprinted ones are the most beneficial, because the originals can sometimes be 100 or 200 years old. With this time frame, towns have come and gone, and many may no longer exist.

Lineage Lingo

A **gazetteer** is like a dictionary for places. Instead of having definitions like a dictionary, a gazetteer gives you details about the place, including its county.

Genie Goodies

Many of the records that genealogists use that date back to the 1700s and 1800s are found on microfilm. As genealogists, we are encouraged to use these microfilmed versions of the records to protect the originals, wherever they may be. If you are fortunate enough to have papers dating back into the 19th century, use copies of the records, rather than the originals when working with those records or sharing with others.

Gazetteers are one important resource on which genealogists should rely, but they usually don't. Because gazetteers vary in contents from single volumes to tens of volumes, they can be difficult to manage. Also, some may only list towns and cities, while others will include meadows, streams, and hamlets. Genealogists have difficulty knowing with any predictability what they can discover from these resources.

In the past, you either had to purchase the gazetteers or find them at your local library. Now, though, we have some great resources online. Some online gazetteers include maps, as well as other features. With some of the current online gazetteers, you can search not only names, but also zip codes.

One of the most powerful online gazetteers for the United States is the U.S. Geographical Survey's Geographical Names Information System (www-nmd.usgs.gov/www/gnis/index.html/). With this Web site, you can search on

➤ Feature name

➤ State or territory

➤ County

➤ Feature type

➤ Population

➤ Elevation

Some of my ancestors lived in Marrowbone, Moultrie, Illinois. However, I have long been intrigued to discover if any other states have similarly named townships.

Heritage Hints

Few genealogists realize that their local Family History Centers usually have microfiche collections that include items like gazetteers from many countries around the world. Many of these gazetteers were published in the early to mid-1800s.

Just as we discussed in a previous chapter, keep in mind that when you do searches, computers are very literal. So, when I searched the USGS site, rather than entering the complete town name of Marrowbone, I instead entered the partial term *Marrow,* and then generated a search. The USGS site showed a list of 46 "features" with the term *Marrow* in them, including a number of Marrowbone Creeks, and a couple of Marrow Bone localities as well. And don't forget that the county as it appears in an online gazetteer may not be the same county where your ancestor lived. If you want to find a place from long ago, you will want to access older gazetteers, which may be available at your local Family History Center.

Many of what genealogists consider to be resources "off the beaten path" are just now becoming available on the World Wide Web. As Internet technology improves, we can expect to find more and more of these special and highly useful resources online.

The Least You Need to Know

➤ The National Archives keeps up with technology.

➤ Online National Archive microfilm catalogs list what information is available.

➤ With the NAIL Web site, you have the opportunity to view some very old records.

➤ With online newspapers, you can see what is going on elsewhere, and keep your fingers clean at the same time.

➤ Some maps you don't have to refold.

➤ Gazetteers are directories of locations, and a resource that every genealogist should use.

Databases Galore

If you could get anything you wanted online, what would it be? For most genealogists, it would be the chance to run wild through databases with millions of names, dates, and places. As a volunteer at my local Family History Center, I know that the first thing visitors to the center do is head for the computers. Most of them aren't searching for microfilms. They are using the Ancestral File and the International Genealogical Index, two of the databases available on CD at the center.

Genealogists love databases. I love databases. If you are new to genealogy, you may not yet know enough about them, but in time you will love databases, too.

Of course, until the introduction of the Internet, most of the genealogically related databases in which we were interested were only available at local Family History Centers or on CDs you had to purchase.

But now, many databases are available online, and many of them are devoted to genealogy. We looked at smaller databases when we discussed vital records that are available online. Any of the searchable vital records indexes are databases. However, now we are going to look at some of what I like to call the "major league" databases. Like everything else in genealogy, the more information available, the better your chances are of finding an ancestor.

RootsWeb Is the Granddaddy of All Databases

RootsWeb (www.rootsweb.com) has a twofold mission that it proudly displays on its front page:

1. To make large volumes of data available to the online genealogical community at minimal cost.

2. To provide support services to online genealogical activities such as USENET, newsgroup moderation, mailing list maintenance, surname list generation, and so on.

Lineage Lingo

A **database** is a searchable, compiled, and computerized list. It could be death records, or people researching certain names or pedigrees.

Over the last decade, RootsWeb has grown considerably. This site is striving to achieve its mission, and doing admirably. And best of all, from a researching standpoint, the information in these databases is open to all researchers. You don't have to be a member or pay a subscription fee to access the data.

We have already mentioned mailing lists, and RootsWeb is currently responsible for maintaining a little more than 6,000 of them. Considering the number of messages any given mailing list can have, this is a major undertaking in the hardware department. And to make the mailing lists even more beneficial, they are archived on RootsWeb in a searchable database.

Genie Goodies

RootsWeb is the brain child of Brian Leverich and Karen Isaacson. It began, like most things, as a small sideline housed on the Rand Corporation servers. However, it wasn't long before genealogists recognized the benefits of what they were trying to do. Today, they boast their own servers and continue to strive to offer genealogists new databases and new methods of sharing genealogy with the rest of the community.

This means that if you are just coming online and you stumble onto a mailing list of interest, you have the opportunity to search past messages to see if anyone else is researching your family. It is likely they are still online and you may be able to get in touch with them if you do find someone.

However, they have other searchable databases that you will find very beneficial.

RootsWeb Surname List (RSL)

The RootsWeb Surname List (RSL) is a registry of surnames. Individuals online can elect to fill out a form and submit the surnames, as well as the dates and places for those surnames.

When you submit your names to the RSL, you first must request a nametag and password.

When you are getting your RootsWeb nametag, the Web site asks you to supply a primary and then two alternates. This is in case the one you want is already taken. Once you have filled out the form and submitted it, the next screen will confirm for you what your nametag is, and instruct you how to get access to their database.

When you have completed your registration to RootsWeb, you finally come to the point where you get to enter your surnames, dates, and places. On the RootsWeb Surname List, the site uses the term *migration* to mean places. With this feature, you can show the migration of the family through the years.

For instance, I have a couple of entries at the RSL for my SICKAFUS and STANDERFER surnames:

Heritage Hints

RootsWeb uses the nametag to more easily track the information you supply. The Web site does not use your e-mail address as a form of identification on the list, to help dissuade people who collect e-mail addresses to send spam.

Lineage Lingo

Spam is the online term for un-wanted e-mail. It generally refers to the advertising e-mails that you are likely to receive. One example of spam that you no doubt have seen is the e-mail telling you how to get rich quick.

Surname	From	To	Migration
SICKAFUS	1810	1920	Maryland, Michigan, Ohio, Illinois
STANDERFER	1840	1990	Illinois

By looking at the chart, you can see that my SICKAFUS family began in Maryland in 1810 and traveled through Michigan to Ohio, and then onto Illinois, where I *daughter-out* in 1920.

The great part about the RootsWeb Surname List is that your updates are added to the database instantaneously. So, the next person that comes along searching on a surname you typed in will see your information in the list.

When you are typing in your surnames, pay attention to the abbreviations you use for provinces, states, and countries. The RSL has a table of abbreviations that you can check. Many of them are three-letter abbreviations. You will want to make sure you use those abbreviations, so that when someone searches for your surname and puts in a locality, he will not overlook your entries. Remember that computers are extremely literal. If you type in *IL*, then that is precisely what it looks for.

Cousin Counsel

Generally, you should not post your home address on the Internet. Unfortunately, for every 10 helpful genealogists who will appropriately respect your privacy, someone else who is neither helpful nor a genealogist will be collecting addresses for unethical or possibly illegal reasons. Selling addresses to mailing house companies is one example.

Searching the RSL is even easier. You can type in a surname from the main RootsWeb page. Or you can select the link to the RSL page and include additional information about your search. The RSL page allows you to further narrow your search by including a location, type of search, and update period.

The type of search section allows you to search on the surname exactly as you spell it. You can also have the Web site do a soundex search. This is the same soundex coding that was used in the census research we discussed. They also offer another search, the metaphone search. This is another "sounds like" search.

Finally, with the update period feature, you can search for only new entries. If you are in the habit of searching the RSL on a weekly or monthly basis, you can tell the search engine you only want those entries that have been added or updated in the last week, the last month, or the last two months. By selecting one of these options, you prevent yourself from contacting the same people repeatedly. The following figure shows how the RSL brings you into contact with other online researchers.

Lineage Lingo

The term **daughter-out** refers to when you descend from a daughter. At that point the surname you are tracing, for her children, changes from her maiden name to the name of her spouse. My SICKAFUS married a STANDERFER, so I then concentrated on the STANDERFERs from that point forward.

At the time I was writing this book, the RootsWeb Surname List had more than half a million surnames and an impressive number of individuals submitting new information. The RootsWeb Surname List is a really great way to discover just who might be researching the same family as you. However, RootsWeb doesn't stop its usefulness here.

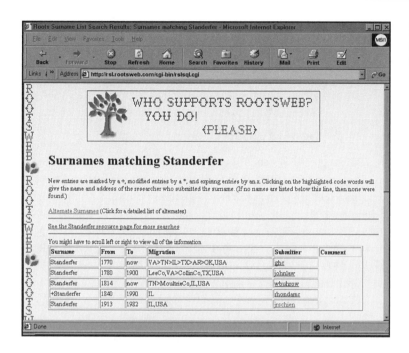

The RSL brings you into contact with fellow online researchers.

RootsWeb Search Engines

As though the RSL isn't enough to keep genealogists busy, RootsWeb has a number of other useful search engines. Perhaps the most useful is the Surname Helper. After all, as genealogists, we naturally think first in terms of surnames. With the Surname Helper, you can search on surnames either by themselves or with the following qualifiers:

➤ Sites to search   ➤ Date of posts

➤ Type of posts   ➤ Geographic areas

➤ Wild cards

The Surname Helper's benefits are that they are not limited to a single Web location where people have submitted their names, dates, and places. The Surname Helper will search posts and messages found on

➤ USGenWeb

➤ WorldGenWeb

➤ Personal genealogy pages (some, not the entire Internet yet)

➤ Surname pages

➤ GenConnect Bulletin Boards

Heritage Hints

To be organized, you should create some type of correspondence log for those you contact online. You will want to include columns or fields for the contact dates, the person's name, the e-mail address, the surnames of interest, and the results. You will end up corresponding online with so many people, you'll find such a list is essential.

Genie Goodies

When you use wild cards, you can greatly enhance your searches. You can use wild cards to replace a specific letter and broaden your search. This feature can be useful when you are searching for surnames that have multiple spellings. Very often, the wild card characters are * or ?. However, on the Surname Helper, the wild card characters are _ and %. Wildcard characters can be substituted for one character or many. The most common wildcard is the *, and it is used at the end of a word. If I wanted to find variant spellings on STANDERFER, I could type in STAND and find STANDERFER, STANDIFER, and STANDIFORD, if these variations were all present in the database I was searching.

The Surname Resources page is another powerful way to search for possible connections within the RootsWeb data. You start by selecting a letter of the alphabet and then a surname. The page that is displayed shows links to many different items and also includes searches for many sites as well. Those included are

➤ Personal Web Sites at RootsWeb

➤ Major Projects Sponsored by RootsWeb

➤ Transcription Projects

➤ Primary Records at RootsWeb

➤ General Links and Search Engines

➤ Mailing Lists

➤ GenConnect Boards

Heritage Hints

The Surname Helper will not search the RSL for you. So, when you visit the RootsWeb page, you will want to be sure to search both places.

The number of ways that you can search for your surnames at RootsWeb can keep you busy for months. Just remember to keep your goal in mind. It's too easy to jump from surname to surname. First concentrate on the surnames you are researching right now. Then, you can branch into searching for the other surnames you have.

GenealogyLibrary.com

It's great that the RootsWeb sites are open to anyone, but the costs of acquiring information, converting it into a digitized format, and making it searchable is very expensive. Many online databases, like GenealogyLibrary.com, seek to recoup some of that cost by charging a subscription fee.

We think nothing of purchasing a book or magazine that might help us in our genealogical research. So, similarly, we shouldn't think about purchasing a database subscription. When people ask me if paying a database subscription fee is worth the price, I have to say only if you find something. If I find worthwhile information, I'll feel that the subscription fee is well worth the price. However, if I find nothing useful, I will see the fee as a waste of money. With the database's subscription fee, you cannot actually try the database before you pay the fee (although some have free trial periods). But, you can at least do a search of the site to see what might be available in the subscription area.

GenealogyLibrary.com (www.genealogylibrary.com) is part of the Family Tree Maker structure. This Web site has been aggressively acquiring published genealogies and other resources to aid genealogists in their search of family history.

When I was writing this chapter, I decided to snoop at this site. It featured 1,788 databases, including

➤ History: 15 databases

➤ Libraries and Archives: 3 databases

➤ Magazines, Publications, and Television: 12 databases

➤ People: 832 databases

➤ Places: 187 databases

➤ Records: 739 databases

As I mentioned, GenealogyLibrary.com is a subscription service. The service offers both monthly and yearly subscriptions. So, if you wish to see what is available at this Web site, you can try it

Lineage Lingo

The **GenConnect boards** are bulletin boards with a specific focus. At present there are separate surname boards for the subjects of queries, Bible records, biographies, deeds, obituaries, pensions, and wills. These boards are moderated and follow the threaded message system.

Cousin Counsel

If you travel and use a notebook computer to access the Internet, you may want to sign up for GenealogyLibrary.com using your notebook. Unfortunately, the way you presently access the site is limited to use on a single PC. (You can't sign up for the service and access it from any PC you may want to use at the time, like e-mail or CompuServe.) This service does not give you a user name and password; instead, the service creates a link between itself and only one of your PCs.

for a month and then decide. With any online database, though, remember that the database and Web site will always be changing.

Among the holdings in the GenealogyLibrary.com databases are

➤ Indexed and scanned images of some of the 1850 census

➤ Dawes Final Rolls (for researchers of Cherokees)

➤ Published genealogies

➤ Other census indexes

Lineage Lingo

OCR stands for Optical Character Recognition. OCR programs take a document that has been scanned by your scanner and convert the text from that scanned image into a text document. Such PC programs have been used heavily in the digitizing of books; however, they are not 100% accurate, especially with text that is not clearly legible.

When you search this Web site's holdings, you will want to remember to come back at another time to see what new records the Web site has added. GenealogyLibrary.com generally adds about three new books each day to its system—a total of 15 new books a week. Keep in mind, though, that books are all secondary sources (see following figure). And because the books have been scanned and run through an OCR program to digitize the text, there is always the possibility that something may not have translated correctly.

Digitized resources are secondary sources.

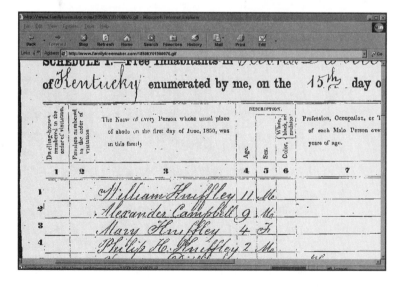

The reason I stress the importance of digitized books being secondary sources is because these records often lull folks into a false sense of security. Because they are books and resources we readily recognize, we tend not to follow up on the information they contain. Even if you are using the original book format of these resources, you still must verify as much information as possible, ideally through primary sources.

Ancestry.com

Another subscription service is Ancestry.com (www.ancestry.com). Like GenealogyLibrary.com, this service offers scanned books and resources to make the information available online.

This service is also striving to add new databases on a daily basis. In June 1999, the service had 1,612 databases containing more than 240 million names. Ancestry.com has several interesting databases, including

➤ Ancestry World Tree (family trees by submitters)

➤ Census indexes

➤ Abstracts of graves of Revolutionary Patriots

➤ Mortality schedules

➤ How-to books

➤ Obituaries

The Ancestry World Tree is one of Ancestry.com's free, searchable databases. You can do a surname search, or search for a specific individual. This database displays a list from which you can then display a pedigree form for the individual you select. When this process is complete, you can then download a GEDCOM file and also find out who supplied the information, so you can contact them directly.

Ancestry.com also has two extremely important databases:

➤ PERSI

➤ American Genealogical Biographical Index (AGBI)

PERSI is the *PERiodical Source Index*. It is an ongoing indexing project from the Allen County Public Library in Ft. Wayne, Indiana. The Genealogy Department of the library began to index these periodicals by surname, record type, and locality. They index the following types of periodicals:

➤ Genealogical publications

➤ Historical publications

➤ Ethnic publications

➤ Family and surname publications

Lineage Lingo

An **abstract** is an abridged version of a document highlighting only the main points of the document.

Heritage Hints

Whenever you download a GEDCOM file from the Internet or elsewhere, do not just dump it into your database. Keep it separate until you have verified the information and know for certain that the individuals contained in the file do connect to your family line. Waiting until you confirm whether an individual is your ancestor before adding that person to your database is much easier than taking him or her out.

This project began in 1984. The amazing aspect of the PERSI index is that the information indexed can be requested from the Allen County Public Library, if you are unable to locate the periodicals in your local genealogical library. The following figure shows PERSI, the index that adds about 100,000 names each year.

PERSI indexes about 100,000 names each year from periodicals.

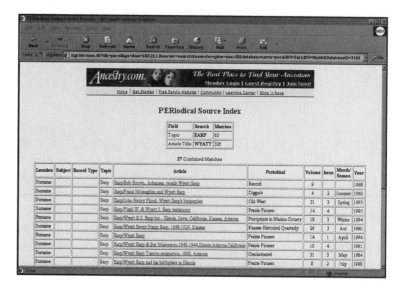

Although PERSI charges a small copy fee, you can take comfort in knowing that you can obtain the periodical you need.

Genie Goodies

I just recently got my first chance to visit the Allen County Public Library, which was a great deal of fun. Located on the second floor, the Genealogy Department takes up almost all of the second level. This library has what is known as "closed stacks." This term means that you have to request the books you want, instead of getting them from the shelves yourself. The library uses runners to retrieve the books requested by patrons, and they are very speedy and quite efficient. In addition to books and periodicals, the library has a great deal of microfilm. The library has the entire U.S. census and the indexes to the censuses. You could easily get lost in this library!

The American Genealogical Biographical Index is more commonly referred to as the AGBI. I was fortunate enough to have access to this index when I was first starting out in genealogy. However, it wasn't until recently that I realized why I was always asked about this index when I mentioned it to other researchers in online messages.

For those who remember the first volumes of this index, it will often remain *Rider's Index* to them. It was the brainchild of Fremont Rider of the Godfrey Memorial Library in Middletown, Connecticut. It began in 1952 and was due to be completed in 1999. When completed it will include more than 200 volumes.

As I mentioned, I was used to having access to this superior index at my local public library. However, I recently discovered that there are only 200 libraries in the United States that have the AGBI. This is primarily due to the length of time it has taken to complete. Most libraries that now recognize the importance of this resource could not get the earlier volumes because they are out of print.

However, Ancestry.com has recently acquired the electronic rights to this massive index. And it is now a part of the Ancestry.com site.

The AGBI's entries come from a wide variety of resources including

➤ The "Boston Transcript" (a genealogy column from the early 1900s)

➤ 1790 census

➤ Published Revolutionary War records

➤ Published family histories

In all, the AGBI contains some 850 sources that have been indexed in this work.

Each entry in the online AGBI may include the following:

➤ Surname

➤ Given name

➤ Maiden name

➤ Birth date (usually just year)

➤ Birthplace (usually a state or country)

➤ Biographical information

➤ Reference

Although many of the sources pertain to the original colonies, the AGBI also contains some useful information for Midwest states, as well.

Heritage Hints

The AGBI offers a major benefit that many other indexes don't, because it includes the maiden name for women whenever they are known. This feature lets you search on both a woman's married name and her maiden name.

Lineage Lingo

The "Boston Transcript" was a genealogy column found in the *Boston Transcript* newspaper in the early 1900s. It consisted of queries, answers, and notes. The answers and notes generally went into great depth. Your local genealogy library may have it on microfiche.

Once you have used this index, you will want to check your local genealogical library to see what else it has. And the Family History Library has about 96 percent of the works that were indexed. You will want to check the Family History Library catalog to see which of them may be on microfilm.

Cousin Counsel

Just because the primary focuses of the AGBI are the original colonies and the Midwest, don't ignore it. In any genealogical research, it is important to leave no stone unturned, including this one.

Heritage Hints

Only microfilms and microfiche can be ordered at your local Family History Center. Anything that is in book format is not circulated. You can ask the FHC staff for a "Request to Microfilm" to see if the work you want can be microfilmed. This does take some time though, as the original author is notified of the request.

Whenever Ancestry.com unveils new databases, the Web site makes one of the new ones available in its free search area for a limited time. Ancestry.com also has a number of other digitized resources available for free all the time, including The Source, A Guidebook of American Genealogy, which gives you in-depth information on a variety of the record types that genealogists use all the time.

In addition to these databases, genealogists also use many databases that fellow researchers have created.

GENDEX

GENDEX (www.gendex.com/gendex/) is an index to some of the genealogical data available on the Internet. Gene Stark's site claims to have indexed "hundreds of World Wide Web databases containing genealogical data for over eight million individuals …."

The site offers a searchable database that brings you a list of those indexed sites that pertain to your surname. A search I did on the surname STANDERFER showed me a list of 15 entries. Each of these entries was located on a different Web site.

Some of the pages may display in a pedigree format, while others limit the information to a single individual, forcing you to select additional links to locate information on the father, mother, spouse, or child.

Many of the indexed sites appear to work with GEDCOM files that you submit. Some of the GENDEX-indexed sites mention that they will work with GEDCOM files. For instance, www.my-ged.com (www.my-ged.com/) is set up so visitors may donate their GEDCOMs so they are available to other researchers for free. Presently, this site has more than three million individual data pages, and these are all GENDEX-indexed.

In addition to the GENDEX site, the Internet also features some other searchable databases, but most of them require that you become a subscribing member. I am listing these sites here, so that you can check them out for yourself and decide whether they will be useful to you:

➤ Kindred Konnections (www.kindredkonnections.com/) has more than 30 million names in its database. While you can search to see a list of this database's names, you cannot view the pedigrees unless you are a member.

➤ GenServ (www.genserv.com/) has more than 16 million names. You can do one free surname search. However, to access the data beyond that point, you must submit a GEDCOM file and pay a subscription fee.

➤ Everton's On-Line (www.everton.com/members-info.htm) has about 50,000 pedigree charts and about 80,000 family group sheets. Like most of the others, in order to access this data, you must be a member.

You will need to evaluate these types of databases to see if they are worth their subscription fees. Most of these databases offer both a monthly and yearly subscription fee. As a result, you can try some of the subscription databases for a month to see if these online services offer you any valuable information.

Cousin Counsel

Whenever you are sharing a GEDCOM file, please be sure to omit any living individuals from the file. You can omit these individuals with a program like GEDClean, which is available for free and can be downloaded at www.raynorshyn.com/gedclean/. This program removes all information about living people. You can even omit that person's name completely, should you wish.

The Least You Need to Know

➤ RootsWeb's long history and large databases make it a dream for genealogists.

➤ Commercial (subscription required) database sites can be valuable, if they help you find your ancestors.

➤ Some databases don't show you pedigrees, but point you in the right direction, so you can continue your research.

➤ With GEDCOM database sites, you may be able to download files.

➤ Don't dump new GEDCOM files into your personal database until you confirm that the individual(s) you've researched is truly related to you.

Part 5
Mining for Family Gold

Often, in our genealogical research, we overlook an important aspect of our research: the history aspect of family history. Our ancestors lived through such momentous events as the War of 1812, the Seven Years War, and World War I. They have braved hardships to migrate from one place to another. They have endured persecution. In Part 5, I'll show you how to find sites that put our family history in the context of overall history.

Part 5 also includes how to access resources for anyone who is researching his or her ethnic ancestry. I'll also show you how to take a tour of the world without needing to pack—through the convenience and ease of the Internet, which lets you contact information repositories and researchers in other countries.

Chapter 18

Using History in Family History

In This Chapter

➤ Helping family history with diaries and other family papers

➤ Sleuthing family style is almost as good as Sherlock Holmes

➤ Using the Web as your time machine

➤ Putting your ancestry into history

Most of us are not actually genealogists. We are really family historians. While we strive to gather the names, dates, and places, we are equally interested in the day-to-day life of our ancestors.

And I find that by learning about the history of the time, that I get a glimpse into what they were going through. I won't pretend that I can really comprehend what their daily life entailed, but I enjoy reading and learning about what was taking place around them.

At times I am astounded at what my families have had to endure. Many people hope to claim a famous person on their family tree. However, if you take the time to read the stories of life during that time, you may find yourself glowing with pride that your family survived at all.

Our Ancestors' History

Once in a while we discover a diary or other family remembrance that gives us insight into the life of one or more of our ancestors.

One of my friends had a diary of her grandfather's travel from England to Philadelphia. He described the trip and his thoughts about what might be waiting for him when he got off the ship in a different land. And we read with fascination as he decided what name he would use when he got off the ship. When he got on the ship he was Edward Newth. And when he got off the ship, he was George Morris.

Heritage Hints

If you are fortunate enough to have family Bibles, diaries, letters, or other remembrances on paper, you will want to be sure to preserve them. There are articles online and companies devoted to the preservation of documents.

We discovered that he wasn't running away from anything. For personal reasons he decided he wanted to be a new person in that new land he was heading to. And through the years, Edward would lead us on a merry chase, marrying under his legal name, disembarking and joining the army with his new name. However, we have his recollections to read even though he is long gone.

For many of us though, there are no diaries, letters, or other shreds of a time gone by. While we may not be able to discover something written by our ancestors, it is possible to locate similar documents on others who lived at the same time.

I just happened to stumble across one of my more colorful ancestors. Having shared information with a fellow researcher online about the brick wall of my STANDERFER line and Benjamin STANDERFER, I began to search any indexes, records, anything I could find on him.

And it was with a little temerity that I mentioned online what I had discovered. It was a statewide index of miscellaneous records for Illinois, and among other more upstanding records were entries in the governor's papers from the 1860s. Unfortunately, my Benjamin was not in there for his being a model of society. The Illinois governor wrote the Iowa governor a letter asking that the fugitive Benjamin be returned to Illinois for trial. Further research on this led us to court records. The State of Illinois had charged Benjamin and another person with stealing $11, which at the time was grand larceny.

The State of Illinois found Benjamin guilty and put him in the state penitentiary for a year. (The first five days of his term he spent in solitary confinement for running away.)

We'd discovered a second marriage for Benjamin, but his first wife had no death date. I was certain Jane, Benjamin's first wife, could not be too happy with Benjamin's "extracurricular activities," especially those resulting in jail, so I thought we'd better look for divorce records.

Married couples in the 1800s didn't have what we now call "no-fault" divorce. Regardless, we found a divorce record, but it wasn't for Benjamin and Jane; rather, the document was for Benjamin's second wife. When I read through this divorce court transcript from 1870, I knew significantly more about Benjamin's life.

Now, for some people, finding these facts would not be a good thing. Maybe the way I look at these old fiascoes, I can see him in me more than I should admit. By seeing these records, I have much more meaningful historical insight into these ancestors' lives than the researcher who would be ashamed or discouraged by the actions of my ancestors. So, regardless of content, I'm always happy when I find any records of my family history.

What did those records tell me? Well, I know that Martha, the second wife, was a strong person. She was willing to go through the traumatic court process to divorce Benjamin. She had to come up with witnesses who would recount what Benjamin had done. By reading the information in the court records, I learned more about when and where Benjamin and Martha were born.

But, what if you have not discovered any letters, court records, or other documents that give you an insight into your ancestor's life?

Cousin Counsel

Should you discover such colorful characters as I have, you will want to be selective about sharing the information if it has happened recently. Many times, it can be upsetting to those members who are closer to the incident than you are, especially if they were alive when the incident took place.

Through the Time Machine

I certainly have wished on several occasions that the fabled H.G. Wells's time machine did exist. While I wouldn't want to actually participate in the history, I sure would love to look on as it took place.

If you don't have records from your family, it might be possible to locate remembrances, pictures, or other resources online with an account of life and times in the town or country where your ancestor lived.

We have already looked at the NAIL database, in Chapter 16. Imagine searching there and discovering a picture of your ancestor working his land. How priceless would that be to you? How real that ancestor would suddenly become.

Recently I was working with the World War I draft cards. These are on microfilm and are available from the Family History Library through your local Family History Center. Among other things, the cards give a description of the men filling out the cards. I recently looked at some of my new STANDERFER men information. But now I knew a little more about them. In fact, my ancestor was described as having a hip out of place and one leg was shorter than the other.

Lineage Lingo

A **remembrance** is anything pertaining to your ancestors. It could be a diary, a manuscript, or a photograph. Very often these articles have found homes in private collections, museums, or historical societies.

Genie Goodies

The World War I draft cards are available on microfilm. Unless your ancestor lived in a small community, it is possible that there will be multiple draft boards in the area. The cards are alphabetical by draft board. There is a microfilm of maps to some of the larger cities with multiple draft boards. You may want to order that first before ordering multiple films for the many draft boards where your ancestor may have been. The cards supply you with name, age, birth date, birthplace, physical description, and naturalization information for immigrants.

As family historians, we should be thorough. We should plan to search any type of record or resource that even remotely connects to the localities of our ancestors.

More frequently, these types of records are making their way online, such as

➤ Diaries

➤ Journals

➤ Letters

➤ Manuscripts

When I was recently randomly searching the Web, I discovered some wonderful diary sites, including

➤ Civil War soldiers

➤ Doctors

➤ Immigrants

➤ Women who lived through the Civil War

➤ Those who went West

Although the letters and diaries may not actually be from one of our actual ancestors, the letter may be from someone who traveled the Oregon Trail with one of our ancestors. Even if the person traveled in another group of wagons, we still have their eyewitness reports to give us an idea of what our ancestors may have experienced on the trail.

If these sites interest you, you can find more of them by using one of the various online directories. In addition to finding diary-related sites, you can also benefit if the directory organizes the site's links in some subject order. Depending on which of the directories you use, you might find History sections, whereas other sites will intermix the historical links with other Web sites specifically related to the locality, such as repository sites.

Searching for sites specific to our ancestors may not yield as much information as we would like. So instead, you may want to look for sites on history in general.

Genie Goodies

Diaries and journals have long been kept. While the settlers may not have stopped to record their experiences while actually traveling the Oregon Trail, such stories were often set down on paper after the travelers settled in the new community. Visit a bookstore and you are likely to see more and more of these reminiscences being published.

Searching Some Great History Sites

If you do a search on the Internet for *history*, you will find it as unwieldy as a search for *genealogy*. Therefore, you need to have a focus. After all, this world has been making history for more years than we can trace our ancestors.

Just as there are thousands of books on every aspect of history, there are an equal number of Web sites. Interested in Ellis Island? Ever wondered what life was like in Colonial America? Did your grandparents help found the Western states?

Once you have decided what you want to learn about, then you can go out and begin to search on that subject.

Ellis Island Remembered

One of my fondest memories when I was growing up was looking at pictures of Germany through a stereoscopic (an antique stereo "Viewmaster"). The stereoscopic had slides that actually had the picture twice on the card. When you put the card into the viewer and put it up to your eyes, you got a 3-D image of the picture. These were quite popular in the early 1900s in schools and libraries. I am not sure why we had one, but I can remember whiling away the hours going through the pictures.

Heritage Hints

Looking for famous events can help you to find sites that will prove useful in general. Instead of looking for Lexington, Massachusetts, you would look for the American Revolution. Or combine the famous event with the place in question.

Recently, I discovered a wonderful site devoted to Ellis Island. At this site, you can view scanned, electronic images of these highly collectible stereoscopic cards. Although you can't get the true three-dimensional effect, these pictures give you a real idea of what Ellis Island was like as a popular port of entry. Images include

➤ Various ships

➤ Ellis Island itself

➤ Disembarking immigrants

➤ Immigrants going through their inspections

➤ Christmas held for the detainees

➤ Images of the SS *Lusitania*

Genie Goodies

Ellis Island was not opened until 1892. Prior to this time immigrants to New York went through the Castle Garden station located in Manhattan. However, to many people Ellis Island is indelibly linked as the entrance point for many of our immigrant ancestors. A search of the Family History Library Catalog will reveal many books about Ellis Island as well as interviews with those who came in through or who worked at Ellis Island.

Pictures make history seem more realistic for us.

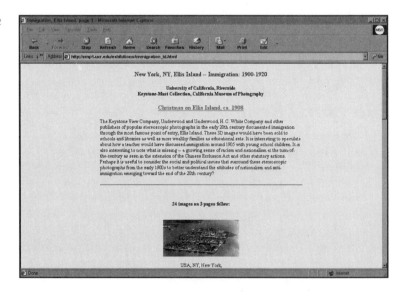

Suddenly the bustle of Ellis Island is right there in front of you. The University of California Riverside made available this site: New York, NY, Ellis Island, Immigration: 1900–1920 at cmp1.ucr.edu/exhitbitions/immigration_id.html. The photographs are from the Keystone-Mast Collection, a derivation of the Keystone View Company that originally created the various stereoscopic photographs.

Many of us who are researching our family may discover at least one ancestor who came through Ellis Island. While you probably couldn't pick your grandmother or great-grandfather out of these photos, you have something tangible of a place that was of major importance to your ancestor.

Another great Ellis Island page is the home page for the Statue of Liberty-Ellis Island Foundation (www.ellisisland.org/). This group began restoring the torch, and its members have taken an active role in restoring the island. While this site doesn't have any family history information, you can search through the entries in The American Immigrant Wall of Honor. Descendants submitted those whose names appear on the wall. There was a fee involved, so not everyone's name is there, but it may get you one step closer to your immigrant ancestor.

Cousin Counsel

While the Ellis Island Museum is open and they have some information on family heritage, they do not have the actual passenger lists. These are on microfilm and are available from the Family History Library and the National Archives.

Canadian History

Despite my colonial New England roots, my maternal grandfather's family spent about 100 years in New Brunswick, Canada. The timing of this little trip was right around the start of the American Revolution. My grandmother, the one that wanted to join the DAR so badly, never pursued this line for fear that she would find her husband was descended from a Tory.

Because I researched this line further, my grandmother need not have worried. While the family did move to New Brunswick, it was in search of land, rather than disagreeing with the newly emerging country. Surprisingly, the family helped fight with the Americans, even though they lived in Canada.

Because of this connection, Canadian things intrigue me. Therefore, I was quite thrilled to see an encompassing site devoted to links to sites on Canadian history: Canadian History on the Web (www.interchange.ubc.ca/sneylan/cdnhist.htm). Some of the links will send you in search of

Lineage Lingo

A **Tory** was a British sympathizer. You will also find them referred to as **Loyalists** in many of the records. Moreover, some of the Canadian records show pensions paid by England to these Loyalists who displaced to Canada.

➤ Archaeology in Kingston and Eastern Ontario

➤ Canadian Women in History

➤ Ghosts of the Klondike Gold Rush

➤ Hudson's Bay Company Digital Collection

➤ Pier 21 Society (Canada's Ellis Island)

If you have Canadian ancestry, you will want to just wander through the many links available on the Canadian Women In History Web page.

Heritage Hints

Land was one of the forces motivating our ancestors to move. It was why some of them moved west and why others migrated north to Canada. With land, they had the chance to create a better life for their families.

The Wild Wild West

I'm not sure what it is about us, but as a people, we have often gone off in search of the unknown. For most of us, this search resulted in us not having been born in the old country. However, for many in the United States, we marvel at what took place in the West during its settlement. The tales of the Wild West have given us such larger than life characters as

➤ Wyatt Earp

➤ Doc Holliday

➤ Bat Masterson

➤ Belle Starr

➤ Wild Bill Hickok

➤ Buffalo Bill Cody

Genie Goodies

Surfing the Web opens doors to how others perceive ideals, localities, and historical happenings. We learn as much by exposing ourselves to this different way of thinking as we do from all the how-to and history books we may read. One of my favorite philosophies is found on Jim Janke's Old West Page (homeages.dsu.edu/jankej/oldwest/oldwest.htm), in which he expresses his belief that the Old West is neither a time or place, but a state of mind.

In fact, our fascination with the West would help Bill Cody make a living for many years, as he brought his Wild West Show to your hometown—or should I say the hometown of your grandparents? Buffalo Bill Cody's Wild West Show began in 1883 and toured around the world until 1902.

Each of these Wild West characters was much more than an icon. They had parents and grandparents and, in some cases, children. Whereas most people remember them for their historical activities, family members remember them as a part of the family tree. Many people who share those surnames work hard trying to find a connection to them.

When we think of the Wild West, we think of the cow towns that popped up west of the Mississippi where the only law was the one with the fastest six-shooter. Of course, if we dig a little deeper we find that this is more Hollywood hype than reality, but it is this kind of thinking that keeps us wanting more.

Living history reenactors not only want more, they have figured out how to get it. The Old West Living History Foundation (www.oldwest.org/) brings the West of the 1800s back to life again.

Cousin Counsel

In our enthusiasm to put a famous person on the family tree, we sometimes don't follow correct research protocols. We try to force the round ancestor into the square family tree, so to speak. Even if you find a "famous" surname on your tree, make sure you continue to follow the procedure of working from the known to the unknown.

Genie Goodies

Living history reenactors devote their time, energy, and money to bringing back to life a bygone era. Walking through a Civil War camp gives you insight into what your ancestors might have experienced. Many living history reenactors are also interested in genealogy; the two subjects go hand-in-hand.

There are living history groups for the Civil War and other historical times. Not only are they educational, it is fun to learn this way. In addition, these living history organizations are usually open to anyone interested in the historical period for that group.

But how do such sites help you with your family history? Although you cannot be descended from Wyatt Earp (he never had any children), it is possible that your ancestor was trying to make it day to day in the same cow town that Earp or Masterson came through. This gives you a story to tell. And while it isn't possible to be descended from Wyatt Earp, his brother Virgil did have a daughter. Researchers of the EARP family have traced the EARP descendants all over the country. In fact, anyone with the EARP surname in their family tree can possibly make a connection to the famous Earp brothers.

Even in this time of technology we are drawn to the stories of the Old West.

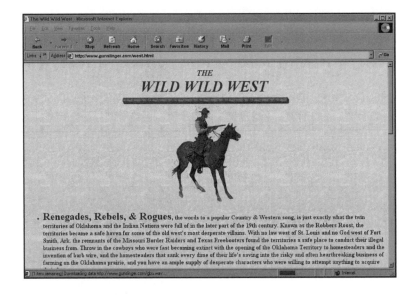

Sites for the Historically Addicted

Those of us who are fascinated by history are always in search of some new aspect of it, whether it is an individual, time, or activity. No matter how often we read about events, it is not always easy to understand them.

The Salem Witch Trials of 1692, the U.S. Civil War, and the assassination of President John F. Kennedy all touch many of us in different ways. As we attempt to come to terms, we continue our search for articles, Web pages, books, or reminiscences of the historical events our ancestors lived through.

I have traced my maternal side back to colonial New England and do have some accused witches on the family tree (we won't use the word *hanging* here, thank you). In my research, though, I have also discovered I had some accusers in my family tree. I am delighted by this—this hysteria fascinates me.

For years, I traced my mother's side of the family tree, since I had access to living relatives and information. So, for the longest time I thought I was a Yankee when it came to the Civil War. However, now that I have begun to research my father's side more thoroughly I discover that this isn't exactly true.

Some of his lines have headed south, although I do not know yet whether any of them fought for the Confederacy during the Civil War. I find myself fascinated by the Civil War, especially by the idea of brother fighting brother. Although I've not yet found such a connection, I realize the family heritage that I hold so dear may have at one time been at odds with itself.

There are some great Web sites available for history buffs. I've listed just a few below.

Since 1996, The History Place, The Past into the Future, at www.historyplace.com/index.html, has been devoted to teachers, students, and anyone interested in history. This site is full of digitized images and some great articles. And for those who are interested in visiting some of the historical spots around the United States, they have some links to various tourist areas.

By far, one of my most favorite history sites is The History Net (www.historynet.com). They have articles from many different periodicals. You can search their site or select articles from an index. While not every article of every periodical is online, they have some fascinating stories. And they have links to some of the most interesting sites on the Internet as well. One of my most recent traipses through their site led me to an interesting Web page devoted to Alcatraz (www.alsirat.com/alcatraz.html).

The History Channel (www.historychannel.com/) is another great site. When you search their site, they supply you with information from their pages, but then include links to

➤ Related people

➤ Related historical places

➤ Related Web sites

➤ Related videos (from their collection)

Cousin Counsel

Just as with family history Web sites, you will want to try to verify any information you find online that pertains to a specific period in history. Some of these sites will be regurgitating already disproved myths, while others will have new hypotheses and perhaps newly discovered details.

Cousin Counsel

Historical sites such as HyperHistory Online have some powerful information stored in their databases. If you do not want in-depth scholarly information about history, this site may not be for you.

HyperHistory Online, at www.hyperhistory.com/online_n2/History_n2/a.html, is another great world history site. On this site's front page, it claims "over 1,400 files, covering 3,000 years of world history." In this site's People Index, the Web page owners have entries for more than 1,000 individuals through 1996, and from all walks of history:

➤ Science and Technology

➤ Culture and Philosophy

➤ Religion

➤ Politics

➤ War

And finally, another great University of California, Riverside, site (www.ucr.edu/h-gig/horuslinks.html) has links to History Resources (www.TK). This site is designed to supply you with information on worldwide historical events.

Making History with Your Family

I could go on forever with the sites that are available on the Internet for those of us that never get enough of history. The great part about history is that you can put your family smack dab in the middle of it.

Adding history to the dry dates and places you have discovered for the family tree brings it alive. If you point out how Uncle Ted was involved in D-Day, or how Great-Great-Grandpa James was in Dodge City at the same time as Wyatt Earp, then you pique their interest. Even those in the family who claim to hate history find something that will catch their interest.

After you've put all your great information into one of those genealogy software programs we examined earlier in the book, don't just concentrate on relatives' and ancestors' names, dates, and important places. Enhance the events of your ancestors' lives by dropping in tidbits such as

➤ Day-to-day life

➤ Today's history

➤ Famous folks who may have done the same thing or who were in the same area

Heritage Hints

Visiting historical societies in the town, county, or state in which your ancestors lived may prove fruitful. Historical societies are repositories for such items as old newspapers and manuscripts and other personal collections. In such collections you may find a hint or clue about your ancestor.

Heritage Hints

Want a real look at what your ancestor's life was like? See what living history/reenactor groups are near where you live. These folks really get into character. Sometimes, the genealogical resources currently available are good enough to convince yourself that the wished-for H.G. Wells time machine really does exist.

Above all, don't forget to put in some computerized form the stories you uncover about your ancestors. Share quotes from the family diaries or letters. If you are one of the lucky ones who can find a picture or other memorabilia about your ancestors, digitize it and include it in the family history.

Family history is just that, the history of the family. The stories, the trials, the joys, and the sorrows all make up the family as it was. The events happening around the family had a direct effect on their lives. It may have been the deciding factor in following others on the Oregon Trail or standing and fighting. Give your ancestors this one last chance to shine and live, in your heart.

The Least You Need to Know

➤ Diaries, letters, and other family papers hold family history.

➤ Be thorough in your research.

➤ Surf back in time; there are great historical sites out there.

➤ You can show how history affected your families.

Chapter 19

The Melting Pot

In This Chapter

➤ They came in ships, but which ship was it?

➤ Taking pride in your ethnic heritage

➤ An overview of what's available online to help your research

---

External to this country and as children, we learn that the United States is a melting pot. What happened to the poor immigrants who believed this cliché? How did they feel, and what did they do when they saw the "huge pot" into which we put everyone? Like no other country, the United States has mixed ethnic origins, traditions, and beliefs from many lands. In fact, immigrants founded this land.

A friend of mine has traced one of her lines back to Native Americans. So we often joke with each other. "My ancestors got off on the *Mayflower*," I always say. And she always answers, "And my ancestors were there to greet them." Old joke, yes. Corny joke, perhaps. But it sort of sums up the tradition of the United States. From its recorded beginning, America has been the destination of ships filled with people seeking a better life, and there have always been people here to meet them.

They Came in Ships

While I can trace one of my lines back to the *Mayflower,* it isn't the line my grandmother would have liked. While she did make it into the DAR, she also had dreams of making it into the Society of Mayflower Descendants as well. Unfortunately, though all her family can be traced back to colonial New England, it was on my father's side that I discovered the connection to the *Mayflower.*

I have often thought I could picture my grandmother's response to this little find. She always maintained that my father wasn't good enough for her little girl, or for her grandchildren for that matter. So had she not already been dead when I made this discovery, I am not sure I would have had the courage to tell her.

Although the *Mayflower* was not actually the first immigrant ship to reach America, it is the one that most people are familiar with. There was the already established settlement in Jamestown, Virginia. And that was actually where the passengers of the *Mayflower* were heading.

By the 1630s, it probably looked like there was an unstoppable tidal wave of immigrants. After all, there were more than 60,000 European immigrants who arrived during that decade. Of course as would be seen later, that was just the beginning. The peak year for U.S. immigration was 1907, when almost 1.3 million flooded into the United States, and most of them came through Ellis Island. For more information about the tide of immigrants, read the chapter on Immigrant Ancestors found in *The Source, A Guidebook of American Genealogy*, edited by Loretto Dennis Szucs and Sandra Hargreaves Luebking (Ancestry, 1997). This flood forced a tightening of restrictions on "unqualified" immigrants. Not everyone who came through the various ports got to stay. These restrictions seemed to be tougher in Ellis Island, probably because of the astronomical numbers of immigrants flocking in on an almost daily basis.

Lineage Lingo

The Society of Mayflower Descendants is a lineage society that accepts membership only of those who have proved their descent from one of the passengers on that original *Mayflower* voyage.

Genie Goodies

The History Channel can be a good source of information. Recently, it aired a program about how the *Mayflower* ended up where it did. Apparently, they absolutely had to make land because they had run out of beer. Funny, that somehow never makes it into the stories they tell the kids in school—which is probably a good thing.

We already looked at a couple of sites that give you insight into the history of Ellis Island. But as genealogists we want to learn what ship our ancestors arrived on. We hope to find out if they traveled with family. And of course we hope to discover where in the old country they came from.

Genie Goodies

To begin searching for immigrant ancestors, a good resource is the federal census records. From 1870 on, they have had columns that deal with immigrant information. Some of the census years even have columns for year of immigration and year of naturalization.

In the last 400 or so years there have been some 57 million immigrants to the United States. And unless you are Native American, you will eventually trace your family line back to one of those immigrants.

For those who have immigrants that did come after 1820, you will want to try to find the passenger lists. These lists will vary from supplying you with very little information in the early years to practically chronicling the passengers' prior life by the late 1800s and on into the 1900s.

Before 1893, the passenger lists included just

➤ Name

➤ Age

➤ Gender

➤ Occupation

➤ Nationality

However, after 1893, the passenger lists for those disembarking in the United States changed dramatically. By 1907, the information found on the passenger lists included

➤ Name

➤ Age (in years and months)

➤ Gender

➤ Occupation

➤ Whether that person could read and write

➤ Nationality

➤ Race

Heritage Hints

While it is true that our ancestors have been traveling the high seas to finally rest on these shores since the early 1600s, it wasn't until 1820 that the federal government began requiring passenger lists. For records before then, you will have to use other resources to trace your immigrant.

➤ Last residence (including country and city or town)

➤ Name and address of nearest relative

➤ Final destination (state and city or town)

➤ Whether they already had a ticket to that destination

➤ Who paid their passage

➤ Whether they had $50 (if not, how much they did have)

➤ Whether they had ever been in the United States at a previous time (if the answer was yes, then the individual was asked to give the year he arrived and where)

➤ Whether the person was joining a relative, and where that relative lived

➤ Whether the person had ever been in prison, the poorhouse, or a mental institution

➤ Whether the person is/was a polygamist

➤ Whether the person is/was an anarchist

➤ The person's general health condition

➤ The person's deformities, if any, or if he was crippled

➤ Height (in feet and inches)

➤ Complexion

➤ Hair color

➤ Eye color

➤ Any identifying marks

➤ Birthplace (country and city or town)

Cousin Counsel

There are no relationships listed in the earlier passenger lists. Although it is tempting to assume that people of the same name are related, you want to be careful in assuming they are father, mother, and children. The children could be nephews and nieces, for instance.

Heritage Hints

Don't just concentrate on the one page of the passenger list that your ancestor is listed on. At the end of the sheets for the given ship that your ancestor arrived on are additional pages that include information about who was detained and why, who was deported and why, and other irregularities.

For those with ancestors who arrived in the United States after 1893, you see why you would want to find them on the passenger lists. And if the ancestor was deported for any reason, then you would see the word *deported* stamped on the entry line for your ancestor.

Like many of the other records we search to locate our family history, many of the passenger lists can be found on microfilm. They are available at the National Archives and the Family History Library. And like most of the other records we use on a day-to-day basis these are not always indexed. There are some ongoing projects to index additional passenger lists, but at this time, these are the indexes available on microfilm, most of them as part of the WPA projects:

➤ Atlantic, Gulf Coast, and Great Lakes ports (1820–74)

➤ Alabama, Florida, Georgia, and South Carolina ports (1890–1924)

➤ Baltimore, Maryland, port (1820–97; 1897–1952)

➤ Boston, Massachusetts, port (1848–91; 1902–06; 1906–20)

➤ Detroit, Michigan, port (1906–54)

➤ Galveston, Texas, port (1896–1906; 1906–51)

➤ Gulfport, Mississippi, port (1904–54)

➤ New Bedford, Massachusetts, port (1902–54)

➤ New Orleans, Louisiana, port (1853–99; 1900–52)

➤ New York, New York, port (1820–46; 1897–1902; 1902–43; 1944–48)

➤ Pascagoula, Mississippi, port (1903–35)

➤ Philadelphia, Pennsylvania, port (1800–1906; 1883–1948)

➤ Portland, Maine, port (1893–1954)

➤ Providence, Rhode Island (1911–54)

➤ San Francisco, California (1893–1934)

But how do you find your ancestor on a passenger list when they arrived during one of the periods that is not indexed? If this happens to you, then your ancestors are traveling with mine. And they are once again getting some weird pleasure out of watching us try to locate them now.

One of the best ways to narrow down when your ancestor arrived is through naturalization records. Even before the United States existed, the colonists decided they needed to have a way for the new immigrants to swear allegiance to what was now their permanent home. So, before the existence of the United States, you may find your ancestor giving an *Oath of Allegiance*.

However, in 1790, things began to change. There was not a country per se prior to this time, and Congress now began to pass acts to naturalize those who were immigrating. Over the last 200 years these acts and laws have changed for many reasons:

Cousin Counsel

The index cards include different formats for different time periods, and in the case of New York, there are four or five different index cards used in the 1904–54 time period. The numbers are extremely important in locating your ancestor on a passenger list.

Lineage Lingo

The **Oath of Allegiance** denunciated any claims by "pretenders" to the throne England and denied the right of the pope to outlaw Protestant monarchs. Generally these oaths were signed as the passenger disembarked from the ships once they arrived in the colonies.

➤ Length of time of residence before eligible

➤ Who was eligible

➤ Who had to go through the process

➤ What steps were required

And just like the passenger lists have improved and become more useful to us, the same is true of the naturalization records. Over time, the records have required more information about the person wishing to seek naturalization.

Two valuable books that will aid you in your quest for naturalization records are:

➤ Schaefer, Christina K. *Guide to Naturalization Records of the United States*. Baltimore, Maryland: Genealogical Publishing Company, 1997.

➤ Szucs, Loretto Dennis. *They Became Americans, Finding Naturalization Records and Ethnic Origins*. Salt Lake City, Utah: Ancestry Inc., 1998.

Szucs's book takes you through the myriad of records and papers generated during the naturalization process over the years. There are lots of great examples so you can get a feel for the records you will be using and what to watch out for with regard to the information.

Schaefer's book looks at record availability within each state. One of the major benefits to the books by Christina Schaefer is her inclusion of Family History Library film numbers. This alerts you to the fact that you may not need to travel to a given courthouse, that the records you seek are on microfilm and therefore available to your local Family History Center.

Genie Goodies

In many ways the United States has been a work in progress. And when it comes to naturalization records, there is no exception. Before 1906 there was no central authority for the naturalization process. Therefore the individual could accomplish each of the three steps involved in the process in different places. And you would have to search for these records in county courthouses and other repositories. After 1906, the process was centralized in the Immigration and Naturalization Service. You would contact them directly about an ancestor naturalized after 1906.

For more information on passenger lists and what is available, you will want to get a copy of John P. Colletta's *They Came In Ships, A Guide to Finding Your Immigrant Ancestor's Arrival Record* (Ancestry, Salt Lake City, 1993). He has some great suggestions on how to determine when your ancestor arrived.

Like all other types of records that genealogists find useful, passenger lists are making their way onto the Internet. Lucky us.

One of the best Web sites for transcribed passenger lists is the Immigrant Ships Transcribers Guild (istg.rootsweb.com/). While their site is searchable, I was amazed at the number of ways in which they have the information organized. You can see lists listed by

➤ Date of arrival

➤ Ship's name

➤ Port of departure

➤ Port of arrival

➤ Surname and captain's name

Please realize that the guild concentrated on the major countries of departure, including

➤ Argentina

➤ Australia/New Zealand

➤ Belgium

➤ Brazil

➤ Canada

➤ Cape Verde Islands

➤ Columbia

➤ Cuba

➤ Denmark

➤ England

➤ Far East

➤ France

➤ Germany

➤ India

➤ Ireland

➤ Italy

➤ Mediterrania

➤ Mexico

➤ Netherlands

➤ Nicaragua

➤ Norway

➤ Pacific Islands

➤ Panama

➤ Portugal

➤ Puerto Rico

➤ Russia

➤ Scotland

➤ Spain

➤ Sweden

➤ Venezuela

➤ Wales

➤ West Indies

Obviously some of these ports at present only have one or two transcribed passenger lists, but when you first venture into the land of the unindexed passenger lists, you may want to check this site first to see if they have your ancestor on one of their lists. This massive undertaking is a major resource for those of us researching our immigrant ancestors.

But what of those ancestors who came on the ships in search of a better life? Does researching them differ from the research you have done already?

Heritage Hints

There are two excellent books to help you in researching your Jewish ancestry. The first genealogy-specific book you'll want to buy is Dan Rottenberg's *Finding Our Father: A Guidebook to Jewish Genealogy,* published by Genealogical Publishing Company. The second is Arthur Kurzweil's *From Generation to Generation, How to Trace Your Jewish Genealogy and Family History,* published by Harper Perennial.

Cousin Counsel

The Holocaust may be a very painful part of your grandmother or grandfather's personal histories. You will want to respect Holocaust survivors' wishes, and those people may not be able to say much about this period in their lives.

Jewish Research

While your initial research will be much the same as for anyone else researching his family history, eventually you need to turn your attention to resources unique to the Jewish heritage.

Among the unique resources that you may find in your research are

➤ Mohel books (records kept by the *mohel,* or circumciser, of the boys he circumcised)

➤ Ketubot (a marriage document, often handed down from generation to generation)

➤ Approbations (a "seal of approval" written by a rabbi in regards to the author of a manuscript)

➤ Yizkor books (memorial books, they tell the story of Jewish community)

➤ Shtetl finders (books to locate Jewish communities, many of which no longer exist)

It's very possible that if you are researching Jewish ancestry, it will have some connection with the Holocaust. Although entire communities were wiped out by the Nazis, institutions such as Yad Vashem (www.yad-vashem.org.il/) have made it their goal to perpetuate the memory of all the Jewish people who lost their lives in the Holocaust.

Bookmark the following two Web sites, so that you can return to them often.

Avotaynu (www.avotaynu.com/) is a major publisher of information and products of interest to those researching their Jewish genealogy. Their quarterly periodical, *Avotaynu,* is a must-have for all Jewish researchers. Begun in 1985, it is in its 14th year. And they have recently released a CD containing the back issues for the first 11 years.

In addition, since genealogists must have databases, Avotaynu has made available the Consolidated Jewish Surname Index, a searchable database of 28 databases including

➤ AJGS Cemetery Project Burials

➤ JewishGen Family Finder

➤ First American Jewish Families

➤ National Registry of Jewish Holocaust Survivors

Although not all of the databases are online, this tool lets you know which databases you will need.

The JewishGen (www.jewishgen.org/) is the other stop online. According to their Web site, JewishGen is "the primary Internet source connecting researchers of Jewish genealogy worldwide." And they really can make that claim. Some of their current projects and activities include

➤ ShtetLinks (includes links to Web pages devoted to many of the individual shtetls [villages])

➤ Yizkor Book Project (includes translations of some of these Memorial Books)

➤ Holocaust-Global Registry (a searchable database of Holocaust survivors and child survivors searching for identity)

Lineage Lingo

A **shtetl** was an individual village in the old country.

African American Research

Sad to say, but many of the original African American immigrants were brought to the American colonies and then the United States against their will. They were treated like property rather than people. As such, researching African American ancestry poses its own research problems.

After 1870, you will rely on the same records as for any other genealogical research. However, for the 1860s and earlier, locating and identifying African Americans is somewhat problematic. Some of the records you will want to find are

➤ Military records (about 180,000 African Americans served in the Civil War)

➤ Freedmen's Bureau records

Heritage Hints

An excellent, and recently published, book for those researching their African American ancestry is Dee Parmer Woodtor's *Finding a Place Called Home, A Guide to African-American Genealogy and Historical Identity*, published by Random House.

➤ Bills of sale

➤ Court records

➤ Will records

➤ Old newspapers

➤ Slave manifests

➤ Family Bibles

Because of the nature of the records, you may not find many records that spell out John, son of James and Mary; however, you can make inferences. The most important step in the researching of your pre-1870 ancestry will be in determining who the owner was of your ancestor at the time of emancipation. Some of the records you will use in this search include

➤ Census schedules 1850–80

➤ 1850 and 1860 slave schedules

➤ Deed books

➤ Tax lists

➤ Maps

➤ Records from the Freedmen's Bureau

There are some great genealogy sites available on the Internet that make it possible for you to begin the search of your African American ancestry.

Probably the most recognized is the AfriGeneas site (www.afrigeneas.com/). In addition to some great tips for getting started, and a searchable surname database, they also have a searchable Slave Data Collection that includes data from

➤ Wills

➤ Inventories

➤ Bible records

➤ Slave manifests

➤ Vital records

➤ Letters

➤ Plantation records

Another good Web site to visit is Christine's Genealogy Website at www.ccharity.com, which is devoted to information and links to African American genealogy.

Heritage Hints

Some of the records generated in running a plantation may have survived. Collections of personal papers may have found their way to historical societies, libraries, and private manuscript collections.

Cousin Counsel

Remember that during the time of slavery, marriages between slaves were not officially recognized. It is very possible that you will never find any proof of a marriage between two slaves.

An anthology that you may want to investigate is the American Slave Narratives: An Online Anthology (xroads.virginia.edu/~HYPER/wpa/wpahome.html). The interviews in this online collection were the art pieces of the 2,300 former slaves who were interviewed between 1936 and 1938, as part of the Works Project Administration interview project. This is just a sample. The complete collection of narratives can be found in *The American Slave: A Composite Autobiography,* edited by George P. Rawick. Greenwood Press published these narratives over a period of seven years beginning in 1972.

Lineage Lingo

An **anthology** is a collection, such as a collection of poems, short stories, or interviews.

Native American Ancestry

Like other ethnic groups, there was a movement to stamp out the ties and connections that Native Americans had with their ancestry and their heritage. For some time it was felt that to "civilize" them, they must be forced to forsake all their traditions.

One of the most important aspects of researching your Native American ancestry is that you must determine the tribe from which you are descended. The records are separated based on the tribes.

Some of the records most useful to genealogists are the census rolls taken at various times for the different tribes. And the enrollment cards for the Five Civilized Tribes are wonderful if you can find your ancestor in them. Very few of them are indexed.

One of the best places to begin your online research of your Native American ancestry is Native American Genealogy (hometown.aol.com/bbbenge/front.html). In addition to links to other sites, they have pages devoted to the following Indian Nations:

- ➤ Cherokee
- ➤ Choctaw
- ➤ Lakota (which most people know as Sioux)

For those of you who are researching the Ottawa, Chippewa, or Potawatomi tribes, you may want to see what the Native American Research in Michigan site (hometown.aol.com/roundsky/introduction.html) has to offer. (Note that this URL has no www.)

If you are more interested in the historical aspects of your heritage, then you will want to stop by the Native American Research Page (maple.lemoyne.edu/~bucko/indian.html). (Note this URL has no www.) This site's emphasis is on history and heritage.

Lineage Lingo

The U.S. government, with the aid of its troops, moved the **Five Civilized Tribes** into a portion of Oklahoma that originally was called "Indian Territory." The tribes that made up this group included the Cherokee, Chickasaw, Choctaw, Creek, and Seminole.

Hispanic Research

Hispanic Americans were among the earliest settlers in the United States. As early as 1565, there were Hispanic settlers in St. Augustine, Florida.

Like any society that has records dating from the 1500s, you will find that as you progress in your research, you are met with a unique obstacle—that of reading the older styled writings. This is one of those projects that you can't zip through in an hour. So make sure you parked in the long-term lot when you go to read those records.

Heritage Hints

There are two books to help you with your Hispanic research. Gale Research Company published Lyman D. Platt's *A Genealogical Historical Guide to Latin America* in 1978. The other one is *Tracing Your Hispanic Heritage,* by George Ryskamp, published by Hispanic Family Research in 1984.

There are a couple of Web sites to get you started on your research. The first is the AOL Hispanic Genealogy Special Interest Group (users.aol.com/mrosado007/index.htm). Their library page has some excellent links to what is available in books. And they have a database of Hispanic surnames that you might find helpful.

Another good starting point is Al Sosa's Hispanic Genealogy (home.att.net/~Alsosa/). Here, you are taken step by step into the process of researching your Hispanic heritage.

Another book that you can order online is George Ryskamp's *Finding Your Hispanic Roots,* published by Genealogical Publishing Company. You can find out more about this book by visiting the GPC Web site at www.genealogybookshop.com.

Asian American Research

While at different times legislation was passed to limit the number of Asians allowed into the United States, there are still many who can trace their ancestry to either Asia or the Pacific Rim. There aren't too many books available to help you in your endeavors. However, you may want to visit the Oryx Press site (www.oryxpress.com/), as they have books for both Chinese Americans and Japanese Americans. While written for younger researchers, they will hold some insight into where you need to go and what you can hope to find.

Online, your first stop should be to the AsiaGenWeb site (www.rootsweb.com/~asiagw/), as they have pages devoted to the Asian countries from a genealogical standpoint. When you visit there, you will see that, unfortunately, some of the areas still need a volunteer to help bring them to life.

The Tip of the Iceberg

The topics we covered in this chapter were only briefly covered, so after you learn the basics from this book, you will want to make additional book investments. There are complete books on how to research most of the various ethnic groups at which we looked. As you begin your research, I hope that if you discover unexpected ethnic connections, you'll research them with great interest.

The Least You Need to Know

➤ All genealogical researchers will most likely need passenger lists at one time or another.

➤ You will find the naturalization records to be helpful in finding your immigrant ancestor in ship records.

➤ Ethnic research presents its own unique difficulties, each of which can be worked around, provided you are resourceful.

Chapter 20

Around the World in 80 Seconds

In This Chapter

➤ If it's 10 P.M., this must be England

➤ Mastering sites devoted to the old country

➤ England, Italy, Germany, and Norway: Help is available

➤ *Sprechen sie Deutsch?* Translators needed

One of the Internet's most amazing features is that it provides the opportunity for you to visit foreign countries from the comfort of your home. With the click of a mouse button, you can see information pages from England, Germany, or Canada without so much as an airline reservation.

The Internet offers us a real view of a small world. In a matter of minutes, you can make contact with a fellow researcher half way around the world. Cousins and re-searchers who share common localities are finding each other like never before.

But, how can you tell just where you're "located" in this World Wide Web? Remember to look at the URL. With the exception of sites housed on servers in the United States, all other countries have a two-character country code as part of their domain.

One of the benefits of using the World Wide Web is the capability of checking records and resource contacts in other countries. Pre-Internet, you would have to have ac-cessed a published directory containing this information, or you would have to have made expensive long-distance phone calls. Now, you can visit a Web site, and, at the very least, get the address information for requesting a record or a search. Increasingly, I am finding searchable databases. Some are free, but others charge an access fee.

Genie Goodies

Domain names clue you in to where the sites are from. Some examples of the two-character country codes include **uk** (United Kingdom), **be** (Belgium), **au** (Australia), and **de** (Denmark).

The British Isles at Bedtime

Information abounds if you are researching ancestors in England, Ireland, Scotland, and Wales. There are easily some 1,000 sites on the Internet for genealogy and family history of the United Kingdom.

If you are researching English, Irish, Scottish, or Welsh ancestors, you will want to make sure that GENUKI is your first step on the Internet.

Cousin Counsel

Be sure to read all the requirements when signing up for a fee-based searchable database. Some of them will charge based on the number of searches. Others charge only if you request additional information after the original index search.

A visit to the GENUKI Web site (www.genuki.org.uk/) is a treat for British Isle researchers. According to the GENUKI site, the "aim of GENUKI is to serve as a comprehensive virtual reference library of genealogical information that is of particular relevance to the U.K. and Ireland."

A Web site is only as good as the information being presented. GENUKI's site has extensive pages on every aspect of genealogy for the British Isles. In addition, they have broken down the information under easy to understand headings:

➤ Archives and Libraries   ➤ Land and Property

➤ Bibliography   ➤ Manors

➤ Cemeteries   ➤ Maps

➤ Census   ➤ Medical Records

➤ Chronology

➤ Church Records

➤ Civil Registration

➤ Colonization

➤ Description and Travel

➤ Directories

➤ Emigration and Immigrations

➤ Gazetteers

➤ Genealogy

➤ Handwriting

➤ Heraldry

➤ History

➤ Merchant Marine

➤ Military History

➤ Military Records

➤ Names, Personal

➤ Newspapers

➤ Occupations

➤ Periodicals

➤ Population

➤ Postal and Shipping Guides

➤ Probate

➤ Societies

➤ Taxation

Although the list gets you started, the GENUKI site then breaks into country categories for England, Ireland, Scotland, and Wales. Some information is specific to the entire country, and some information is county-specific, as you can see from the following figure.

If you select to link to any one of the given counties, you can see what GENUKI has for that county, including

➤ Archives

➤ Church records

➤ Census records

➤ Civil registration

➤ Genealogy

➤ Societies

The links for the various subjects may include actual raw data or they may include the addresses and phone numbers for contacting given repositories.

While GENUKI is probably the best site, there are other sites that should be kept in mind when researching the British Isles.

Lineage Lingo

GENUKI is the premier genealogy site for the United Kingdom and Ireland. They got their name by combining the GEN from genealogy with the abbreviation UK and the first letter from Ireland. It is a very fitting name for a site that brings genealogists plenty of information on the United Kingdom and Ireland.

*GENUKI also offers
information for the specific
counties.*

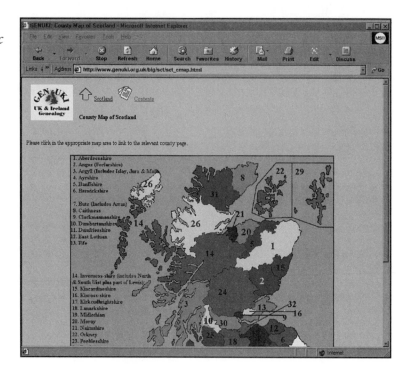

Genie Goodies

There are many good books on how to research your British, Scottish, and Irish ancestors. Both Genealogical Publishing Company, Inc. (www.genealogybookshop.com) and Ancestry, Inc. (www.ancestry.com) offer some excellent volumes, including Angus Baxter's *In Search of Your British and Irish Roots* (GPC) and *Irish Records* by James G. Ryan, Ph.D. (Ancestry, 1998).

Genie Goodies

The Family History Department of the Church of Jesus Christ of Latter-day Saints has recently released two new CD database products that can be beneficial to those researching their British family history. The *1881 British Census* is a transcription of the census on 33 CDs. In addition to being searchable, you can view additional information about each individual and see him or her in household units. The other CD is the *Vital Records Index British Isles,* which is on five CDs and includes extractions from vital records for the years 1500–1888.

The Public Record Office (www.pro.gov.uk/default.htm) is the National Archives for England. The holdings of this repository are astounding. Finding out what is available and how to use it can sometimes require a little homework. Not to worry though, as the PRO has more than 100 information leaflets available on their Web site on a wide variety of topics including

Heritage Hints

Many of the pages on the GENUKI site are informational. You will find that if you have a question about a records type or repository, this is a great place to begin.

➤ Military records

➤ Bankruptcy records

➤ Common lands

➤ Domesday Book

➤ Genealogy

➤ Heart tax

➤ Oath Rolls

For those beginning their Irish research, you will want to make sure that you visit Irish Ancestors (www.ireland.com/ancestor/). This is a comprehensive guide to those researching their Irish ancestry. This site includes pages devoted to

➤ Identifying the family's place of origin

➤ Finding out about surnames

➤ Learning about emigration

➤ Understanding heraldry

If you are researching Scottish ancestry, then you will want to check out the Gathering of the Clans Web site (www.tartans.com/). This site deals with all things Scottish, including

➤ Clans

➤ Tartans

➤ Famous Scots

➤ Genealogy

If you are new to researching your British Isles ancestors, begin with these valuable books on the topic:

Lineage Lingo

The **Domesday Book** was a general survey, taken in 1086, of those who owned land in England. It has sometimes been referred to as the first English census. However, it is not a census of everyone, only those who owned the land. It was named so as it was the final judgment or final proof of legal ownership of the land.

➤ Baxter, Angus. *In Search of Your British & Irish Roots*. 4th Edition. Baltimore, Maryland: Genealogical Publishing Company, Inc., 1999.

➤ Cory, Kathleen B. *Tracing Your Scottish Ancestry*. Edinburgh, Scotland: Polygon, 1991.

➤ Irvine, S. *Your English Ancestry: A Guide for North Americans*. Salt Lake City, Utah: Ancestry, Inc., 1993.

Germany from Your Office

Many of us are researching our German ancestry. Some of us are related to German immigrants, and the rest of us are researching another ethnic group, the Germans from Russia.

If family folklore says your family came from Germany, you cannot just immediately jump into researching German genealogical records. You will need to exhaust all records available in the United States or other country where your more recent German ancestor emigrated.

Cousin Counsel

When working with German research, it is important to keep in mind that the country of Germany did not exist until 1871. Before that time each of the states was a separate entity.

What are some of the records that might help to supply you with this vital piece of information?

➤ Family stories

➤ Obituaries

➤ Tombstones

➤ Passenger lists (primarily after 1893)

➤ Naturalization records

➤ *International Genealogical Index*

➤ County histories

➤ Fraternal or cultural organizations

➤ Vital records

Many of these records are going to be on microfilm or will need to be requested through agencies and repositories in the United States. While you are waiting for records from repositories, you will want to talk with any older relatives. It's a good idea to write down, or tape, those family stories.

Once you have some records, you will want to sit down with them and begin to evaluate what they tell you about the old country.

1. Try to determine who the immigrant ancestor was.

2. Determine what you already know about that ancestor.

3. Decide what additional records you may need to order.

The ultimate goal with these records is to determine the parish from which your immigrant ancestor came from.

Of course, just because you have a parish name does not mean that you will know where it is. If you are lucky, the records will supply you with not only the town but also the state. However, if your luck runs akin to mine, then you will want to turn your attention to gazetteers and maps to help you pin down where the parish is likely to be found. There are some excellent gazetteers on microfiche through your local Family History Center.

If you are just beginning to research your German ancestry, you no doubt have many questions. The Internet offers you some great resources that you can access when it is convenient to you. One of the best Web sites is the German Genealogy Home Page (www.genealogy.net/gene/index.html). This site has many valuable pages that cover subjects such as

➤ Beginners' tips

➤ General research

➤ Regional research

Cousin Counsel

Try not to have any preconceived notions during your evaluation phase. Lay out all the records and notes you have compiled on the individual and methodically construct a timeline. This will help you in establishing a pattern for his life, and will show you where the gaps exist in your record keeping.

Lineage Lingo

A **parish** can refer to either an ecclesiastical (church) or civil government division.

➤ German emigration to America

➤ Links to other Web sites

The general research section offers you insight into

➤ Getting started (a must-see site for new researchers)

➤ History

➤ Genealogical and historical societies

➤ Libraries

➤ Bibliography

Lineage Lingo

Ortsfamilienbucher are printed books that duplicate all the births, marriages, and deaths listed in the handwritten parish registers for a given town. These books do not exist for every community nor are they necessarily easily available.

Heritage Hints

When researching your family history in Germany, if you find yourself in either Holstein or Ostfriesland, it is possible that the surnames you will be researching will be patronymics. **Patronymic** surnames change with each generation. The last name is taken from the first name of the father with an extension. So the son of Peter, would have the last name Peters.

Remember, not all genealogists know everything about researching their own family trees. What they do know is where to find the answers to their questions. Bibliographies are one of the best ways to learn what books are available to help you with your questions. The bibliography page here includes books by some of the best known in German genealogy:

➤ Angus Baxter

➤ Larry O. Jensen

➤ Kenneth Lee Smith

➤ Ernst Thode

The Bibliography page also includes a link to information and listings of Ortsfamilienbucher.

For those of us who have not yet been able to convince our spouse that reading the PC screen in bed is just like reading a book, there is hope. A great resource that you can read in bed is Angus Baxter's *In Search of Your German Roots,* which is in its third edition and was just this year reprinted by Genealogical Publishing Company.

Angus Baxter's book is especially useful to those who do not have plans to visit Germany any time soon. He talks about records that you can write for or microfilms you can get through your local Family History Center.

Of course, increasingly we are beginning to find raw records that are located on the Web. This is one of the advantages that the Internet brings to us. There are some passenger lists available through the Immigrant Ships Transcribers Guild (istg.rootsWeb.com/). In addition, other records such as naturalization records are beginning to make their appearances, as shown in the following figure. You will find many of these sites listed through the following sites:

➤ German Genealogy Home Page (www.genealogy.net/gene/index.html)

➤ German Roots: German Genealogy Roots (home.att.net/~wee-monster/)

➤ Cyndi's List for Germany (www.cyndislist.com/germany.htm)

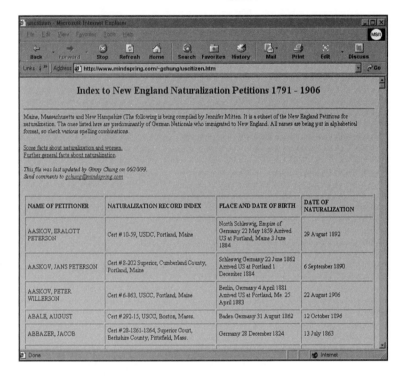

More records, such as this naturalization index, are making their way onto the Internet.

Scandinavia or Bust

Ask some people what countries are included under the heading of Scandinavia, and it is likely that they will not be able to list them all. Scandinavia includes the following countries:

➤ Denmark

➤ Finland

➤ Iceland

➤ Norway

➤ Sweden

For a lifelong student like myself, genealogy is the perfect hobby. I can keep learning. Each time my ancestors move onward or backward, I find myself getting the chance to learn about a new town, county, or country. When I start delving into a new country, there are often new records to learn about as well.

Genie Goodies

One of the things you will discover about genealogy is that there are many books available on a variety of aspects of genealogy. The genealogy subject has how-to books devoted to record types, ethnic research, regional research, and electronic genealogy. You will want to get familiar with the various genealogy book vendors such as Genealogical Publishing Co. (www.genealogy-bookshop.com), Ancestry (www.ancestry.com), and Everton's (www.everton.com). You will find a wide variety of how-to books available through these vendors.

Some books to help you with your Scandinavian research are

➤ Johansson, Carl-Erik. *Cradled in Sweden*. 5th edition. Logan Utah: Everton Publishers, Inc.

➤ Kowallis, Gay P., and Elly M. Poulsen. *The Danish Genealogical Helper*. Logan, Utah: Everton Publishers.

Cousin Counsel

It is important that you do not just assume that because someone has the same surname as you that he is related. It wasn't until about the 1200s (in some countries) and even later (in others) that surnames began to be used. Individuals often selected their surname based on their occupation, the name of their farm, or their location.

➤ Vincent, Timoth Latila, and Rick Tapio. *Finnish Genealogical Research*. New Brighton, Minnesota: Sampo Publishing, 1994.

At the present time, there are not that many records available online. However, if you can find an address for people with the same surname or for the archive that you need to contact, then you are once again on your way.

However, start with these few sites if you are researching your Scandinavian ancestry:

➤ Nordic Web Index (nwi.dtv.dk)

➤ Tracing Your Danish Ancestors and Relatives (www.denmarkemb.org/tracing.htm)

➤ Danmark Genealogy Resources (http://members.tripod.com/~Youda/denmark.htm)

➤ Family History Finland (www.open.org/~rumcd/genWeb/finn.html)

➤ Beginner's Guide to Finnish Family History Research (members.aol.com/dssaari/guide.htm)

➤ The Icelandic GenWeb (http://nyherji.is/~halfdan/aett/aettvef.htm) (this page currently has no English translation)

➤ Icelandic Names (www.itn.is/~gunnsi/family.htm)

➤ Ancestors from Norway (http://members.xoom.com/follesdal/)

➤ Swedish Research (www.familytreemaker.com/00000386.html)

Heritage Hints

When working with the Scandinavian countries, you may find yourself working with patronymics. This naming convention always gives you a clue to the given name of the father of the individual. It also guarantees that the surname will change with each generation.

Italy by Moonlight

Like many of the other countries we have already looked at, it is important to know the town your Italian ancestors are from. To locate the civil vital records, it becomes important to understand the divisions in Italy:

1. Regions (similar to states)
2. Provinces (similar to counties)
3. Communes (similar to towns)
4. Frazioni (similar to villages)

Heritage Hints

When trying to determine where your ancestor was from, it is possible that the place name you will discover will be the *frazione* rather than the commune. Most of the records you will need will be on the commune level.

Civil registration in Italy actually creates two copies of the birth, marriage, or death. One copy remains at the commune level. The other is sent to the province level, to the *procurra della repubblica,* which is similar to a county courthouse in the United States. When requesting vital records, you will need to write directly to the commune, but once you obtain the records you need, you'll see that Italian records can supply you with significant information.

Civil registration records are a wonderful source for genealogical information. After all, it is the main records that genealogists like to find the most: births, marriages, and deaths. The wonderful part of these records is that you will almost always find full names for all those involved, including maiden names for women, and places of residence. This is the type of information we drool over.

Italian records can supply you with lots of useful information.

Church and parish records may be accessible to you on microfilm. However, these are not nearly as prolific or as easily accessible as the civil registration records. When delving into these records, you will want to keep in mind that the civil registration records will be in Italian, while the church records will be in Latin.

An excellent resource, full of examples of the different record types, is Trafford E. Cole's *Italian Genealogical Records* published by Ancestry, Inc. This book includes examples of the record types for a number of different time frames. This offers you a view of the variations for records by time.

Cousin Counsel

Before writing directly to a commune or church in Italy, or any country actually, first visit your FHC and see what records have been microfilmed by the Family History Library. If the records you need have been micro-filmed, use these instead of contacting the officials in the old country.

Another good resource for the researcher that does not live in Italy is Sharon DeBartolo Carmack's *Italian-American Family History,* published by Genealogical Publishing Company. This book looks at the records that can be accessed from the United States.

Some of the other records that you might find yourself working with include

➤ Census records

➤ Conscription and military records

➤ Notary records

➤ Passenger records

➤ Passport records

➤ Tax records

Online, you will find some sites that can help you get started. The first one to stop by is The Italian Genealogy Homepage (www.italgen.com/). Here you will find pages devoted to

➤ Italian given names

➤ History and culture in your genealogy

➤ Getting started

➤ Introduction to Italian records

➤ Understanding Italian records

➤ Transcription, translation, and presentation

Another valuable Web site is the D'Addezio Italian Genealogy Web site at www.daddezio.com/index.html. This site includes a number of articles that you will find informative.

Lineage Lingo

Notary records can trace their roots back to ancient Rome when a slave would keep notes and correspondence for his owner. They now record land transactions and other property (such as a car), loans, new businesses, and the collection of state taxes.

Translator Needed

We have looked at a number of countries now, some of which you may find yourself visiting, at least to see the records they might have online. But, you'll be surprised to find out that these records in these other non–English-speaking countries are also generally not in English.

It is true, folks: English is not spoken everywhere, even in the world of genealogy. You will need to assume that as you branch out into foreign countries, you will need to learn a new language, or at least some core words.

Now, before PCs, this generally meant that you would need to visit your local bookstore and purchase an English-French or English-German dictionary. Nowadays, though, there are PC programs that can help you learn a new language.

For genealogists, there is also a great CD that includes word lists specifically designed for genealogists. This CD, the *Family History SourceGuide*, is available from the Distribution Center of the Church of Jesus Christ of Latter-day Saints. This CD compiles a number of reliable genealogical resources. We will look more at this and the other offerings of the Family History Library later on.

Heritage Hints

Whenever you are researching records from a foreign country, don't try to do it when you are pressed for time. Because of the language difference, you might need to spend extra time reacclimating your mind to the language in question.

Word lists allow you to see in an instant important terms and words you would need to keep an eye out for when looking through records of foreign countries:

➤ Days of the week

➤ Months of the year

➤ Occupations

➤ Relationship terms (mother, father)

Using these word lists, you will find that you can more confidently take that leap and begin researching in records from the old country.

Lineage Lingo

Word lists are compiled lists of important terms of use to genealogists, as opposed to a general language dictionary, with the foreign language word and the English translation. Word lists are available for Danish, French, Latin, Spanish, and German.

What do you do online though? We have already looked a little bit at the fact that the domain name of a Web site clues you in to the country of origin of the pages. Sometimes, the language of the site is a little more apparent. When you begin to visit sites from other countries, it is likely that the pages will be in the language of the country.

Fortunately for us, many of these pages have also included an English equivalent. Once in a while I have also seen other language choices as well. But what do you do when the Web site you visit doesn't have an English translation equivalent? You can let your PC and the Internet help you out with this and other aspects of researching foreign records, including

➤ Letters

➤ Documents

➤ Words on certificates

Cousin Counsel

When working with any kind of translation software or Web site, you want to keep your sentences simple. Slang terms may not have an equivalent in the foreign language. The translation software may misunderstand the point of the sentence, and translate it incorrectly. If that happens, you have defeated the purpose of your efforts.

There are two types of Web sites available for this type of translation problem. There are dictionaries such as those that we have always had access to. The other sites offer a way to create translations, from English to the foreign language.

If you are going to require a lot of letters or documents translated, you may do better to hire a translator. You can find many of these on the Internet as well, usually by visiting the same sites that offer limited translation services. Another option would be to purchase translator software in the language you will be relying on the most. If you purchase your own translator program, be sure to keep your sentences simple and free of slang expressions.

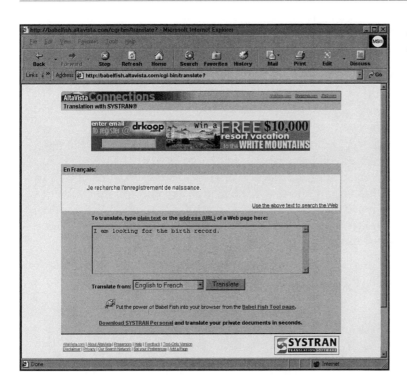

Keep your sentences simple and free of slang when using a translator.

As I mentioned, there are both dictionaries and translation sites available. The sites support translations to/from

➤ English
➤ French
➤ German
➤ Italian
➤ Portuguese
➤ Spanish

FreeTranslation.com (www.freetranslation.com/) claims to be the fastest, Web-based language service. It will not always translate verbatim, but will give you the gist of the text from the page. This site is sponsored by Transparent Language, a developer of translation software. You can translate to/from the following languages:

➤ Spanish to English
➤ French to English
➤ German to English

Heritage Hints

When trying to translate information from a Web site, you will want to copy and paste small pieces of the text from the Web site in question to one of the translator sites. This is done easily by opening two browser windows and having the Web site in one and the translator site in the other.

➤ English to Spanish

➤ English to French

➤ English to German

➤ English to Italian

➤ English to Portuguese

AltaVista brings its translation service to the Web at babelfish.altavista.digital.com/cgi-bin/translate?. AltaVista, as you probably already know, is the World Wide Web's largest search engine. The translation service also offers you a way to add a button to your browser to directly link you to AltaVista's translation capabilities. AltaVista uses translation software developed by Systran, a software vendor that also sells an independent version of its software for use at home. On the site, you can translate plain text (has to be typed in at the site) for the following:

➤ English to French

➤ English to German

➤ English to Italian

➤ English to Portuguese

➤ English to Spanish

➤ French to English

➤ German to English

➤ Italian to English

➤ Spanish to English

➤ Portuguese to English

To translate a Web page, you will want to type in the URL of the page, rather than copying and pasting the text as you find it in the Web page.

While the translation sites may be limited to just a few languages, there are many other sites that offer translating dictionaries.

Cousin Counsel

Just as spell checker dictionaries do not have every word that exists in them, the online translators do not have every word for any given language, either.

One such dictionary site is Dictionaries and Other Useful Sources (www.cis.hut.fi/~peura/dictionaries.html). Here you will find dictionaries for

➤ English

➤ French

➤ German

➤ Finnish

➤ Italian

➤ Russian

➤ Spanish

Genie Goodies

Don't get discouraged if you do not see the language of your ancestors above. A great site with a wide variety of dictionaries is Online Dictionaries and Translators (http://rivendel.com/~ric/resources/dictionary.html). In addition to the more common languages, you will find dictionaries here for Arabic, Cheyenne, Hebrew, Hindi, Persian, and many more.

The Least You Need to Know

➤ When you are beginning your research into your foreign country ancestry, the Internet has specific sites to help you.

➤ You can learn online about the peculiarities of certain repositories and records.

➤ Sites for records and research in foreign countries may not be in English.

➤ Online dictionaries and translation sites can help you get familiar with the language of your ancestors.

Part 6

PJs and Slippers Time

Because everyone is so busy these days, many would-be family history researchers probably feel that researching their family lineages is almost impossible because libraries aren't open when they have time to do their research. However, the Internet and electronic communications are changing how everyone researches family history and when—sometimes, an activity that you can now do comfortably in the time after you've put on your PJs and slippers.

In Part 6, I'll teach you how to search online library catalogs before you visit any physical libraries. Plan a complete research trip from online resources even before you see the library doors. Part 6 shows you the amazing resources available through the online access available from the Family History Library.

Finally, in Part 6, I introduce you to the methods you can use to create your own family history Web site. Whether you want to learn HTML or just put together a less elaborate Web site and have a software program do the technical stuff, Part 6 will offer you the information and direction you need.

Rifling Through Library Catalogs at 2 A.M.

You may not realize it yet, but libraries will become one of your favorite places to hang out. In fact, you are likely to want to be there even more than the librarians, who will be the ones shooing you out when the library closes each evening.

There are libraries all over the world that have resources for genealogists. The trick is finding the library and then seeing what it has to offer.

I often joke about doing my research at 2 o'clock in the morning. Of late, that hasn't been quite the joke it used to be, as I have become a little night owl. However, there are very often times that I need to know if a library has a certain book or other resource. Naturally the question does not come up until after the library has closed for the evening, even if I could just hop in my car and drive to it.

Online library catalogs are the next best thing to being there. And in fact, they offer you the chance to plot your research and get an idea of what is available before you even visit the library.

A couple of years ago I had the opportunity to visit the Newberry Library in Chicago. While the trip to Chicago had been in the works for a few months, I had not realized that I would have any time to do genealogy while we were there. This was a family trip, which in my life often has translated to "No genealogy allowed." So when my husband suggested I go ahead and enjoy a day at the library I jumped at it.

Of course this posed a slight problem. What could I research? I hadn't planned to do anything while I was there. Fortunately I did have my notebook PC, which meant I had all my data with me. So, I began looking through my database for questions I had in my Illinois lines. Then I began to wonder what the library had.

My motto now is "When in doubt, head to the Internet." I logged on and headed for the Newberry Library page. While they did not have all of their holdings available in an online database, they had enough to whet my appetite and allow me to put together a tentative research plan.

But just how do you find available online library catalogs?

Cousin Counsel

Just as there are differences in the many Internet search engines, you will find that the various online library catalogs will work differently as well. If you are not certain about the catalog, read any online help files that are supplied. You don't want to miss an entry in the catalog because you don't know the correct way to run the search.

Finding Online Libraries with WebCATS

The WebCATS site (www.lights.com/WebCATS/) is devoted to amassing links to those libraries that have online catalogs. Keep in mind that not all libraries with online catalogs will be found here in WebCATS. This is an ever-growing site and they are constantly adding new links. If you don't find a particular library listed, check back.

Genie Goodies

When trying to locate something online for the first time, it is a good idea to rely heavily on directories. Start with those that you are most familiar with and then branch out. If you didn't know the URL for WebCATS, you could start with the *Libraries, Archives & Museums* section of Cyndi's List (www.cyndislist.com) to locate the WebCATS site. Then once you are at the WebCATS site, you can use their services to locate available online library catalogs.

On the WebCATS site, they have a What's New link where you can see what has been added in the last three months. I was interested to see libraries from different countries being added. The United States is not the only country taking advantage of the Internet.

On the WebCATS site, there are different ways to locate a particular library. I have already touched on the What's New section, which lists the newly added libraries by the date they were added. Other ways include

➤ Search for keywords

➤ Geographical index

➤ Library type index

Lineage Lingo

Library type refers to the specialty for that particular library. Some library types include armed forces, college and university, government, law, public, and religious.

It is likely that you will tend to lean toward the Geographical Index. At the present time, WebCATS has the following regions in the Geographical Index:

➤ Africa

➤ Americas

➤ Asia/Pacific Rim

➤ Europe/Middle East

Under each of these regions, the various countries are listed alphabetically.

To locate the Newberry Library, I began by selecting the Geographical Index, and then United States (found under the Americas region) and then I selected Illinois.

The list of libraries displayed was arranged alphabetically by first word of the library's name. It wasn't too difficult to locate the Newberry Library that way.

If I hadn't known that the Newberry Library was in Illinois, or if I just wanted to see if a particular library offered an online catalog, I could have used the Search for Keywords option and typed in the word *Newberry*. Doing this reveals a list of possibilities:

➤ Illinois (rank: 1,000; 3,943 bytes)

➤ VTLS Inc. (rank: 721; 5,678 bytes)

➤ Special (rank: 200; 17,973 bytes)

➤ United States (rank: 24; 143,856 bytes)

Heritage Hints

When working with the search option in the WebCATS site, the higher the rank number, the more specific the page.

Heritage Hints

Don't discount any type of library. Genealogists rely on such a wide variety of record types that the different specialty libraries may be just what we need. And it is much better to search the catalogs from home rather than to have exhausted money and time to get to the library only to discover it has nothing of use to you.

The word *Newberry* shows up on each of these links. The trick is to select the highest ranking number as your first choice. Notice that as the rank number gets smaller, the number of bytes for the page gets bigger. That is because the "topic" gets broader. Obviously the list of libraries for Illinois is going to be much smaller than the list of libraries for the United States. The Newberry Library appeared on each of the above listed pages, but was easiest to scroll to using the Illinois page.

Locating the libraries using something such as WebCATS offers you the ability to locate the library quickly on the Internet. The benefit of such a site is that it is not limited to just a specific type of library. As genealogists, we often develop such tunnel vision that we overlook reliable alternative resources. University libraries often have valuable records, for instance. Therefore, with WebCATS you can see all different types of libraries that are online, and you can then search those catalogs.

Other Online Avenues

Of course, we also like to know where the genealogical libraries are located. At the present time, WebCATS does not offer a special library type heading for genealogy libraries. These libraries are generally interspersed in with the public or special libraries, depending on how large their genealogical focus is.

One Web site that genealogists will find useful in locating genealogical libraries is the Directory of Genealogy Libraries in the U.S. (www.greenheart.com/rdietz/gen_libs.htm). This comprehensive list of genealogical libraries is not limited to just those with online catalogs. Each library includes the address and for those that do have online sites, they have included a link. Keep in mind that a link does not guarantee a database, just a known Web site devoted to that library.

Probably one of the most overlooked repositories for genealogists is the state library. Many times the holdings of the state library are just what a genealogist is looking for.

Recently I had an intriguing research question. A fellow genealogist had been told that her grandmother was supposedly sent to Florida by train because she was suffering from tuberculosis. She wanted information about rest centers for these patients.

In researching this, I decided to call the Florida Department of State, Division of Library and Information Services. The woman that I talked with was very helpful. Not only did she suggest some possible avenues for my research, but within a week she sent me copies of annual reports from Florida's Health Department and other resources. These copies allowed me to answer the question for the individual.

Of course had I received such a question now, I could have done some of the preliminary research online before calling to request copies or to see about getting such copies. In comparing the PC catalog printouts that were sent to me with the search results on the Florida State Library's Web site, it was nice to be able to compare and see that both have the same information.

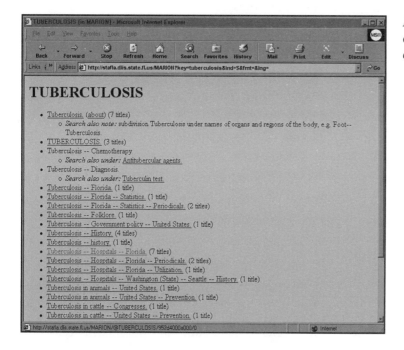

It was nice to see that the online catalog was so complete.

Finding the online state libraries has gotten very easy, thanks to the Library of Congress. The Library of Congress has set up a Web page devoted to links for the state libraries. This site, the Library of Congress: State Library Web Listing (lcWeb.loc.gov/global/library/statelib.html), lists the states alphabetically and includes links to

➤ State libraries

➤ State archives

➤ Public library systems

➤ State library networks

Most of the states have just a single link to their state library or other state repository. However, there are a few with links to the state library and another library or catalog site.

Cousin Counsel

It is important not to contact state libraries for basic how-to questions. You should turn to other avenues such as online help, how-to books, and fellow genealogists for answers to basic questions. Reserve the phone call to the State Library for requesting information about specific records held in that repository.

The Alabama Department of Archives & History has separated out their Family History & Genealogy. After selecting this from the front page, you are given the following subject headings to select from:

➤ Federal census

➤ Land records

➤ City directories

➤ Historical and genealogical societies

➤ State census

➤ Military records

➤ African American

➤ Related links, genealogy

➤ Vital records

➤ Military discharge records (DD214s)

➤ Native American

➤ County records

➤ Surname files

➤ Immigration and naturalization

➤ Newspapers

Heritage Hints

Not all state libraries are created equal. Some offer searchable databases, others have organized their holdings under subheadings. Still others will only have a Web page devoted to information about the library.

You can select these links to see a display of available records housed at the archives. You can also do an online request for reference help. They offer you the chance to fill out a form that includes

➤ Date of request

➤ Your name

➤ Mailing address

➤ Phone number

➤ E-mail address

➤ Information on the person to research (name, date or birth, county in Alabama, name of spouse)

➤ Type of record to search

➤ Information known to locate that record

Cousin Counsel

Do not forget to include the county when corresponding with a state library. Remember that many of the records you will work with in your research will have been created originally at the county level. Also, when corresponding with another researcher or a library, you want to be sure to give them as much information as possible.

Once you have supplied the details, you can then submit the form. Remember to include your phone number and e-mail address so that they can easily contact you if there is a problem with the data you supply.

Not all state libraries offer an online reference request service. Some of the libraries, while having their catalogs online, still require that you mail them any requests. However, their online site offers you the chance to first search for available records and then second, to educate yourself as to how to request information from them, including any costs involved with that request.

Genie Goodies

Always assume there will be some charge involved when requesting materials from state libraries. The people that reside in a particular state fund that state library. Therefore, very often there is no research fee charged to the in-state researchers. Out-of-state researchers, though, can expect some sort of a research fee. And everyone can expect photocopy costs. It is important that we remember that the state library is experiencing high costs for electricity, paper, and toner when they make photocopies for us. It is only right that we should offset that cost. After all, we would have paid for the copies had we gone to the library in person to do the research.

Know Before You Go

Online library catalogs are not just for researching that far away library. If you are like me, your library time is precious, as it is hard to come by. You want to make the most of your time and you don't want to have to waste any of it searching a library catalog if at all possible. The next time you are getting ready to head to your favorite library, check to see if they have an online catalog you can search. It might save on the disappointment.

While I am going to describe some of the libraries you are likely to travel to, I did want to point out that these same thoughts could and should apply to using the online catalog of your local library.

Have you ever gone to a library and discovered that they had nothing for what you had planned to research? I know that I have. With notebook PCs, it is a little easier to switch gears at a library since you can have your entire database handy. Of course, not everyone has a notebook PC, and there are still some places where all you can take with you is a pencil and notebook paper. So it is important to know what is available before you get there.

Cousin Counsel

More and more library Web sites are relying on the user-friendly capabilities of Web page coding. However, there are still some online catalogs that rely on less user-friendly interfaces such as TELNET to search the catalog. You will want to be sure to follow all directions supplied on these sites. Otherwise you will have a very frustrating search session.

Heritage Hints

Just because the book you want is in another library does not necessarily mean you cannot gain access to it without visiting the library that it is housed in. An interlibrary loan is very often an option for getting some records to you locally. Microfilmed records and non-rare books are sometimes available this way.

Some of the larger libraries that you will want to search before you get there include

➤ The Library of Congress (www.lcWeb.loc.gov/)

➤ The Daughters of the American Revolution Library (dar/library.net)

➤ The New York Public Library (www.nypl.org/)

➤ The Los Angeles Public Library (www.lapl.org)

➤ The Allen County Public Library in Fort Wayne, Indiana (www.acpl.lib.in.us/)

While I have mentioned some larger libraries of the United States, you will also want to keep this in mind if you get the chance to travel abroad. You can always start by selecting Cyndi's List (www.cyndislist.com) and finding the link to the country you will be visiting. If there are libraries online, she is likely to have them listed.

We talked a lot about how to conduct searches using Web site search engines in Chapter 12, when we talked about locating family Web pages. These search principals still apply when using the online catalogs.

➤ Always start out with less information.

➤ Try to search on the least common word first.

➤ Doing a search on *genealogy* is not effective.

➤ Have a goal in mind before you begin the search.

➤ Learn how the catalog handles word combination searches (Boolean searches).

One more thought about searching online catalogs. There are times that a library may not include its entire collection. Very often periodicals will be omitted or cataloged separately. When searching the Los Angeles Public Library's online catalog you will find that they have separated out their magazines and other periodicals into a separate searchable database.

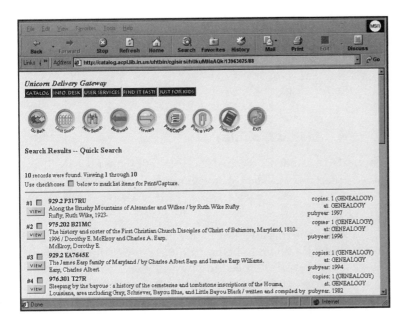

You can make the most of any research trip, such as a trip to the Allen County Public Library, by searching the catalog before you get there.

Genie Goodies

We have mentioned Boolean searches before and described how they affect your searches. This type of search was named after George Boole, a British mathematician who was born in 1815. His Boolean algebra was the basis of the design of modern computers.

Libraries in the Twenty-first Century

I have been involved in online research for more than 10 years. In the world of PCs that time encompasses the changes of 100 years when compared with the evolution in other fields. Every day brings us new capabilities and better technology.

Five years ago, searching for information online was a pipe dream. A couple of years ago, even those libraries that had their catalogs on computer did not have them available online. Today there are digital libraries. Look at all the interesting documents the National Archives is placing online through its NAIL site. The Library of Congress has begun to digitize some of its holdings. And now The New York Public Library offers some digitized collections.

Lineage Lingo

Manuscripts generally consist of groups of papers. They can be a person's private papers, log books, or drafts. Usually a manuscript has a common theme and is created by or around an individual or family.

Where is this all going? For genealogists, I suspect that it can only go on to better things. While I strongly believe that we will still need to physically visit courthouses, libraries, and archives, I also believe that resources coming out online and in other digitized mediums can only help us to push our lineages back further.

I wouldn't begin to prophesy about where computers are going. The technology is progressing at lightning speeds. However, the genealogical community is always looking for new ways to apply the technology of the future to aid them in searching for the past.

Even as I write this, there are CDs available with the scanned images of the census on them. These CDs have taken the pages of the census and enhanced them and placed them on CDs to be viewed on our PC. These are not indexes or transcriptions or some other human alteration of the original record. These scanned census pages on the CDs are just like cranking the films on a microfilm reader. Of course by using the CDs you won't get quite the tired arm as you do when using the microfilm.

More and more we see items online. While I don't know where it is headed, I am eagerly looking forward to the ride.

The Secrets Held by NUCMC

Believe it or not, NUCMC (pronounced nuck-muck) is not a PC term. It is an acronym that stands for the National Union Catalog of Manuscript Collections.

The National Union Catalog of Manuscript Collections began in 1959. The point of this was to catalog the manuscripts housed in repositories through the United States. The value of such a catalog to genealogists is great.

Manuscripts are very often one of the hardest things to track down. While there are usually guides published by the library for the manuscripts it holds, if you don't know that the manuscript exists, you won't know to look for it. NUCMC is not a catalog of all manuscripts, though. The holdings of certain libraries are excluded, including

➤ Holdings of federal libraries (National Archives and Library of Catalog)

➤ Holdings of presidential libraries

➤ Some holdings at state level archives (items you would expect to find at the state archive are excluded)

➤ Manuscripts held by the repository that created them

If you keep this in mind, then you won't expect to find certain items in NUCMC and end up being disappointed. While NUCMC was originally in a published book form, with the first volume published in 1962, you can now search an online version. The NUCMC site can be found at lcWeb.loc.gov/coll/nucmc/nucmc.html.

What types of records are you likely to find indexed in the NUCMC catalog? Basically, it includes just about any type of record. With more than 65,000 collections from more than 1,300 repositories, it is easy to see that anything is possible. Some of the records you are likely to find include

➤ Personal papers

➤ Correspondence

➤ Legal documents

➤ Property records

➤ Letters

➤ Diaries

➤ Photos

➤ Newspaper clippings

Cousin Counsel

Because NUCMC does not hold the key to all the manuscripts, don't overlook the other searchable databases such as NAIL, which is the catalog to the National Archives. Presidential libraries each have their own online sites where you can get more information about their holdings.

Heritage Hints

One of the aspects to searching databases is that I often come across subjects or items that I hadn't even considered until they were displayed there in front of my eyes. When you keep your searches simple you will be surprised at some of the interesting resources and records that might be included.

Now, I have already admitted to being addicted to history. I am always finding new periods in history that intrigue me. Usually it is because my ancestors were somehow involved, but there are times it is just because the people or events pique my interest. However, for as long as I can remember I have been interested in the Earps—yep, that's Wyatt Earp and his brothers.

Cousin Counsel

While there are times that we would love to limit our search to just three or four Web sites or entries from a search, you don't want to omit any possible useful sites. So if you can get the total number of finds down to fewer than 50, you probably don't want to limit the search any further.

Cousin Counsel

It is important to note that the online version of NUCMC is an ongoing project and not all-encompassing. It does not include the information cataloged from 1962–1993. It currently has information from 1986 and 1987 only.

When visiting the NUCMC site, I used the Earps to discover what types of records I could uncover using their online search engine.

The NUCMC search engine showed me 16 entries that included the word *Earp*. Not all of them had to do with Wyatt Earp and his brothers, but that was easy enough to determine as I read the descriptions. I learned that the Bancroft Library of the University of California has a small collection of records on the Earps and that the University of Idaho had some interesting items as well.

Had the search resulted in a larger number of entries, say more than 100, I would have wanted to add an additional term to the search. It is always best though to begin with just a single term or surname and then you can add to it if need be.

While it is likely that you will still have to physically visit the repositories that house the manuscript you are interested in, you have saved yourself some time. Using the online NUCMC site, you have

➤ Determined that a manuscript collection exists.

➤ Established where it is housed.

➤ Learned of any restrictions on the collection.

NUCMC is one of three databases that compile information about the manuscript holdings in repositories around the United States. It is currently the only one that is searchable online by anyone.

The National Inventory of Documentary Sources (NIDS) is newer than NUCMC and does not include as many repositories. However, it does not exclude some of the items that NUCMC does. It includes the information in the National Archives, Library of Congress, and the presidential libraries. NIDS is available on fiche and now on CD.

Finally there is the Research Libraries Information Network (RLIN). RLIN (pronounced r-len) is an electronic database that lists manuscript material. Originally RLIN was only available to libraries and archives that belonged to the Research Library Group. This group consisted primarily of students and faculty at certain academic institutions. Now you can join the CLASS (Cooperative Library Agency for Systems and Services) network that allows you to search the database. Membership in CLASS requires certain one-time and yearly fees.

Genie Goodies

For more information about these databases, you will want to access an article found in the *National Genealogical Society Quarterly*. Bell, Mary McCampbell, Clifford Dwyer, and William Abbot Henderson, "Finding Manuscript Collections, NUCMC, NIDS, and RLIN," *National Genealogical Society Quarterly*, Vol. 77–3 (September 1989), pp. 208–218.

The Least You Need to Know

➤ Libraries are a major resource for genealogists.

➤ Some libraries offer online catalogs to search.

➤ Take advantage of these online catalogs to plan your research.

➤ WebCATS can help you find online library catalogs of all kinds.

➤ The NUCMC manuscript database helps you find the hard-to-find records.

Family History Library

Everyone who researches his or her family history dreams of at least once visiting the Family History Library in Salt Lake City, Utah. This tremendous repository of genealogical information seems to be something magical. The Family History Library consists of five floors, four of which are open to the public, free of charge. Even though the library is privately owned, there is no charge to visit. And, the costs for copies and computer printouts are minimal.

I remember my first visit to the Family History Library. I'd prepared for weeks before by visiting my local Family History Center. At that time my local center didn't have a photocopier for the microfiche or microfilm. As a result, I had handwritten everything that I thought was important on the items I wanted to go through while I was there.

One of the things that makes genealogy a natural for me is my attention to detail. I write down everything. In research this is a plus. When preparing to go to Salt Lake City this resulted in giving me a hand cramp. Of course now I can type a lot of it into my PC, but back then, even the laptops were a bit heavy and a bit expensive. So every Tuesday night you would find me scribbling away in a notebook for three hours.

I also spent the weeks before, and the plane ride too, reading Nancy Carlberg's *Researching in Salt Lake City,* which prepared me not only for the library, but also for Salt Lake City. And through that preparation I felt like I could really accomplish my research goals.

Families Really Are Forever

For most of us our local Family History Centers (FHCs) are our lifeline to the Family History Library. The more than 3,000 branches to the main library in Salt Lake City are stocked with microfiche and CDs that hold millions of names as well as the catalog to the library's holdings.

Unfortunately, the hours of operation for FHCs vary from center to center and often they are only open a few hours each week. This is because volunteers staff them. If the director of the center cannot get enough volunteers, then she or he must cut back on the hours of operation.

Genie Goodies

The Church of Jesus Christ of Latter-day Saints, often referred to as Mormons, owns the Family History Library. Latter-day Saints, or LDS, members have strong religious beliefs that motivate them in the search of their family histories. It is this religious belief that has helped build the impressive library that genealogists are encouraged to visit. FHCs are generally located in local LDS chapels. However, like the main library, they are open to anyone interested in researching his or her family history. Locating your FHC can usually be done by looking in the yellow pages of your phone book under the Church of Jesus Christ of Latter-day Saints.

When you visit your local Family History Center for the first time, it is a good idea to ask them to show you around. Some of them even have a video they can show you that outlines what you can expect in researching your family history and in using your local FHC. Because of the records made available, it is as though your family goes on forever.

Just as you need to have a goal when you are online or going to any other library, when you visit your Family History Center, you need to have a goal there as well. If you go in empty-handed, you are likely to go home empty-handed. Each Family History Center has some standard resources that you can expect to find whether you visit one in Los Angeles or Orlando. Those resources include

➤ FamilySearch

➤ Fiche version of the International Genealogical Index

➤ Fiche version of the Family History Library Catalog

➤ Microfiche Reference Collection, Part I

➤ Microfiche Reference Collection, Part II

➤ Fiche version of PERSI

➤ Fiche version of Everton's Family Cellar

➤ Fiche version of AIS census indexes

When you first visit your local FHC, you are likely to find yourself using their PCs. The FamilySearch CDs offer you millions of names in different databases. Presently the FamilySearch system includes names in the following:

➤ Ancestral File

➤ International Genealogical Index

➤ Social Security Death Index

➤ Military Index

➤ Scottish OPR Index

➤ Family History Library Catalog

Each of these databases offers different data in different formats. Some of them group people together in family units and display lineages of multiple generations. Others show a single individual's birth, marriage, or death.

You may wonder why, in an online genealogy book, I'm telling you all about the Family History Library. In April 1999, the Family History Library put some of its most used databases online for searching at anytime, including two o'clock in the morning if you so desire. The FamilySearch site (www.familysearch.org) was in a testing phase until its official launch. It was more popular than anyone expected. A lot of genealogists have been waiting for the unveiling of this site.

Cousin Counsel

Keep in mind that at the present time the Ancestral File database does not include source documentation. You will want to correspond with the submitters to discover the sources they used in compiling the lineages.

Lineage Lingo

The Scottish OPR Index is the Scottish Old Parochial Register index. This is an index of entries in the old (pre-1855) church registers from the Church of Scotland. It was originally on microfiche and required that you know the shire from which the family came. The CD version combined them, making searching that much easier.

Index to the World—Almost

The International Genealogical Index (IGI) was originally created as a means for LDS individuals to track religious ordinances done on behalf of their deceased family. However, genealogists soon discovered that this index was a valuable tool, as it had the potential to be an index to the world. What made it so valuable was that it listed specific information for each person. As it grew, it encompassed more individuals and more localities. Currently the IGI has more than 100 million names in it.

Genie Goodies

The LDS members believe very strongly that families can be together forever. Marriages in the LDS faith are not until death do you part, but are sealed together for eternity. Another belief is that these sealing ordinances must be completed here on earth in one of the LDS Temples. So the LDS practice proxy work on behalf of their ancestors. These sacred ordinances are done in the hopes that the deceased individual will accept them in the spirit world. Because there are so many ancestors who need these ordinances done for them, the IGI was created to help keep track of which individuals have already been done.

Entries in the IGI include

➤ Name of the individual

➤ Name of parents or spouse

➤ Event (usually birth, christening, or marriage)

➤ Date of event

➤ Place of event

➤ LDS ordinance dates

➤ Batch number and serial sheet (identification for locating the original)

➤ Microfilm number (available only in the CD version)

When originally released in microfiche format, it was necessary to know a specific division:

➤ The United States is divided into states.

➤ Canada is divided by province.

➤ Ireland and Germany on a country basis.

➤ The CD version just requires you to select a region such as North America, the British Isles, or Germany.

Information found in the IGI gets there from two possible sources. Patron submissions make up the bulk of the index and were supplied by fellow genealogists, primarily LDS. Other entries are from the library's extraction program.

Part of the International Genealogical Library is now available through the FamilySearch Web site. At the present time, the online version includes entries from North America, the British Isles, and Finland.

If you type in the name of your ancestor on the main page of the FamilySearch site, it will automatically search all the currently available regions. However, by selecting the Custom Search tab, you can further limit the search to a specific region or a specific event.

Heritage Hints

You can tell the difference between patron submissions and extractions by looking at the batch number. If it begins with a **C** or an **M**, then the entry is from the extraction program. Entries from the extraction program are generally more reliable, having been extracted by two people and then compared by a third. It is still important to look at the original record.

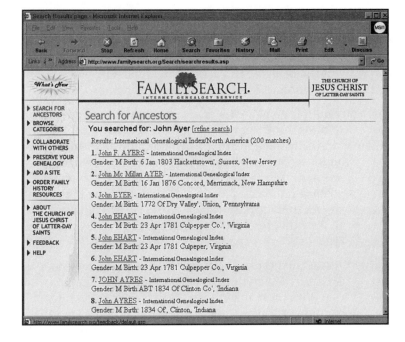

The IGI is an index that can help narrow down your search.

From the list of possible matches, you can then click on one of them and the IGI Record will be displayed. You will get

Cousin Counsel

When working with the IGI, keep in mind that this index is only for deceased individuals. The majority of individuals included in the IGI are those who were born prior to 1900. However, as more LDS converts begin this work, the number of post-1900 individuals is increasing. Those who have their Temple ordinances done while they are alive are not presently found in the IGI.

➤ The name of the person

➤ The date of the event

➤ The place where the event took place

➤ The name of the parents or the spouse

➤ Source information (the microfilm that has the original record)

While you may know a lot about your ancestor, remember that less is better when supplying data to the search fields. If you supply too much information, it may turn out that you know more than the index does or that your data disagrees with what the index has. By supplying all you know, you run the risk of eliminating the very person you were searching for. A good rule of thumb is to begin by searching on the first and last name. If that results in too many possible matches, you can then begin to narrow it down. Start with the birth or marriage year (available online in the custom search); then you can add information on the father or spouse if further narrowing is still necessary.

Lineage Online

By far the most popular database available in the FamilySearch databases is the Ancestral File. This is a lineage-linked database that can display the pedigree of a given individual. You can then print out the pedigree and accompanying family group sheets. You can also save this information to a floppy disk to use at home.

Because it is likely to show you multiple generations, many people start and end their research at a Family History Center, or through the FamilySearch site with the Ancestral File database. I once had an individual tell me that he couldn't do anything more on his research. When I questioned him on where he was in his research and then made suggestions about possible resources, I discovered that all he had used so far was the Ancestral File database. He was unaware of all the other resources at his fingertips through his local FHC.

Lineage Lingo

Information that is **lineage-linked** is connected by family relationship. In the Ancestral File this is displayed in the form of a pedigree or a family group view.

This is the norm, unfortunately. Many people assume or expect that everything available at the FHL should be on CD. With more than two million reels of microfilm containing copies of records from around the world, there would have to be a lot more CDs than are currently available.

The Ancestral File should be used in conjunction with all the other databases and resources found at your Family History Center.

When you search the Ancestral File, it is very similar to other searches in FamilySearch. You first supply a name. If you have selected the Custom Search, in addition to the first and last name of the individual you are searching for, you can also include the

Heritage Hints

When working in the Ancestral File, living non-LDS individuals are listed with the word LIVING and no other information. Living LDS individuals will have their name but no additional information.

➤ Spouse's name

➤ Parent's name

➤ Birth and/or death year

➤ Christening year

➤ Burial year

➤ Marriage year

➤ File number (AFN)

Once you have supplied your search fields, you will be supplied with a list of possible matches, or a message saying there are not matches if it does not find anything for you. Each match will show you the

➤ Name of the person

➤ Gender

➤ Birth date

➤ Birthplace

You will then need to select one of the people from the list. FamilySearch will then display the Individual Record for that person, which will also include the name of the parents of that individual, if known. To the right are a number of buttons:

➤ Pedigree button

➤ Family button (with individual you selected as a child)

➤ Details button (displays the name and address of the individual that supplied the lineage)

In the Pedigree view, you will see that there are additional family buttons. You can click on any individual to view that person's Individual Record or you can click on the Family button to view the complete family for that individual. Once you have done your initial search, you can then use the buttons to move back further and further through the generations.

In the pedigree view you can select other individuals to view their Individual Record.

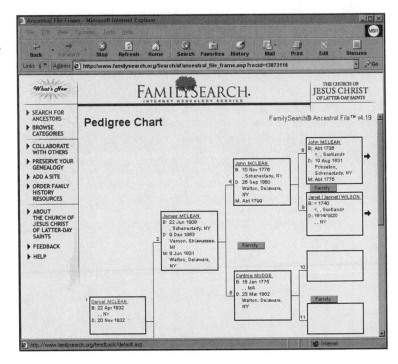

The Ancestral File grows only as individuals submit GEDCOMs of their families. While it is good to submit accurate information, don't hold up your submissions waiting for everything to be done. You can always submit additional information later. You do not need to submit your entire database at once. You can be selective, sharing just the line that you have compiled complete details on. Then as you work on another line, you can submit that one.

Cousin Counsel

When using information from the Ancestral File, whether it's the online or the CD version at your local Family History Center, be sure to keep it separate from your personal family database until you have been able to verify the names, dates, places, and relationships. If you do put something into your personal database, be sure to cite the Ancestral File as your source.

Your local Family History Center has a handout, "Contributing Information to Ancestral File," that shows you what is necessary for contributing to the Ancestral File. Once your contribution has been received, it will be included in the next release of the Ancestral File.

You can also read this handout online.

1. Visit the FamilySearch site.

2. Select Browse Categories.

3. Select Research Support.

4. Select SourceGuide.

5. Select How-to Guides.

6. Scroll down until you find the "Contributing Information to Ancestral File" handout and select it.

There are also ways to correct information in the Ancestral File. You will want to read the handout "Correcting Information in Ancestral File" which is available at your local Family History Center or by following the above steps and selecting the link to the guide on correcting, rather than contributing.

Genie Goodies

In 1998 the Church of Jesus Christ of Latter-day Saints released the Family History SourceGuide. This CD included an electronic version of all their published research outlines on the U.S. states, Canadian provinces, and various countries. They also included word lists and other useful handouts. These are now all available online at the FamilySearch Web site. You can scroll through the list of available handouts or you can get help by using the Catalog Helper. You tell it what you hope to find and it suggests possible handouts to help you.

Catalogs at Dawn

You know my penchant for searching online catalogs in the middle of the night. Because of the massive holdings at the Family History Library, I have often found myself looking in their catalog first. Of course, until recently, this meant usually waiting until the next time I was at my local Family History Center.

While people flock to their local Family History Centers and to the new FamilySearch Web site to search the Ancestral File, the library catalog is indeed the backbone. It is through the Family History Library Catalog (FHLC) that you can determine what records might be available.

At the present time there are more than two million reels of microfilm housed in the Family History Library. Each of these films contains

➤ Vital records

➤ Census records

➤ Probate records

➤ Family histories

➤ Cemetery records

➤ Newspapers

➤ Bible records

Because these microfilms often contain more than a single source, there are more than two million records available through the Family History Library. Many of the microfilms contain multiple records. This is especially true with books, where sometimes 5–10 or more books may be found on any given film.

Heritage Hints

There are times when it will actually save you time and money to hire a professional genealogist, especially when the records you need are available only at the county courthouse or other unique repository. To find professional genealogists, you may want to visit The Association of Professional Genealogists Web site (www.apgen.org/~apg/).

I confess that my favorite part of researching my family history is the search. Don't get me wrong, I am just as excited as the next person when I find a new ancestor, but that excitement stems from the payoff of the search. Somehow the name means more to me when I have had to work to find it. While I won't turn down generations found in something like the Ancestral File, I don't feel the connection to them that I do with those I have worked hard to pin down.

The Family History Library Catalog is your key to the records of the Family History Library. By searching the FHLC, you can begin to see what records are going to be easily accessible and which you are likely to either have to write for or visit in person.

It is important to know what you need to look for when you begin to use the FHLC. You need to know what records you can expect to find in each governmental jurisdiction.

For instance, if you are researching your family in Massachusetts, it is important to know that most of the records for that state are actually kept on the town level. Therefore, if you were to search the FHLC at the county level, you would be disappointed.

Probably one of the best ways to get familiar with the records that are available and on what level you are most likely to find them is to read about them. There are a number of published resources that can help you with this:

➤ Val D. Greenwood's *The Researcher's Guide to American Genealogy*

➤ Ancestry's *RedBook, American State, County & Town Sources*

➤ Loretto D. Szucs and Sandra Hargreaves Luebking's, *The Source, A Guidebook of American Genealogy*

➤ Everton's *The Handybook for Genealogists*

These books will tell you about the records, what information they will supply, and on what level you are most likely to find them. They will also tell you when they were first created, which is very important.

In addition to these books, you will also want to use the SourceGuide. The handouts for the various states, provinces, and countries can save you hours of frustration. The

SourceGuide research outlines also include information useful in using the Family History Library Catalog.

Under each heading in the research outline, you will be given information about a specific record type, which may include

➤ Titles of compiled records based on that source

➤ Years of availability

➤ Addresses of other repositories for those records

➤ Differences between various records of that particular group

➤ Library microfilm or book call numbers

Lineage Lingo

The experts at the Family History Library have developed **research outlines.** They detail the history of the locality or record type and include information about the record availability, including addresses for repositories other than the Family History Library.

By using these outlines, and the other books mentioned, you will find yourself learning about the locality of your ancestors along with how to use the Family History Library Catalog.

Once you know how to search for the records, you will know when to concentrate on the county, the town, or the state. Once you type that in, you will then see a list of record types displayed for that locality. Selecting the record type will display a list of resources under that record type. You can then select one of these resources and get details on what the resource is and in what format the Family History Library has it.

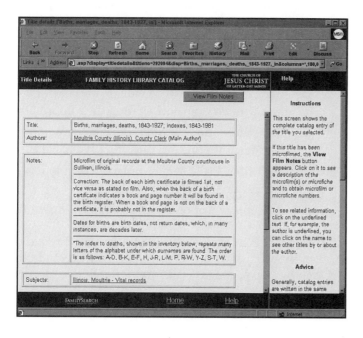

Searching the FHLC online helps you to learn what you can get from your local FHC.

Preserving Your Family History

One of the amazing aspects of the Family History Library is their endeavor to preserve the records they have microfilmed. In addition to making the microfilms available to the public for use, they have also stored these microfilms in the Granite Mountain Records Vault. This vault is said to be able to protect the microfilms from every known natural and man-made disaster, thus ensuring their preservation for generations to come.

Genie Goodies

The Family History Library has begun to release some valuable databases on CD for use by researchers in their homes. Each of their databases includes millions of names. Best of all, these CDs have been reasonably priced for any researcher. One of the most recent releases was the 1881 British census, which is not just an index, but a transcription of that census.

Cousin Counsel

While many records that we rely on have been microfilmed, there will be times when you need to visit actual courthouses and other repositories to find additional records on your ancestry. However, it is a good idea to check the holdings of the FHC first to see if they have what you need.

One of the features of the FamilySearch Web site is to include your family information in what is stored in the Granite Vault. The information you submit will be made available to fellow researchers in one of the current or future databases available on CD or through the FamilySearch site.

➤ If you include living individuals, you must have their permission before sharing their information.

➤ You understand that the FHL will incorporate your data into one or more of their databases.

➤ You will be listed as the contact person in regard to those lineages.

➤ Your entry must be submitted as a GEDCOM file.

You can upload your GEDCOM to the FHL through the FamilySearch Web site. They have a very easy to follow step-by-step page that walks you through this process.

FHCs—Yes, You Still Need Them

Although I would love to tell you that everything can be done from the comfort of your easy chair through the Internet, the realities are that this has not yet occurred. You will still need to plan visits to your Family History Center. You will find yourself cranking microfilm.

Many of the records that you will be using are not in a digitized format. The records, such as land and probate records, are found in large ledger books often with hard-to-read handwriting and atrocious spelling. Records such as these become secondary sources as soon as someone transcribes them for use on the Internet.

Perhaps at some point the same technology that is being used to scan the census records will be used on other records.

The Least You Need to Know

➤ The Family History Library is a vast repository for genealogists.

➤ The FamilySearch Web site brings you closer to those holdings.

➤ Searching the FHLC has never been easier.

➤ Submit your family history so you can preserve it for others.

➤ Yes, you still need to visit your Family History Center.

Chapter 23

Online U

In This Chapter

➤ Learning where to learn

➤ Online education, at your own pace

➤ Expanding your genealogical knowledge

➤ Going to the experts for insight

While it is certainly not required in order to research your family history, learning about genealogy, different record types, and the localities your ancestors were from can make the search even more enjoyable.

Like many researchers just starting out, when I began I had people I could ask questions. They were very giving of their knowledge as far as they had it. I was one of the lucky ones. As I mentioned earlier, my grandmother wanted to join the DAR. When I got interested, I wrote and asked her for anything she had on the subject. She sent me copies of her DAR application and a few other papers. I set about re-creating the information she'd supplied me with. Fortunately, because my public library has an excellent genealogy department, many of the books I needed to re-create her research were available to me.

From there I moved on to the Brigham Young University's Independent Study. They have a number of programs for genealogists. I was fascinated with what I was learning.

While I was involved in the independent study course, I went online for the first time. This was long before the Internet was for anyone outside of the military and the universities. However, I was coming into contact with other genealogists. These genealogists had different research experiences from me. Some were professional genealogists while others had just been exposed to different resources.

Help Is Just a Link Away

Education comes in many forms and this is especially true in the online world. Because of the way in which the Internet brings genealogists together, you will come in contact with others that you would not necessarily have met in any other way. And through that connection you have the opportunity to learn from others.

In addition to this way of learning, the Internet also offers a more structured learning experience as well.

Like everything else on the Internet, you will get to those sites by one of the various techniques we have learned so far:

➤ Using search engines

➤ Using directories

➤ Posting a question on a bulletin board or a mailing list

So, just what is available on the Internet to help you learn about genealogy?

➤ Online university classes

➤ Work at your own pace lessons

➤ How-to articles

➤ E-zines

Each of these offers you a different approach to learning about genealogy. Some of them are interactive, having you answer questions. Others are articles that you read.

Study at Your Own Pace

One of the great aspects of independent study is the ability to largely work at your own pace. Usually there is some deadline, but it is generally far enough down the road that you feel comfortable going as fast or as slow as you like. Unlike regular college courses, you generally can start the class at any time you like. Online, these classes usually don't have an expiration date.

There are a number of sites that offer some form of online classes. These are just a few of the sites that have classes:

➤ Free Genealogy Classes (www.rootsWeb.com/~genclass/)

➤ FamilyTreeMaker.com Online University (www.familytreemaker.com/university.html)

➤ National Genealogy Society Online Course—Introduction to Genealogy (www.ngsgenealogy.org/)

Free Genealogy Classes

In keeping with the traditions of the RootsWeb mission, where the majority of the resources are available free to genealogists, this Web site also offers a number of free classes. Each of these classes offers short lessons that you can read and print out for future reference. Registering for these classes is done through a mailing list. It is also through this mailing list that you can ask questions of the instructor and of fellow students and find out about new classes. Currently they offer the following classes:

➤ Beginning Genealogy

➤ England Genealogy

➤ African American Genealogy

➤ Ireland Genealogy

➤ Iowa Genealogy

➤ German Research

➤ Scotland Research

➤ Hispanic Research

➤ Information about Professional Genealogist Certification Course

They are also working on an Australian Research class.

These classes concentrate on the various record types and the information you are likely to get from them. For those classes that deal with a specific locality, the classes also look at the history of the locality and unique research strategies for the tracking of immigrant ancestors.

Cousin Counsel

The class on Professional Genealogist Certification should not be confused with the certification offered through the Board for Certification of Genealogists, which remains independent of all other genealogical societies. The BCG emphasizes high standards of competence and ethics. For more information on the BCG, you can visit their Web site at www.genealogy.org/~bcg/.

FamilyTreeMaker.com Online University

The Online University at the Family Tree Maker Web site offers a large number of classes. They are one of the few sites that include classes about online genealogy.

Genie Goodies

The FamilyTreeMaker.com Online University has gone to experts in their fields for the creation of their online classes. Karen Clifford, A.G., has been involved in genealogy and genealogical societies for some time. She is the author of a number of books including *Becoming an Accredited Genealogist*. Marthe Arends is the author of the online genealogy classes. She is the author of the *Genealogy Software Guide*.

The Online University offers classes in Beginning Genealogy, Tracing Immigrants, and Internet Genealogy.

The Beginning Genealogy class offers the following lessons:

➤ Mapping the Course and Equipment for the Hunt

➤ Vital Records

➤ Vital Records Substitutes

➤ Trail Guides for Ancestral Hunters

➤ Shedding Light on Your Clues

➤ Your Best Ally in the Hunt—The U.S. Federal Census

Lineage Lingo

Karen Clifford is an **A.G.,** an accredited genealogist. While certified genealogists go through the Board for Certification, accredited genealogists take their test through the Family History Library in Salt Lake City, Utah.

The Tracing Immigrant Origins class offers the following lessons:

➤ Introduction to Immigrant Investigation

➤ Identifying the Immigrant, Part 1

➤ Identifying the Immigrant, Part 2

➤ Identifying the Immigrant, Part 3

➤ Discovering the Most About Your Immigrant

➤ Reading the Place Name, Part 1

➤ Reading the Place Name, Part 2

➤ Overview of Immigrant Origins Research Strategies

➤ Twentieth-Century Immigrants—Home Sources and Vital Records

➤ Immigration Passenger Lists

➤ Modern Naturalization Records

➤ Other Federal Records

➤ Clues from the Census Records

➤ Clues from Church Records

➤ Dying to Be Found, Part 1: Immigrant Obituaries

➤ Dying to Be Found, Part 2: Cemeteries

➤ Evidence in Print: Local Histories and Biographies

➤ Enlisting the Help of Others

Heritage Hints

These online classes are each about 11 pages in length. At the end of each one, you will discover an assignment. These assignments are designed to help you take what you have learned and apply it.

The classes at the FamilyTreeMaker.com Online University are specific and informative.

The Internet Genealogy class offers the following lessons:

➤ Usenet Newsgroups

➤ Creating Effective Queries

➤ Online Reference Sites

➤ Genealogy Data Online

311

➤ Using Newspapers for Research

➤ Libraries in the Digital Age

➤ Genealogy Files Online

➤ Conducting an Oral History

➤ GEDCOM Mysteries Revealed

➤ Geographic Tools and Resources

➤ Finding People Online

➤ Armchair Travel for Genealogists

➤ Search Engines—Sorting Through the Web

➤ Organization Is the Key!

➤ Internet Genealogy Chat Via IRC

➤ Historical Timelines and Resources

➤ Help from Societies

As you can see by these lessons, the Online University offers detailed subjects to help you. Each of the lessons averages about 10 screens of information that you read through. There are very often links to other useful sites included in each of the lessons.

Genie Goodies

Another site where you will find online lessons is RootsWeb's Guide to Tracing Family Trees (www.rootsweb.com/~rwguide/). These lessons are useful to genealogists of all levels, from beginner to experienced. The beginner will find useful how-to information about specific records types and methodology. The experienced genealogist will appreciate the links to other pertinent Web sites, including sites with raw data available.

NGS Online Course—Introduction to Genealogy

The NGS Online course is the only one of the three that I have included here that has a cost involved with it. However, it also offers you quizzes and evaluations to aid you in understanding the lessons you are working on. Should you complete the course, you will be mailed a certificate of completion.

The course itself consists of six lessons. You are allowed 90 days to complete it. However, should you not be able to finish it in that time frame, you can request an extension. The lessons are very thorough and truly cover the basics when it comes to genealogical research.

Lesson One: Genealogical Basics covers

➤ The basics of genealogical research

➤ Terms of relationship

➤ Recording the information (including numbering systems for your ancestors, the recording of names, dates, and places)

Lesson Two: Family and Published Sources looks at

➤ Family sources (relatives themselves and papers such as letters and diaries)

➤ Published sources (family histories, record transcriptions, and genealogical periodicals)

➤ Locating published sources (using library catalogs, both published and online, and purchasing books)

➤ Proper source citations, which are critical in genealogical publishing

Lesson Three: Birth, Death, and Marriage Certificates examines

➤ The different vital records

➤ How to obtain those records (locating, gaining access to, and ordering copies)

➤ Proper source citations for vital records

Lesson Four: Finding Birth Information looks at

➤ Finding birth dates through other records (records created at the time of the birth, records created at the time of the death, estimating birth dates)

➤ Finding birth places through other records (records created at the time of the birth, records created at the time of the death, suspected birthplaces)

➤ Finding parents

➤ Citing sources properly

Heritage Hints

The National Genealogical Society has long offered an intensive study-at-home course that gives you experience with different record types and feedback from professional genealogists.

Lineage Lingo

Register style and **NGSQ style** refer to the two numbering schemes most often used in publishing a genealogy. Register style assigns consecutive numbers to those individuals who had issue (had children). NGSQ style assigns consecutive numbers to each individual and then adds a plus mark (+) next to those who have children. You then look further in the published volume for these continuing generations.

The NGS Online Course is very thorough.

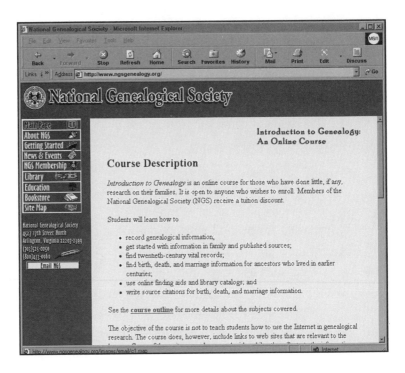

Cousin Counsel

Whenever it becomes necessary to estimate a date or place for an event, it is always a good idea to make a note of this for yourself. It is even more important for those who will use your research to help in building their family tree.

Lesson Five: Finding Death Information offers insight into

➤ Finding death dates (records created at the time of the death, estimating death dates)

➤ Finding death places (records created at the time of the death, suspected death places)

➤ Citing your sources

Lesson Six: Finding Marriage Information covers

➤ Different types of marriage records (civil and church)

➤ Locating wives (finding given names, finding maiden names)

➤ Finding marriage dates (records created at the time of the marriage, estimated marriage dates)

➤ Finding marriage places (records created at the time of the marriage, suspected marriage places)

➤ Citing sources of marriage data

As you can see, this class is very big on source citation. It is an important aspect of your genealogy. Without the source citation, no one else can follow your trail. And your work may hold the very key they need. Without that source citation, they are left spinning their wheels.

The NGS Online Course is one of the most in-depth of the online self-paced courses. When you have completed it, you will certainly have a sense of accomplishment.

Online Classrooms

If you stop by any of the Web sites for colleges and universities, you are likely to discover that they are also offering classes online. This is especially true of those schools that offer independent study courses. While getting a degree isn't for everyone, many of these online classrooms offer you the chance to just take a class or two. For genealogists this is a great way to get some additional knowledge on a subject near and dear.

The most important aspect of the online classes offered through universities is that these are more likely to have set start times or set lengths of time for completing the course.

While more and more universities are taking some of their classes online, there are few of them with genealogy courses, and of those, even fewer with advanced classes in genealogy.

Genie Goodies

Unlike most self-paced online courses, the university courses are usually available for a fee. Some charge by the semester hour (if the course is a university-level course). Others may have a flat fee or the fee may be based on the number of modules or lessons included in the class. You will want to investigate this thoroughly if you are interested in taking such courses.

I mentioned taking courses through Brigham Young University's Independent Study. And they have a number of classes that they offer at coned.byu.edu/is/index.html. Of those offered, there is one devoted to beginning genealogy and a few others that would be of interest to genealogists:

➤ F HIST 70 Finding Your Roots (personal enrichment course)

➤ ENGL 220 Writing Personal History (university course)

➤ GERM 101 First-Year German 1 (university course)

➤ REL C 261 Introduction to LDS Family History (university course)

The Brigham Young Independent Study courses are thorough and include feedback from your instructor. Some of the tests are given online. When I took the REL C 261 course from BYU a few years back, the lesson assignments were mailed through the postal service and the instructor's comments were then mailed back. When I enrolled, I had to wait for the course syllabus to arrive. They now offer such amenities as:

➤ Complete at your own speed (you have up to one year)

➤ Choose the time and place you work on the lessons (even 2 A.M. in your pajamas; I am not the only one doing that, obviously)

➤ Explore course-related Web sites

➤ Multimedia resources on CD (no more syllabus)

➤ Optional discussion with others (through an online bulletin board, something I would have liked when I took the course)

➤ Online grading (of all assignments except exams; no more waiting like I had to do for the letter carrier to bring me the graded paper)

➤ Immediate instructor feedback (you get statements written by the instructor on questions you got wrong)

➤ Course progress tracking (online tracking of your grades for the course)

➤ University credit

Another college that offers online continuing education courses is Bellevue Community College Continuing Education (www.conted.bcc.ctc.edu/users/online/) in the state of Washington.

Heritage Hints

If you are new to online genealogy, you may find the type of class offered by Bellevue will give you a sound footing on which to venture out onto the Internet.

Bellevue Community College offers some courses at any time, while others are at scheduled times. The index to their courses includes

➤ The title of the course

➤ The item number

➤ The cost for the course

➤ The number of modules (lessons)

➤ Number of weeks to complete (for some courses)

Marthe Arends is the instructor for Bellevue Community College's Introduction to Genealogy Online. There are eight modules in this class. Each of the lessons includes a section on related online resources. However, you can see that, in addition to online aspects, the class also deals with the records and research all genealogists must undertake:

➤ Resources and tools

➤ Name changes

➤ GEDCOMs

➤ Interviews and letters

➤ Libraries

➤ Vital records

➤ Court records

➤ Primary and secondary sources

➤ National Archives

➤ Census and soundex

➤ Military records

➤ Land records

➤ Immigrant ancestor research

➤ Writing your family history

➤ Creating a family history Web page

There is a lot of information to read and digest in this class. But think how prepared you will be when you have finished such an undertaking.

Articles from the Experts

I know many professional genealogists that shun the title "expert." I tend to feel the same. We are all constantly learning new things when it comes to genealogy. However, what I have learned may be of help to another and is probably different than what Myra Vanderpool Gormley knows. Someone who has concentrated on Jewish research would be a better source of information on that type of research than someone who has concentrated on researching *Mayflower* descendants.

Articles come in different shapes and flavors. Some can come to you, while others you must go in search of. There is a wealth of information out there. The trick is finding it.

Heritage Hints

A good place to begin to locate sites and e-zines is to start with a directory or search engine. When using a search engine, it is a good idea to have a title, an author, or a focused subject in mind to limit the number of items found.

There are certain Web sites that you will just naturally return to again and again, as your research results in additional questions. Usually these sites have many of the tools you find the most useful. And very often you will use a combination of sites.

For instance, if you were new to census records, it would be a good idea to read up on them. Hitting some of my favorite sites, I found the following articles that deal with this subject:

➤ "Tips on Using Census Records Effectively" by Loretto D. Szucs on the Ancestry.com Learning Center (www.ancestry.com/research/index.htm)

➤ "Information in U.S. Federal Censuses 1790–1920" on the Ancestry.com Learning Center (www.ancestry.com/research/index.htm)

➤ "Every Ten Years" on the How-To Articles of the Genealogy.com site (www.genealogy.com/genealogy/backissue.html)

➤ "Printable Census Forms" (for abstracting info from the census) on the How-To Articles of the Genealogy.com site (www.genealogy.com/genealogy/backissue.html)

➤ "Secrets of the Census" by Donna Przecha on the How-To Articles of the Genealogy.com site (www.genealogy.com/genealogy/backissue.html)

Genie Goodies

One of the hardest things about census research is estimating the year of birth for those you find in the census. There are two excellent charts that can help you out with this. The 1790–1840 Census Birth Year Reference is available at www.genrecords.com/library/birthyear2.htm. The 1850–1920 Census Birth Year Reference is at www.genrecords.com/library/birthyear.htm.

So far, we have talked about Web sites that you go to when searching for information. Another way to learn from the experts is to subscribe to e-zines.

When you search out how-to articles on sites such as those I mentioned above, you have narrowed down the subject to something specific. E-zines arrive daily, or weekly, or some other constant frequency and therefore you cannot limit the subject that you receive. However, I have found that if you don't necessarily need the information of the most recently received issue of the e-zine, it is likely that you will at a later time.

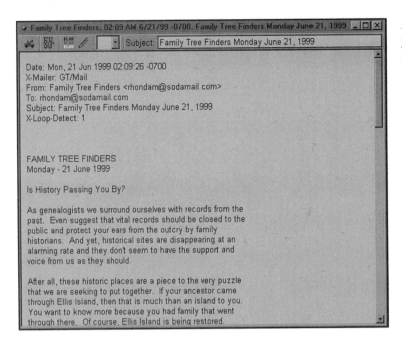

E-zines offer you articles in your e-mail box on all aspects of genealogy.

If you like to print out things you find of interest, you may want to print out the e-zines as they arrive. Then you can organize them by subject. Later, when you need answers or guidance about censuses, numbering systems, or a specific locality, you can flip right to those articles.

Some e-zines that you may find useful are:

➤ Missing Links (www.rootsWeb.com/~mlnews)

➤ Eastman's Online Genealogy Newsletter (send an e-mail to listserv@peach.ease.lsoft.com that has *subscribe rootscomputing Jane Doe* in the body of the text; substitute Jane Doe with your first and last name)

➤ Everton Publishers—Family History Newsline (www.everton.com/FHN/)

➤ Family Tree Finders (www.sodamail.com/site/ftf.shtml)

The Least You Need to Know

➤ Online classes allow you to work at your own pace.

➤ Some online classes can count for college credit.

➤ The educational resources at your online fingertips are bountiful.

➤ You can learn from some of the best genealogists through their online articles.

Chapter 24

A Virtual Canvas

In This Chapter

➤ Finding an online storage place for your family pages

➤ Do you have to learn HTML?

➤ Looking at programs to help create Web sites

➤ Adding graphics to spice up your family Web pages

We've done the research. We've been good and typed all that we know into our chosen genealogy program. We hit all the Web sites we could find, and have been involved in discussions on mailing lists and bulletin boards. We're done, right? Nope. Now we come to the fun part.

Unlike publishing your ancestry in a journal or book form, publishing to the Web offers you total creativity. Moreover, therein lies the problem. Total creativity can be as overwhelming as that initial researching of your ancestry was. Of course, now you're an old hand at that. And soon you will feel like an old hand at designing Web pages as well.

It's Your Turn

Up to this point we've looked at and talked about other people's Web pages. Now it is your turn to create a Web page of your family history.

The great part about publishing to the Internet is that it doesn't have to be perfect. If you discover another child in a generation or you learn that you have some children in the wrong order, it is not the end of the world. Back when everything had to be typeset, this could be a disaster of exponential proportion. Now, we just make the changes in our database and then re-create or update the Web page.

While it is easier to make changes to the information you share on the Web, it is also easier for the misinformation to travel further and faster than if you were to publish the family history in a book.

Here is an example of how quickly Web sites are discovered and read. Recently RootsWeb (www.rootsWeb.com) launched a new set of Web pages to guide people in genealogy. RootsWeb's Guide to Tracing Family Trees (www.rootsWeb.com/~rwguide/) launched its first lesson and within a week it had already received some 14,000 visitors to the site.

Genealogists on the Internet are clamoring for Web sites. Even though we have looked at a number of useful Web pages throughout this book, we have merely scratched the surface. In fact, every day new Web sites are brought online by fellow researchers just hoping to be of help or to make connections with fellow researchers.

Of course, just as you need to research your family history by taking small steps from the known to the unknown, you also need to create your Web page by taking small steps.

The first step is to determine just where you are going to put your Web pages. This may be directly affected by what the requirements are of a particular Web site or by what you are hoping to accomplish with your Web pages.

Finding a Home for Your Page

Just as a book has a shelf in a library where it sits, your Web pages need to have some place to sit as well. We talked about servers a little bit earlier when we looked at mailing lists. Servers can handle more than one thing at a time. After all, they are computers. They can multitask just like the PC you have at home can do more than one thing at a time.

So, you need a server that can hold all the files that you'll show on your Web page. Once you have found a place to put your pages, you can say that you have a home page.

Before you can decide on a place to put your Web pages, you need to keep a few things in mind:

> ➤ Is there a space limitation imposed by the server?

> ➤ Do they require you to include certain graphics on your pages?

Cousin Counsel

While I am encouraging you not to wait until you have all of your genealogy done (here's a tip: it's never really done), it is important to make notations on work still in progress. If you are unsure of a date or a place of an event, include the information, but be sure to add a note that you are still trying to verify it.

Lineage Lingo

Your **home page** is the first Web page on the Internet where visitors can find information about you. Your site will probably have many pages, but everything is accessed from the links on the front page.

➤ Do you have to pay for the Web space?

➤ Do they require you to use their Web creation software?

➤ Do they require you to use their uploading software?

➤ Are you limited to noncommercial pages?

These are just a few items to consider as you look for a server to store and display your pages. The answers to these questions can affect whether or not creating and uploading your Web pages is enjoyable or just a major frustration.

There are three different types of servers on which you are likely to put your pages:

➤ Your local ISP or current commercial service

➤ Free Web site servers

➤ A commercial Web server

Your Local ISP or Current Commercial Service

You may already have server space and just don't realize it. Most Internet service providers (ISPs) offer you limited space as part of your monthly access fee. In order to find out what you may have, you will need to visit the home page of your ISP and see if they detail what you get as part of your subscription. Usually, your ISP has an address where you can e-mail them. And if all else fails, you can call them on the phone.

When talking with them, you will want to make sure to ask them about

➤ Total amount of Web space

➤ Microsoft FrontPage extension support

➤ Limitations on putting things up for sale, or offering research services

➤ Capability of having your own domain name

When I first got involved in the Internet, I looked around and selected an ISP that offered me a local phone call and made Web space available for me to

Cousin Counsel

If your access to the Internet is through Web TV, you are limited to those servers that allow you to create everything online. One such server that you can use is Yahoo! Geocities (www.geocities.yahoo.com/home/).

Heritage Hints

If you access the Internet through AOL, Compuserve, or one of the other national commercial services, you may have Web space available through them.

Lineage Lingo

Microsoft FrontPage extensions refer to specific capabilities found in FrontPage, software to create Web pages developed by Microsoft. If your Web server supports them, you can use FrontPage to its fullest. If they don't, you can still use FrontPage, but not all of its fancy extra capabilities.

create a Web page. At the time, I hadn't given any thought to having my own domain name, and as a result didn't ask anything about that. Once I did elect to get my own domain, I discovered that the ISP would not let me launch a page using that domain without considering me a commercial site, regardless of whether or not I offered any services on the site. Their monthly charges for a commercial site were more than I was willing to pay. So, I elected not to create a Web page using my domain address at that time.

Free Web Space Servers

Several Web servers are willing to let you upload Web pages for free. You may be asking, how can they do this? Usually they can do this because one of their requirements is that you allow them to place advertising on your pages, usually in the form of banners or smaller pop-up windows. The drawback to this is that many people get frustrated when they are trying to visit a site where they are bombarded by flashing ads at the top of your page, or by windows that open by themselves. In fact, to those who are not too comfortable with their PCs, these self-opening ad windows can be a little disconcerting.

One of the major benefits to these free Web servers is their ease of use. When you sign up, not only do they offer you Web space, they also usually offer a number of tools and graphics to make creating a Web page as painless as possible.

Of course, with the good sometimes comes the bad. Some of the free Web space servers will only allow you to use their tools. These can limit you in the capabilities of your Web site. However, if the thought of having to learn HTML or another software program has you cringing in your chair, then you will probably want to check out one of these many free Web space servers:

➤ Angelfire (www.angelfire.com/) offers you fast page creation and a total of 5 megabytes of space.

➤ Channel 21 (www.channel21.com/) offers an online builder, where you point and click to create your Web page, which can add up to 12 megabytes.

➤ CyberCities (www.cybercities.com/) offers, in addition to free Web space, a free e-mail address.

➤ The Express Page (expage.com/) requires that you use only their graphics and has a limit on the amount of text each page can handle.

Cousin Counsel

If you select one of the free Web servers, you need to be aware that they will control what ads appear on your site.

Heritage Hints

Finding the free Web space server that is just right for you can take some time. Fortunately, a site can help you out. The Free Pages Page (freepages.taronga.com/) has listed a number of sites that offer free pages and includes a key to available features that you can incorporate into your site.

➤ Free Sites Network (www.fsn.net/index2.html) offers up to 30 megabytes of space, your own domain, and requires advertising at the top and bottom of each of your Web pages.

➤ Fortune City (www.fortunecity.com/) offers you up to 20 megabytes of free space.

➤ Freeservers (www.freeservers.com/) offers up to 20 megabytes of free space, custom domain names, and custom e-mail addresses.

➤ GeoCities (geocities.yahoo.com/home/) offers up to 11 megabytes of free space, requires either pop-up ads or their embedded banner code.

➤ Tripod (www.tripod.com/) offers up to 11 megabytes of free space, a free e-mail account, and requires no knowledge of HTML.

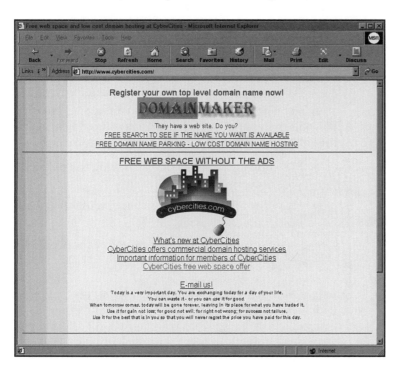

Free Web space servers are a great way to go when you are first putting up a Web page.

Commercial Web Servers

Commercial Web servers offer you certain advantages and additional tools that you may not be allowed to use or have access to through free Web servers. These include

➤ The ability to have your own domain name

➤ No forced advertising placed on your site by their server

➤ Larger amounts of Web space

➤ Guest books

➤ Counters

➤ Support for scripts

➤ Storefronts

➤ Tracking capabilities (individual page hits)

Lineage Lingo

Having a **storefront** is the ability to handle purchasing and money transactions on your Web site. Such capabilities are good for societies and professional genealogists. However, your company must be set up to accept credit cards through a bank. The storefront software only handles the actual orders, not the bank processing of charges.

When you purchase your Web space, they very often assume that you are doing so to set up a commercial online enterprise. As long as your commercial service does not fall outside the scope of their acceptable use policy, you will be fine. Such Web space has come down in price. I was recently pricing the cost of Web space. Many of the Internet service providers that offer personal Web accounts also offer commercial Web space as well. The amount of Web space, additional features, and monthly fees vary. By looking around you can find a set-up that works for you.

Unlike many of the free Web servers, where you can use point-and-click or drag-and-drop type features to create your Web site, the fee-based Web servers assume that you will use your own software. In addition to connecting to the ISP, you will need to become familiar with

Lineage Lingo

FTP stands for **File Transfer Protocol.** FTP software allows your computer, where you have created your Web pages, to easily upload those pages to the Web server where they will be displayed. It offers you a little more control than trying to upload the files through your browser.

➤ FTP software (software for uploading the pages you create on your PC)

➤ HTML or HTML software (what you use to actually design the Web pages)

➤ Other software (tracking or storefront software, for instance)

Before running off to find a major Web server that offers you multiple megabytes of space and all the other features, check to see what your current ISP offers you. Even if they offer you just 1 megabyte of space, that amount should be plenty for testing out your knowledge of Web page publishing.

Sites Just for Genealogists

While you can certainly post your Web pages to any site, there are some servers devoted especially to genealogists. While I have mentioned some of these sites elsewhere in the book because of their other features, we will now look at their Web space options. Some of them are free and others are fee-based.

Ancestry (www.ancestry.com) offers free personal Web space in their MyFamily.com site (www.myfamily.com). This is private space allowing you the capability to share information that you might not ordinarily want to share with the entire world. Web space on the MyFamily.com site is available for free.

Family Origins (www.parsonstech.com/genealogy/registry.html) has a registry where owners of the Family Origins program can upload family Web pages created by the program.

Family Tree Maker (www.familytreemaker.com) offers free Web space for those who own the Family Tree Maker genealogy software. Through the software you can create and upload Web pages to their Web space.

RootsWeb (www.rootsWeb.com) offers Web space to contributors. The amount of Web space made available depends on the total annual contribution. However, unlike other genealogy Web space providers, you are not limited in how you create your pages and you do not need to use a specific genealogy program.

Ultimate Family Tree (www.uftree.com) offers free Web space to owners of its program. Once you have created the pages within the program, you then select an option for automatically uploading the pages to the Ultimate Family Tree Web site.

As you can see, you have many choices about where you can decide to upload your Web pages. You may be asking yourself, though, just how do you create your Web pages?

There's Help Out There

Creating your family history Web pages shouldn't be difficult. It should be fun. It should be something which you look forward to. And it would be if it weren't for one thing—your PC. You have to do it on the PC and other PCs will be looking at it. For some reason, when you put a PC into any activity, you can easily become intimidated and frustrated. Not to fear, there really is help out there.

Help in designing and creating your Web site comes in many shapes and sizes. Some sites will offer you graphics while others will offer you insight into ways to use the real estate of the Web page more effectively. Still others will help to make sure that the HTML code that you have used has been done correctly.

Cousin Counsel

Before uploading to any Web server, you will want to find out what their policies are. Some of them will require you to agree to a usage policy. Read the fine print to see if you are giving them permission to be able to incorporate your data or information into other products that they may offer.

Lineage Lingo

In the Internet world, **real estate** is the space displayed in the browser window. This is where you put your graphics and text. This is where you want to connect with those surfing your site.

You should approach the design of your family history Web page just as you would the design of a poster or book. After all, in a sense, you are creating an online book of your family history.

The computer book publishing world is full of titles explaining anything you might ever want to know about HTML. Some of these books are for professional programmers, while others are intended just for the newcomer.

Finding books on HTML is not going to be your problem. Go to any bookstore and you will discover shelves of them. Visit an online bookseller and again you will have no shortage of books. However, when you are first starting out, it is a good idea to concentrate on those designed specifically for beginners.

I can suggest a couple of good beginner's volumes to get you launched:

➤ McFedries, Paul. *The Complete Idiot's Guide to Creating an Html 4 Web Page.* 3rd Edition. Que, 1997.

➤ Mack, E. Stephen, Janan Platt, and Stephen Mack. *Html 4.0: No Experience Required.* Sybex, 1997.

➤ Wilson, Richard S. *Publishing Your Family History on the Internet.* Compuology, 1999.

Genie Goodies

When I was just beginning, a friend shared the best piece of advice with me. He told me to find a Web page that I liked, and to examine the source code for that page. You can use your browser to view the HTML behind the Web page. You can pull down the View menu and select Source. He told me to switch between the source code and the browser window, so that I could begin to understand how the various HTML codes affected the look and feel of the Web page. It was as though the proverbial lightbulb went on. Try it for yourself.

Online help exists as well. In fact, increasingly, I find myself heading off to the Internet for answers to all sorts of questions in general. And since the Internet uses Web pages, it makes sense to turn there for answers in creating your family Web pages.

The help you are likely to find covers the full range from beginner to expert. The sites listed here will give you enough information, without being too overwhelming.

➤ Cyndi's Genealogy Home Page Construction Kit (www.cyndislist.com/construc.htm) takes you through all aspects of the creation process and includes many useful links.

➤ HTML: An Interactive Tutorial for Beginners (davesite.com/Webstation/html/) is just that, a tutorial. This interactive site will allow you to dig in and get your hands dirty without the world seeing as you learn (as they would if you were posting your Web page).

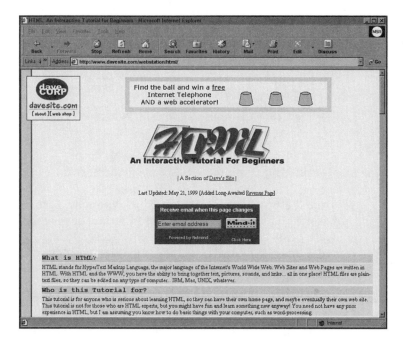

Sites such as HTML: An Interactive Tutorial help teach you the intricacies of Web page coding.

Software to Do the Work for You

Okay, so you have visited the various sites and checked out some of the books mentioned, and you have to come to a single conclusion, "Why do I need to learn how to do this?"

That is a fair enough question. You simply want to get your information out onto the Web so that cousins and fellow researchers can see it and contact you. You don't want to have to jump through hoops, learn technical codes, and spend hours putting it together.

You are not the only one that feels this way. Others out there want the same things. Moreover, you have all been heard. There are a number of programs that you can download and use that can help you out of this particular jam.

Earlier we looked at how genealogy programs can be of help to you in recording and tracing your family history. In addition, in many cases those same programs can generate elaborate family history Web pages for you. We also looked at some of the programs that can generate pages using a GEDCOM file from your genealogical data. But what if you wanted to create an introduction page? What if you want to add information about the history of an area, not just the lineage of your family that lived there?

If you still don't want to learn how to code the Web pages, then you will want to look into one of the many HTML creation software packages. Some of them are free, others are shareware, and still others you can purchase at your local computer store. Some of these programs you may already have access to and just not realize it.

Cousin Counsel

While there are many programs available that can be of help to you in creating your Web page, what you name that first page is very important. The best name to give it is either index.htm or index.html. This way people going to your root domain will always see the first page, and not stumble into your file directory.

Since you are on the Internet, it is very likely that you already have a built-in Web page creator. Both Microsoft Internet Explorer and Netscape Communicator have developed built-in Web page editors:

➤ Netscape Composer (comes in Netscape Communicator) (www.netscape.com)

➤ FrontPage Express 2.0 (comes in Microsoft Internet Explorer 5.0) (www.microsoft.com)

While these Web page editors are fine, you may discover that they have limitations in regard to some of the more creative aspects of Web pages available today. In that case, it may be necessary to look into one of the many other Web page and HTML editors:

➤ Built with BBEdit (www.barebones.com/products/bbedit/builtwith.html)

➤ HomeSite (www.allaire.com/products/HOMESITE/)

➤ HTML Author (www.salford.ac.uk/iti/gsc/htmlauth/summary.html)

➤ Microsoft FrontPage (www.microsoft.com/frontpage/)

➤ WebMASTER Pro (www.galttech.com/Webmaster.shtml)

Lineage Lingo

A **Web page editor** allows you to create Web pages, usually without your needing to have knowledge of HTML coding. An **HTML editor** allows you to work with the actual HTML codes, and is not necessarily going to show you what you are creating in graphics format.

Before deciding on one of them, you will want to evaluate the various features. Some of those that you will want to keep in mind include

➤ Ease of use

➤ True Web page editor, or do you need to know some HTML

➤ Capability to create tables

➤ Capability to create frames

➤ Capability to easily place graphics

While a couple of the programs listed are more HTML editors, there is likely to come a time when you will need to learn something about the world of HTML. Even if you first start out with one of the Web page editors where you can click buttons to create tables and easily add links, understanding the world in which that page will be displayed can help you to grow and design a better page.

Heritage Hints

You may already have Web page capabilities in your word processing program. This is true if you are using Microsoft Word 97 and higher.

Beauty Is in the Eye of the Beholder

I am sure that as you have surfed along the Internet some Web sites have just appealed to you more than others when it comes to colors, placement of pictures, and use of text. We are all individuals and this is never more apparent then when we begin to view family Web pages.

To me, though, in addition to colors, pictures, and text, the amount of time I wait for a page can seriously alter the artistic feel of a site once I finally get there.

There is nothing more frustrating than clicking the link to a site and waiting a minute or more for the site to load. People are generally impatient waiting for a page to load. They often will give up waiting and go off in search of another page. As modems have gotten faster, our patience has gotten even shorter. Even asking us to wait 30 seconds for a page to load is pushing it. And a Web page that is 30 kilobytes could take up to 30 seconds depending on the modem speed and Internet traffic.

Here are some ideas to keep in mind as you begin your family history masterpiece:

➤ Color scheme

➤ Font

➤ Buttons and other small graphics

➤ Pictures and other larger graphics

To help you in putting all the colors and buttons together so that they match, you may want to investigate Web designers who put together theme sets. Theme sets usually include graphics for

➤ Background

➤ Various buttons (including e-mail, back, next)

Cousin Counsel

It is tempting to put many pretty pictures on your Web site. A general rule of thumb, though, is to keep each page under 30 kilobytes in size. This includes the totals of the text on the page, plus the totals of all graphics on that page as well. The easiest way to figure it out is to add up the file sizes.

➤ Bullets

➤ Horizontal rules

Those of you who would like to include some genealogically-specific free graphics on your sites will want to check out these sites. While they have other themes and graphics, they also include genealogy ones.

Lineage Lingo

Horizontal rules are dividers to help break up your text and make it more visually appealing. While you can ask the browser to insert a generic horizontal rule, very often themed sets offer one or more horizontal rules in the color scheme of the theme.

➤ Toadstool Designs (toadstool.2u.to/contents2.html)

➤ The MousePad (www.vikimouse.com/)

➤ Debbie's Free Graphics (members.aye.net/~autumn/graphics.html)

➤ Cherished Memories (www.freecenter.digiWeb.com/arts/cstern/csindex1.html)

➤ Free Graphics from the Timberlake Family Home Page (www.geocities.com/Heartland/Plains/7906/freestuff.html)

By combining graphics with your family history, you can come up with one beautiful site.

Making your family history look good is half the fun.

You're a Publisher Now

Once you have put that first Web page up, you have become an electronic publisher. In addition, with that title come certain responsibilities. We will look at those in a moment, but for the time being, once you have your first pages uploaded, sit back, smile, and enjoy. You have done some good work and deserve the chance now to admire it.

The Least You Need to Know

➤ You will need a Web page server somewhere to post your Web pages to the Internet.

➤ You can use HTML to design Web pages, but you can also use several very popular commercially available programs to create your Web pages.

➤ Please use graphics on your Web pages because they can add a good feel to them.

Chapter 25

Privacy and Copyright

In This Chapter

➤ Learning to be mindful of what information we send where

➤ Exercising caution about information pertaining to living people

➤ Accepting that your obsession may be your family's intrusion

➤ Learning about copyrights

We live in a world that thrives on information. We clamor for it, and companies pay big dollars to learn more about what we all like to do and spend our hard-earned money on. This truly is the information age. As genealogists, we are in the habit of sharing our family history information with anyone who asks about it. However, we need to keep some important issues in mind when we share our information, regardless of whom we share it with or when we share it. Here is a list of ways that we have likely shared our database:

➤ On disk sent through postal mail

➤ In e-mail

➤ As a file attachment in e-mail

➤ On a newsgroup or mailing list

➤ On a bulletin board

➤ On a Web page

All of these listed alternatives have the potential to release into the great electronic world information we had not intended to share with the rest of the world.

Mom's Maiden Name

In the world of genealogy, a woman's maiden name is her identity. We think nothing of listing the females on our family tree this way. Without the maiden name, we cannot trace back to the next generation on that particular line. And yet there is at least one maiden name that you do not want to give out to anyone online.

Genie Goodies

Those of you having trouble locating and discovering your female ancestors may want to see Sharon DeBartolo Carmack's *A Genealogists Guide to Discovering Your Female Ancestors,* published by Betterway Books in 1998.

Have you guessed whose maiden name you do not want to share? I sort of gave it away in the heading to this section. Your mother's maiden name has been used as a means of identification with important companies, like the credit card services. If someone gets that information and a couple of other items, he could have a field day pretending to be you and might be able to drastically affect your credit rating. It is a shame that we must be so careful to protect our privacy and our credit, but is it possible that you have inadvertently shared some information about your living relatives with total strangers?

Cousin Counsel

It is possible that you have already inadvertently shared your family history in one of the above formats. It might be a good idea to contact those people to see what they have done with your data. It is a good idea to know where your information is going.

I would like to tell you a little story now. I do this not to scare you, but to show you how easy it is to get burned. We genealogists are such a trusting group. Some years back on a commercial online service, a newcomer arrived on the genealogy scene. He seemed to be just another genealogist. He'd drop in comments to a number of the topics and even posted some about his own research. A number of us, myself included, mailed him family group sheets and other forms with our genealogy on them. I can't speak for the others, but I had included my home address on mine. And to really round out the picture, my home phone number as well. A short time later, things turned ugly where this individual was concerned. I started receiving messages of the "I know where you live" variety. It was at this point that I vowed to never again share my home address with anyone that I was corresponding with until I knew him or her quite well.

We tend to forget that for every person that posts on a mailing list or newsgroup, there are 10 or 20 or even 100 others who are very quiet. They are just sitting back reading. Now, this is not to say they are all just waiting to pounce. Ninety-nine percent of them will be honest and trustworthy genealogists just like you and me, but it only takes one, as I found out the hard way.

You're How Old?

Having been accused of being a 400-year-old witch, I guess I don't worry about whether someone discovers the truth about my age. See what rumors can get started when you are responsible for keeping discussions on topic and you discover you have way too many witches from Salem and Andover, Massachusetts, on your family tree? So any other posted age for me is just fine. However, I know plenty of people who would prefer not to have their life story splashed out there for the entire world to see. It is our responsibility to make sure when we are sharing our information online or submitting it to an individual or a repository that we do not include information about living relations.

While many times conversations about privacy seem to center on the Internet, there are other places that we need to be as careful.

Some of the places we need to consider what we are sharing with others are in

➤ Online messages

➤ GEDCOM files sent to individuals

➤ GEDCOM files submitted to libraries

➤ GEDCOM files submitted to lineage publishers

➤ Web sites we create

Cousin Counsel

If you are planning on posting a number of queries in genealogical periodicals and will be corresponding with a variety of people, you should consider getting a post office box. This will protect your privacy a little more.

Heritage Hints

Perhaps a yardstick by which you can measure the appropriateness of posting a person's information to the Web is to act as if the information belonged to your child. I know that I guard the privacy of my children fiercely. We should all guard the privacy of those adults who are still living as closely.

I give lectures on a variety of subjects that apply to genealogists, including online and computerized genealogy. I recently stood in front of a group of individuals and asked how many of them had recently shared a GEDCOM disk of their entire family with a newfound possible cousin. I wasn't surprised to see the hands shoot up. I then said why I wouldn't give a GEDCOM of my entire database to anyone, except my brother. With him as the exception, no one else can claim my complete lineage. Oh sure, I have lots of cousins out there, but for each one, we connect through one or two specific lines, and eventually one or the other of us will daughter-out and move on to another line.

Cousin Counsel

As soon as you donate your entire database to someone else, however honorable he seems to be, you run the risk of having your living relatives plastered online or in a CD-ROM database.

Surprise, You're a Star

A dear friend and fellow genealogist was recently tripping along the cybertrail when she was shocked to find herself, her sons, and her grandchildren prominently displayed on a total stranger's Web site. Unfortunately she is not the only one to discover this. For years we have not given security much thought. We shared our GEDCOMs with cousins, who incorporated the data into their databases and passed it along to other cousins. We were still living in that isolated pre-Internet cocoon. Suddenly the Internet was available and we were all clamoring to post our data on it. And we didn't stop to think just what we had done. Too late to close that barn door, the horse is already out.

Genie Goodies

To get more insight into this problem, there are some excellent resources available online and in the local bookstores. Myra Vanderpool Gormley has written two articles on this subject, "Adventures in Cyberspace" (July 9, 1998) and "Exposing our Families to the Internet" (June 19, 1997), in her "Shaking Your Family Tree" column that can be found at Ancestry.com. And there is a book out by Carole Lane, *Naked in Cyberspace: How to Find Personal Information Online* (Pemberton Press, 1997).

So what can we do to protect the information on our living ancestors? We've already looked at some common sense approaches, but there are some computer programs that can help you make sure you don't share living information.

While I have described how I send information, most people do not do this. They could have a much larger database than I do, or are hoping to reach multiple cousins by sharing their entire database. However, software applications have been developed to strip out the living individuals in your database.

➤ GEDClean32 (www.raynorshyn.com/gedclean/) is a program designed to clean out everything about a living individual except the name. It operates on Windows 95/98/NT. It can be purchased for $14.95 (or downloaded for $9.95). There is a freeware 16-bit version of the program.

➤ GEDLiving (www.rootsWeb.com/~gumby/ged.html) is available in a 16-bit and 32-bit version that actually runs in a "dos box" within Windows. However, it allows you to replace living individuals with a message and to set up cutoff years and other features.

➤ GEDPrivy97 (www.hometown.aol.com/ gedprivy/index.html) is a program to make the birth dates of living relatives private. You can also remove sources as well. This is a shareware program available for Windows 3.x/95.

➤ Res Privata (www.ozemail.com.au/~naibor/ rpriv.html) is a privacy program that comes from Australia. It can remove all details about living individuals. A unique feature is its ability to keep the original GEDCOM file intact by creating a new copy of the filtered GEDCOM. This shareware program is available for Windows 3.x/95/98/NT.

Cousin Counsel

While these programs can certainly make it easier to remove information about living individuals, it is a good idea to go through and verify that the GEDCOM file has indeed been cleaned out of all information on living individuals before sending it out.

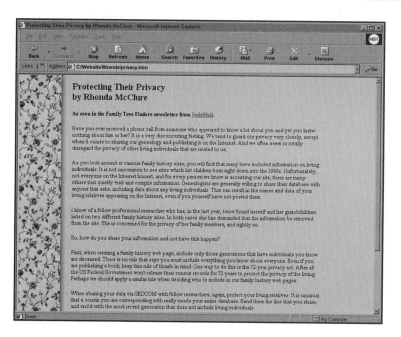

We need to be mindful of the privacy of our living relatives.

Privacy is truly an important issue. In fact, it is so important that when you use the ancestral file CDs at your local Family History Center, you will find that they omit everything on a living non-LDS individual in any pedigree chart. The word LIVING replaces the name. For LDS individuals, the name is present but the word LIVING replaces any dates that would have accompanied that individual. Common sense somehow didn't make it on to the Internet. While we would scoff at anyone who posted family information or secrets onto a real bulletin board in the town hall or the public library, we seem to think nothing of posting that and more on to the Internet, where the world can see it. So the next time you go to share with a cousin, whether online or through postal mail, stop and think about what it is that you are sending.

Copyrights, Now and Tomorrow

Go to the Family History Library and you will see a notice about copyrights posted on the copiers in their copy centers on each floor. When I go to my local public library I see the same notice. Sometimes I think we see it and hear about it so much that we have forgotten what it really means.

Pick up any book or piece of music and you will see a copyright notice. When you see a videotape, you see the copyright notice right at the tape's beginning. And if you stick around long enough after a movie at a movie theater to view all the credits (yes, I said all), you will see a copyright notice there as well.

Over the years there have been changes to the copyright law as contained in Title 17 of the United States Code. And you will be happy to hear that I am not going to quote it verbatim. Nor am I going to interpret it. There is a reason that there are copyright attorneys out there. However, the most recent changes were signed into law on October 28, 1998, which begins to address online copyright infringements as well as other copyright issues. For those interested in reading it and other issues directly related to copyrights, you will want to visit the United Stated Copyright Office at the Library of Congress Web site (lcWeb.loc.gov/copyright/). For the history of the Copyright Office you will want to see the "Brief History of the Copyright Office" found at lcWeb.loc.gov/copyright/cpypub/circ1a.html. It is short but very interesting.

What does a copyright mean to you as you are surfing around the Internet?

➤ You cannot borrow someone else's Web code.

➤ You cannot save their graphics for use on your Web site.

➤ You cannot build upon their work and then call it your own.

Heritage Hints

Most of the genealogy software available on the market today allows you to work with a specific group of individuals in your database. This makes it easy to take the ancestors of great-grandfather AYER or the descendants of your colonial BAILEY ancestor for four generations. Using the capabilities of your software program will allow you to share—and still protect—your loved ones.

Lineage Lingo

A **copyright** offers protection to authors, artists, musicians, and others to help encourage them in their creative endeavors. It does this by limiting what others may do with the works they have already completed and made available.

There are a number of myths about copyrights, especially as it pertains to the Internet.

They don't have a copyright statement on their Web site, so the information is fair game. In the past it was essential to have a copyright statement on everything in order to protect the copyright. However, since 1989, unless the author specifically offers the information as being in the pubic domain, it is copyrighted material.

If it is on the Internet, it must be in the public domain. Generally you will find this to be horribly incorrect. Most of the information you see on the Internet was created by people. Their creativity brought the site to life. Some of them were responsible for the text that you may be reading. Others designed and created the graphics. It is just as much theirs on the Web as if they had put it into a book.

Facts and ideas can't be copyrighted. This is true. While the names, dates, and places of our family history cannot be copyrighted, the format we display them in can be. While the URLs to various Web sites are not copyrighted, how they are included as links in a Web page (the coding and design) is.

What I have used falls under the "fair use" clause. While this may be true of a few things, the fair use clause was intended for the use of small excerpts of works for commentary, such as a book review. And the original source is always attributed. Copyright law is involved and intricate. Like most things that involve the law, you are better safe than sorry. While it is true that most copyright infringements do not get punished, you may want to ask yourself how lucky you feel. Do you really want to be the test case?

When putting together something that you wish to publish, I have found that most people are very willing to give you permission to include some of their work. But do yourself that favor and take the extra few minutes to dash off that e-mail or letter requesting their permission. And be sure to include a notice of permission in the finished product.

Lineage Lingo

Web code is the HTML code the Web browser software reads to display the graphical page we see when we view a Web page. Because this code is created by the compiler of the Web site, it falls under copyright protection.

Lineage Lingo

Public domain is where works go when the copyright laws no longer cover them. Before assuming something is in the public domain, you may want to ask.

Heritage Hints

While your work is copyrighted as soon as you create it, if you find yourself in a position where you need to sue someone, registration with the U.S. Copyright Office is required. In the case of a book, this is just good practice. Even Web sites can be registered these days, though you may want to decide if you wish to go to that extreme.

While it is not necessary, when you create your family Web pages, you may want to include a copyright notice on the bottom of each page for your own peace of mind. While you couldn't sue someone with just this (remember, you have to have registered the work with the Copyright Office), it gives you a much firmer foundation should someone swallow up your hard work. Just make sure what you are claiming a copyright on is indeed your own work.

Additional information on the entire copyright issue and especially how it affects us on the Internet can be found at the following sites:

➤ 10 Big Myths About Copyright Explained (www.templetons.com/brad/copymyths.html)

➤ Copyright FAQ and Copyright Resource Page (www.aimnet.com/~carroll/copyright/faq-home.html)

➤ Copyright in the New World of Electronic Publishing by William S. Strong (www.press.umich.edu/jep/works/strong.copyright.html)

➤ Copyright on the Internet by Thomas G. Field Jr. (www.fplc.edu/tfield/copyNet.htm)

➤ Cyber-Property: Copyright, Citation, and the World Wide Web by Janice R. Walker, (www.cas.usf.edu/english/walker/papers/cyberprop.html)

➤ U.S. Copyright and Genealogy (www.rootsWeb.com/~mikegoad/copyright.htm)

Heritage Hints

If you are putting something together and you have serious concerns about copyright issues, you may want to investigate the costs for meeting with a copyright attorney.

Don't stop working on your family history because of the points made in this chapter. They are included to help you be as responsible with your family history as I know you want to be.

The Least You Need to Know

➤ Living relatives have a right to privacy.

➤ It is your responsibility to protect your living relatives' privacy.

➤ You can buy software programs to help weed out or block information on living family members.

➤ Copyrights are still very much in effect on the Internet.

You're on a Roll Now

It is almost time for me to say good-bye. I have enjoyed sharing this tour of the Internet for genealogists with you. The ever-changing Web is one of the greatest tools to come along for genealogists. And like all tools, it usually takes a little getting used to. Because the technology that runs the Internet is always growing and improving, genealogists are always learning. And the best way to learn is by doing.

I thought it would be a good idea to go over a few aspects of this wonderful resource to further help you get the most out of it.

Do's and Don'ts of Online Genealogy

The Internet reminds me of a game that we played in Girl Scouts. It requires the group to sit in chairs in a circle facing each other. The game begins when someone passes a pair of scissors (when done with small children, you use the "kiddie" scissors), one person to the next. Each person is required to tell whether the scissors are open or closed, which seems simple, right? Nope. If you've played this game before, you know that determining whether the scissors are open has absolutely nothing to do with the scissors. The object of the game actually has to do with the legs of the individual holding the scissors. If the person's legs (or ankles) are crossed, then the "scissors" are closed. If the person's legs are uncrossed, then the "scissors" are open.

Having played this game a few times, I always sympathize with those that don't get it. In many ways the Internet is very much like this game. You know there is a "trick" to the game, but you just haven't figured it out yet.

Here are some do's and don'ts to help you get it:

Do expect to find an ever-growing amount of genealogical data available on the Internet. The Internet attracts new users every day. You may be one of the newcomers for today. However, soon you will be an old hand and will be posting your information.

Genie Goodies

For an interesting look at online genealogy of the future, check out the November/ December 1998 issue of *Heritage Quest Magazine* (P.O. Box 329, Bountiful, UT 84011-0329); "The Internet, The Future, and the Genealogy;" "The List;" "The Future of Genealogy?"; and "Electronics is Changing Genealogy Research" are some of the articles found in this issue.

Heritage Hints

As a reminder, when sharing dates on the Internet, be sure to use the DD-MMM-YYYY format so that regardless of what country a researcher lives in, he or she will know the dates without question. And always include full place names. Not everyone will know that Nashville is in Tennessee.

Don't expect to find everything on your ancestors online. Genealogy wouldn't be much fun if all we had to do to complete our research was to click a button. I like the chase. I like getting lost in those old records. However, I also like surfing the Internet to see who is out there with me searching for my family names.

Do test the waters first before plunging in. Genealogists are by far the most helpful and friendly people I know in general. However, the online method of communication can cause misunderstandings quickly. Whenever you venture into a new area, just lurk for a few days. Get an idea of how some entity manages the area, and what, if any, requirements the area has before you join. It may save you some hurt feelings.

Don't assume that others know what you are talking about. It is easy to forget that your messages and Web pages are likely to reach people around the world. In addition, slang terms that you have used all your life may have another connotation to someone half a world away. While genealogists are notorious for using abbreviations and acronyms, you may want to make it a point to spell out any resource, repository, or other term completely before reverting to the abbreviation or acronym.

Do share as much information as possible when posting a query. Remember that in this medium it is impossible for those reading your post to know what research you have done or what copies you have sitting by the PC. Try to concentrate on a specific generation or individual. This way you will be able to give a detailed message without it being too overwhelming or long.

Don't share information about living individuals. It isn't fair to those of your family who are still alive to have their private details posted for the world to read. They should not have to suffer, or worry, because of your obsession with cemeteries and dusty old tomes.

Do help others. So, you think this goes without saying? I have thought so in the past. Online genealogy works so well because I help you. You in turn help Jimmy. Jimmy helps Rose, and Rose helps me. While you and I didn't see a direct reciprocal exchange, we will receive significant help from other people. We owe it to the genealogical community to share our knowledge. It could be the very tidbit that someone is looking for.

Don't assume that everything on the Internet is free. While a majority of the Web sites you will be using will be free to you, it is important to remember that there is a cost to someone. Some companies pass such costs directly on to you by requiring a membership to access their databases. Others rely on the "kindness of strangers" in the form of donations. Still others have turned to advertising as a way to recoup some of the hard costs associated with a Web page.

Do check out any online commercial enterprise thoroughly before joining, sending money, or giving them your information. Just because someone does business on the Internet does not guarantee that the person is upstanding and trustworthy. Be as smart a consumer online as you probably are offline.

Cousin Counsel

If your message looks like a solid wall of text, it will be passed over by the vast majority of genealogists who come upon it. Regardless of whether you posted your message to bulletin boards, newsgroups, or mailing lists, you will want to be sure to include lots of Web space. Proper punctuation and mixed case are also extremely helpful.

Heritage Hints

It is easy to convince yourself that if you are familiar with a specific record type or repository that every other genealogist is also. This is generally not true. Share what you know. I guarantee that it will help others and is one of the ways in which communicating on the Internet has helped genealogists so much.

Don't take everything you see online as truth. For genealogy purposes, the Internet and 99 percent of its Web sites should be considered secondary sources. It is essential that you remember this when working online. Sure, use the information, but be sure to cite the source and make a notation to yourself to verify the information next time you have access to records for that locality or surname.

Do find ways to help the online genealogical community as a whole. In addition to queries and other ongoing discussions, many of the online areas rely heavily on volunteers. Many times, you do not need to know a lot about HTML or the Internet to volunteer. Very often, they will have a "template" you can use if you are transcribing records. The more that information is made available, the more people will find it, and the more the Internet will grow.

Genie Goodies

A great place for volunteer projects is RootsWeb.com (www.rootsweb.com). They offer server space for a number of transcription projects, and have links from their main site to these various projects.

Heritage Hints

Before posting your information on the Internet, you will want to make sure that you are not infringing on someone else's copyright. If you were to post all the SMITH entries you found in the American Genealogical Biographical Index online, that would be a copyright infringement, especially if you retained the format found in this index.

Don't assume that just because something is on the Internet it is in the public domain and not copyrighted. As of 1989, it is no longer required to put a copyright notice on a work for it to be copyrighted. As soon as you put the information online or on paper it is protected by the copyright law.

Do investigate what is available online to help you learn more about an aspect of genealogy. Because it is easy to publish on the Internet, many people have taken valuable how-to information and posted it to the Internet to share with others. Very often, this information comes from well-respected genealogists whom you have read in periodicals and journals. Sites such as the RootsWeb Guide to Tracing Family Trees (www.rootsWeb.com/~rwguide) can enlighten you on genealogy and on what is available online. Online lessons, like the RootsWeb Guide Lesson shown in the following figure, save you time in the long run.

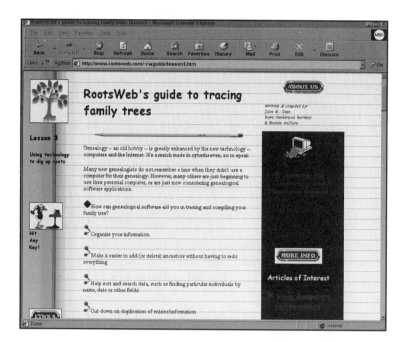

RootsWeb Guide lesson.

Don't give up. Finding things on the Internet very often requires more than one try. The information you are interested in is probably available. Alternatively, perhaps it is there, but the words you used in the search engine need to be changed. Even those who have spent years online sometimes have to try a search more than once.

One Link at a Time

You work your way around the Internet one link at a time. Sometimes you will end up exactly where you intended to be, while other times your destination turns out to be a total surprise.

As we discussed in Chapter 9, there are sites for beginning your research. Directories and search engines are two of the best ways to launch yourself on the Internet.

For instance, you could select one of the USGenWeb locality sites where your ancestors lived. From this site, you will be given a number of links to additional useful Web sites that are pertinent to your subject, the locality.

Heritage Hints

While I have stressed the importance of having a goal, this doesn't mean you can't do a little exploring. If you start out using your goal as the basis for your original Web site, all those that you are likely to surf to will generally have some connection to the search you were originally working on.

By selecting a link, you will be shown another page with additional links. This is really what surfing is all about. You move from one site to the next, using the links supplied from the previous Web page.

As I discover a new site, I try to investigate it thoroughly. The NAIL site available off the National Archives Web site is one that fascinates me. And it was through the NARA site that I also discovered the wonderful links to the presidential libraries.

The more you surf, the more you will find. You limit yourself only by your own thinking and imagination. Yes, I truly believe that some of my best finds have been wishful thinking. But I plugged in a few words or phrases into various search engines and much to my surprise discovered items I hadn't anticipated, but was thrilled to find.

Remember to Have Fun

Whether you are new to genealogy or just to the Internet, there will be times when the frustrations of trying to find a site about your ancestors will overshadow the fun you should be having while online.

Genealogy is a hobby, which means we do it to have fun. It should be an enjoyable way to spend our off-work time. However, there are times when we are working on our more difficult lines that the fun flies out the window.

Don't let the new technology get to you. Just as you have learned what records types will supply you with what needed information, you will learn how the Internet works and how to get from one site to another. And there are plenty of folks out there willing to help you.

Genie Goodies

If you are still having trouble trying to find things on the Internet, then select a single site to always begin your genealogical research. A directory, whether it is the Genealogy Toolbox (www.genealogy.com) or Cyndi's List (www.cyndislist.com), offers you a format that you are likely to be familiar with and with subject headings and links that you select. Sites like this will take the pressure off of having to really search the Internet.

For the most part, I have left behind the families that seem to fall in my lap, as many of you have as well. But because of this, I have come to appreciate all the more those new generations I find. The Internet can sometimes break open the research of those lines you are having the most difficulty with. Remember that you are now exposing your research to a much larger audience and the response can be very positive.

One particular line that had me stumped for some time almost provided me the ticket for my admission to a nice room with soft walls. I'd been pushing at this particular line for 10 years, when I discovered a possible clue. In concentrating on one of the sons of the family, I was trying to determine when he died. I was using an index to probate records. It had a strange index, which turned out to be a blessing, so instead of aiming right for his name, I was forced to look through all the pages for the first letter of his surname.

Well, you could have picked my chin up off the floor (okay, technically it landed on the microfilm reader) when instead of finding the son, I found the name of the father. I had never found any indication that he'd moved on with the two sons that migrated further west from Ohio to Illinois. Nonetheless, here was the name I needed most of all. I was a good genealogist though, I finished searching the index for the son, whom I didn't find listed, though I wasn't quite as disappointed as I might have been.

A letter, a check, and about three agonizing weeks of waiting brought the much desired probate papers. In addition, the choices of administrators gave me one of my biggest finds. It gave me a connection to about 200 years of family. To say I was excited would have been an understatement. Moreover, my children watched as mother danced about the living room clutching papers to her as though they were gold.

This kept me going for quite some time. It spurred on my enthusiasm, even gave me the energy to catch up on my filing from my last research trip.

Genealogy is fun. It should be fun. Yes, it is a science of sorts, but then so are stamp collecting and baseball cards. Each hobby that we find fascinating has its own rules and requirements. Just as a baseball card is anything but to a card collector, our ancestors are much more than just "dead people" to us.

Cousin Counsel

While such a find is certainly possible, you want to make sure that you aren't trying to force someone else's ancestor into the shoes meant for yours. Be very sure that the individual in question is indeed your ancestor.

Heritage Hints

PCs are slowly entering into all aspects of genealogy. You can even find them in the copy centers of the Family History Library in Salt Lake City. These new copiers offer much clearer copies. Often times they even manage to clear up the awful black smudges found on census pages and other older documents.

This fun is highly contagious. I try to infect as many people as possible. Remember, there is strength in numbers.

I hope that you are having fun in the chase of your ancestors. It should be fun. And while the Internet may feel intimidating as you first get online, you will soon find that you are enjoying the hunt for your family in this medium as much as in microfilm.

Online the adventures are always a surprise. With a Web page up for others to find, you just never know who is going to contact you or what they may have that is of help to you.

Don't let the fact that you have to use PCs ruin the true joy of the hunt. The PCs are simply a means to that end: the joy of genealogy.

Family Web pages allow fellow researchers to find you.

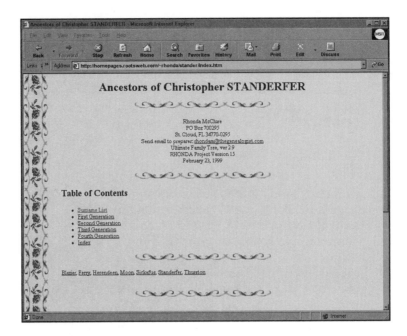

The Ever-Changing World Wide Web

The online world is in a constant state of flux. This can be seen in

➤ Frequent browser updates

➤ The number of new sites appearing

➤ Creative ways to display sites

➤ The introduction of new features, such as frames

➤ The ability to include movement in your site

The online world has gone from straight text to a wonderful world of color, sound, and movement.

This is truly an exciting time to be a genealogist. Each day brings new discoveries and new technology. The publishing of our ancestry never was easier and the amount of information literally available at our fingertips is almost unbelievable.

Sit at your PC, strap yourself in, and enjoy the ride. I know you won't regret it. Just remember that with each ancestor you find, you bring a piece of your personal history back to life. Good luck and good surfing!

Lineage Lingo

Frames offer a way of viewing multiple windows in a single browser window. The browser screen is divided up into two or three blocks, each displaying something different. Each frame usually has a specific function. For instance, one may list the counties of a state. When you click on one of the counties, the other frame may display the books for sale about that county.

The Least You Need to Know

➤ Even with online genealogy, you have a few guidelines to follow.

➤ Only your own lack of adventure can limit you.

➤ Surfing one link at a time can take you anywhere.

➤ Don't throw out the fun with the frustration.

➤ The Internet's constant change makes online resources better for genealogists.

State Resources

You can get in touch with many resources online at the state level of repositories and archives. Below is a list of online state vital records, state archives, and state library sites, where available. Please note that if a state's vital statistics are not accessible directly online, I have not included non-online alternatives.

Alabama

Alabama Department of Public Health (www.alapubhealth.org/frames2.htm)

Alabama Department of Archives & History (www.archives.state.al.us/index.html)

Alaska

Alaska Bureau of Vital Statistics (health.hss.state.ak.us/dph/bvs/bvs_home.htm)

Alaska Division of Libraries, Archives, and Museums (www.eed.state.ak.us.lam/)

Alaska State Library (www.educ.state.ak.us/lam/library.html)

Arizona

Arizona Vital Statistics (www.hs.state.az.us/plan/ohpes/htm)
Department of Library, Archives, and Public Records (www.lib.az.us/)

Arkansas

Arkansas Department of Health (health.state.ar.us/)

Arkansas State Library (www.asl.lib.ar.us/)

California

California State Archives (www.ss.ca.gov/archives/archives.htm)

California State Library (www.library.ca.gov/)

Colorado

Colorado Department of Public Health & Environment (www.cdphe.state.co.us/cdphehom.html)

Colorado State Archives (www.state.co.us/gov_dir/gss/archives/arcother.html)

Connecticut

Department of Public Health (www.state.ct.us/dph)

Connecticut State Library (www.cslib.org)

Delaware

The Delaware Public Archives (www.lib.de.us/archives)

District of Columbia

State Center for Health Statistics (www.ci.washington.dc.us/agencylist_57.html)

Florida

Florida Department of Health (www.doh.state.fl.us/)

The Florida State Archives (dlis.dos.state.fl.us/barm/fsa.html)

State Library of Florida (dlis.dos.state.fl.us/resources/resources.htm)

Georgia

Georgia Division of Public Health, Vital Records (www.ph.dhr.state.ga.us/org/vitalrecords.htm)

Georgia Department of Archives and History (www.sos.state.ga.us/arhives/)

Hawaii

Hawaii Department of Health (www.hawaii.gov/doh/)

Hawaii State Archives Home Page (kumu.icsd.hawaii.gov/dags/archives/)

Idaho

Idaho State Library (www.lili.org/isl/index.htm)

Illinois

Illinois Department of Public Health (www.idph.state.il.us/)

Illinois State Archives (www.sos.state.il.us/depts/archives/arc_home.html)

Indiana

Indiana State Department of Health (www.state.in.us/isdh/bdcertifs/birth_and_death_certificates.htm)

Indiana State Archives (www.ai.org/icpr/webfile/archives/homepage.html)

Indiana State Library (www.statelib.lib.in.us)

Iowa

Iowa Department of Public Health (idph.state.ia.us/pa/vr.htm)

State Library of Iowa (www.silo.lib.ia.us/)

Kansas

Kansas Department of Health and Environment, Vital Statistics (www.kdhe.state.ks.us/vital/index.html)

Kansas State Library (skyways.lib.ks.us/kansas/KSL/)

Kentucky

Kentucky Department of Libraries and Archives (www.kdla.state.ky.us/)

Louisiana

Louisiana State Archives (www.sec.state.la.us/arch-1.htm)

State Library of Louisiana (smt.state.lib.la.us/)

Maine

Maine Department of Health (www.state.me.us/dhs/main/faq.htm)

Maine State Archives (www.state.me.us/sos/arc/general/admin/mawww001.htm)

Maine State Library (www.state.me.us/msl/mslhome.htm)

Maryland

Maryland State Archives (www.mdarchives.state.md.us/)

Massachusetts

Registry of Vital Records and Statistics (www.magnet.state.ma.us/dph/vitrecs.htm)

Massachusetts Archives (www.magnet.state.ma.us/sec/arc/arcidx.htm)

Michigan

Division for Vital Records and Health Statistics (www.mdch.state.mi.us/PHA/OSR/vitframe.htm)

State Archives of Michigan (www.sos.state.mi.us/history/archive/archive.html)

The Library of Michigan (www.libofmich.lib.mi.us/index.html)

Minnesota

Minnesota Department of Health (www.health.state.mn.us/forms.html)

Minnesota Historical Society (www.mnhs.org/)

Mississippi

Vital Records Information (vitalrec.com/ms.html#state)

Mississippi Department of Archives and History (www.mdah.state.ms.us/)

Missouri

Missouri Department of Health (www.health.state.mo.us/BirthAndDeathRecords/BirthAndDeathRecords.html)

Missouri State Archives (mosl.sos.state.mo.us/rec-man/arch.html)

Missouri State Library (mosl.sos.state.mo.us/lib-ser/libser.html)

Montana

Montana State Library (msl.mt.gov/)

Nebraska

Nebraska State Historical Society, State Archives Division (www.nebraskahistory.org/index.htm)

Nevada

Nevada State Library and Archives (www.clan.lib.nv.us/docs/NSLA/nsla.htm)

New Hampshire

New Hampshire Division of Records Management and Archives (www.state.nh.us/state/archives.htm)

New Hampshire State Library (webster.state.nh.us/nhsl/index.html)

New Jersey

New Jersey State Department of Health (www.state.nj.us/health/vital/vital.htm)

New Jersey State Archives (www.state.nj.us/state/darm/archives.html)

New Jersey State Library (www.state.nj.us/statelibrary/njlib.htm)

New Mexico

State of New Mexico Department of Health (www.health.state.nm.us/website.nsf/frames?ReadForm)

New Mexico State Library (www.stlib.state.nm.us/)

New York

New York State Department of Health (www.health.state.ny.us/nysdoh/consumer/vr.htm)

New York State Archives and Records Administration (unix6.nysed.gov/default.htm)

New York State Library (www.nysl.nysed.gov/)

North Carolina

North Carolina Center for Health Statistics (www.schs.state.nc.us/SCHS/)

North Carolina Division of Archives and History (www.ah.dcr.state.nc.us/)

State Library of North Carolina (statelibrary.dcr.state.nc.us/NCSLHOME.HTM)

North Dakota

North Dakota Department of Health (www.ehs.health.state.nd.us/ndhd/admin/vital/)

Ohio

Ohio Department of Health (www.odh.state.oh.us)

State Library of Ohio (winslo.state.oh.us)

Oklahoma

Oklahoma State Department of Health (www.health.state.ok.us)

Oklahoma Department of Libraries, State Archives Division (www.odl.ok.us/oar/)

Oregon

Oregon Health Division (www.ohd.hr.state.or.us/cdpe/chs/certif/certfaqs.htm)

Oregon State Archives (w=arcweb.sos.state.or.us/default.html)

Oregon State Library (www.osl.state.or.us/oslhome.html)

Pennsylvania

Pennsylvania Department of Health (www.health.state.pa.us/)

State Archives of Pennsylvania (www.state.pa.us/PA_Exec/Historical_Museum/DAM/psa.htm)

State Library of Pennsylvania (www.cas.psu.edu/docs/pde/libstate.html)

Rhode Island

Rhode Island State Library (www.sec.state.ri.us/library/web.htm)

South Carolina

South Carolina Health and Human Resources (www.state.sc.us/health/)

South Carolina Archives & History Center (www.state.sc.us/scdah/)

South Carolina State Library (www.state.sc.us/scal/index.html)

South Dakota

South Dakota Department of Health (www.state.sd.us/state/executive/doh/)

South Dakota State Archives (www.state.sd.us/state/executive/deca/cultural/archives.htm)

South Dakota State Historical Society (www.state.sd.us/state/executive/deca/cultural/sdshs.htm)

Tennessee

Tennessee Department of Health (www.state.tn.us/health/vr/)

Tennessee State Library & Archives (www.state.tn.us/sos/statelib/tslahome.htm)

Texas

Texas Department of Health (www.tdh.state.tx.us/)

Texas State Library and Archives Commission (www.tsl.state.tx.us/)

Utah

Utah Department of Health, Vital Records (hlunix.state.ut.us/bvr/home.html)

Utah State Archives (www.archives.state.ut.us/)

Utah State Library Division (www.state.lib.ut.us/)

Vermont

Vermont Agency of Human Services (www.ahs.state.vt.us/)

Vermont State Archives (vermont-archives.org/)

Virginia

Virginia Department of Health (www.vdh.state.va.us/)

The Library of Virginia (www.lva.lib.va.us/)

Washington

Washington State Department of Health (www.doh.wa.gov/)

Division of Archives & Records Management (www.secstate.wa.gov/archives/default.htm)

Washington State Library (www.statelib.wa.gov/)

West Virginia

West Virginia State Archives (www.wvfc.wvnet.edu/history/wvsamenu.html)

West Virginia Library Commission (www.wvlc.wvnet.edu/)

Wisconsin

Wisconsin Department of Health & Family Services (www.dhfs.state.wi.us/)

State Historical Society of Wisconsin, Archives Division (www.shsw.wisc.edu/archives/index.html)

State Historical Society of Wisconsin, Library (www.shsw.wisc.edu/library/)

Wyoming

Wyoming Vital Records Service (wdhfs.state.wy.us/vital_records/default.htm)

Wyoming State Archives (commerce.state.wy.us/CR/Archives/)

Wyoming State Library (www-wsl.state.wy.us/)

Country Resources

You would need an entire book to detail all the online country resource sites available on the Internet, but this list will certainly get you started researching various countries.

Australia

The Australasian Genealogy Web (home.vicnet.net.au/~AGWeb/agweb/htm)

Australian GenWeb (www.rootsweb.com/~auswgw/)

Austria

Austrian Genealogy (AustriaGenWeb) (www.rootsweb.com/~autwgw/)

Belgium

Genealogy Benelux Home Page (www.ufsia.ac.be/genealogy/)

Genealogy in Belgium (WorldGenWeb) (win-www.uia.ac.be/u/pavp/sdv/index.html)

Canada

Canada Genealogy and History Links (www.islandnet.com/~jvienot/cghl/cghl.html)

Canada GenWeb Project (www.rootsweb.com/~canwgw/index.html)

Denmark

Genealogy Resource Index for Denmark (fp.image.dk/fpemartin/)

Denmark GenWeb (users.cybercity.dk/~dko6959/indexuk.htm)

England

EnglandGenWeb (www.rootsweb.com/~engwgw/index.html)

Finland

Family History Finland (WordGenWeb) (www.open.org/~rumcd/genweb/finn.html)

Nordic Notes—Finland Genealogy (nordicnotes.com/html/finland.html)

France

France GenWeb (francegenweb.org/)

Germany

German Genealogy Home Page (www.genealogy.net/gene/index.html)

German Genealogy (WorldGenWeb) (www.rootsweb.com/~wggerman/)

Iceland

Icelandic GenWeb (nyherji.is/~halfdan/aett/aettvef.htm)

Nordic Notes—Iceland Genealogy (nnordicnotes.com/html/iceland.html)

Ireland

Irish Ancestors (www.ireland.com/ancestor/)

IrelandGenWeb Project (www.rootsweb.com/~irlwgw)

Italy

The Italian Genealogy Homepage (www.italgen.com/)

Italy GenWeb (www.rootsweb.com/~itawgw/)

Netherlands

Dutch Research Corner (www.ristenbatt.com/Genealogy/dutch_rc.htm)

Genealogy Links in the Netherlands (WorldGenWeb) (members.tripod.com/~westland/index.htm)

Norway

Norway Genealogy (WorldGenWeb) (www.rootsweb.com/~wgnorway/index.html)

Poland

PolandGenWeb (www.rootsweb.com/~polwgw/polandgen.html)

The Polish Genealogy HomePage (hum.amu.edu.pl/~rafalp/GEN/plgenhp.htm)

Scotland

ScotlandGenWeb (www.rootsweb.com/~sctwgw/)

The Gathering of the Clans (www.tartans.com/)

South Africa

South African Genealogy (home.global.co.za/~mercon/index.htm)

Spain

Spain GenWeb (members.aol.com/balboanet/spain/index.html)

Sweden

Sweden Genealogy (WorldGenWeb) (www.rootsweb.com/~wgsweden/)

Swedish Resources (www.montana.edu/sass/sweden.htm)

Switzerland

Swiss Genealogy on the Internet (www.eye.ch/swissgen/)

Switzerland Family History (WorldGenWeb) (www.rootsweb.com/~chewgw/)

United Kingdom

The UK & Ireland Genealogical Information Service (GENUKI) (www.genuki.org.uk)

Online Library Resources

More and more, genealogists are finding libraries making their catalogs available for searching online. This list is just a short one of some of the more useful libraries for genealogists.

Allen County Public Library (www.acpl.lib.in.us/)

Cyndi's List—Libraries, Archives & Museums (www.cyndislist.com/libes.htm)

Family History Library's FamilySearch (www.familysearch.org/)

Houston Public Library (sparc.hpl.lib.tx.us/clayton/)

Library of Congress (lcweb.loc.gov/)

Los Angeles Public Library (www.lapl.org/)

National Archives, NARA Archival Information Locator (www.nara.gov/nara/nail.html)

National Society of the Daughters of the American Revolution (www.dar.org/index.html)

The Newberry Library (www.newberry.org/nl/newberryhome.html)

New England Historic Genealogical Society (www.nehgs.org/)

The New York Genealogical & Biographical Society (www.nygbs.org/)

New York Public Library (www.nypl.org)

Useful Forms

Even today when the PC rules, sometimes a form we fill out by hand makes the information we view much clearer. Included in this appendix are forms that you may photocopy, if you wish. You can also access these forms and print them by visiting Genealogy Records Service at www.genrecords.com/.

➤ Census History Form

➤ Family Group Sheet

➤ Pedigree Chart

➤ Research Log

➤ Marriage Log

➤ Cemetery Log

➤ Abstract for Soundex Research

Census History of: _____

Date of Birth: _____ Date of Birth: _____

In Household of:		Males			Males						Females				
		To 16	16 & up	Females	0-10	10-16	16-18	18-26	26-45	45 & up	0-10	10-16	18-26	26-45	45 & up
1790-County:	State:														
Name:															
1800-County:	State:														
Name:															
1810-County:	State:														
Name:															
1820-County:	State:														
Name:															

In Household of:		Males												Females												Aliens
		0-5	5-10	10-15	15-20	20-30	30-40	40-50	50-60	60-70	70-80	80-90	90-100	100 & up	0-5	5-10	10-15	15-20	20-30	30-40	40-50	50-60	60-70	70-80	80-90	90-100	100 & up	
1830-County:	State:																											
Name:																												
1840-County:	State:																											
Name:																												

1850-County: _____ State: _____ Postoffice: _____

Dwelling No.	Family No.	Names of each person whose place of abode on June 1 was in this family	Age	Sex	Color	Occupation	Value of real estate	Value of personal property	Place of Birth	Married w/i year	In School	Can't read/write	Deaf, blind, insane etc.

1860-County: _____ State: _____ Postoffice: _____

Dwelling No.	Family No.	Names of each person whose place of abode on June 1 was in this family	Age	Sex	Color	Occupation	Value of real estate	Value of personal property	Place of Birth	Married w/i year	In School	Can't read/write	Deaf, blind, insane etc.

Please distribute this form freely. More FREE forms are available online at: http://www.genrecords.com
Courtesy of Genealogy Records Service

1870-County: State: Postoffice:

Dwelling No.	Family No.	Names of each person whose place of abode on June 1 was in this family	Age	Sex	Color	Occupation	Born this year	Value of:		Place of Birth	Father Foreign	Mother Foreign	Month if born this yr.	Month if married this yr.	School this yr.	Can't read/write	Deaf, blind, insane etc.	Male Citizen	Can't vote
								Real estate	Personal estate										

1880-County: Enumeration District: State: Twp/City/Street Address: Sheet #:   Super. Dist. #:

Dwelling No.	Family No.	Names of each person whose place of abode on June 1 was in this family	Color	Sex	Age	Relation	Born this year	Occupation	Months Unemployed	Deaf, blind, insane etc.	In School	Can't read/write	Place of Birth	Place of Birth of Father	Place of Birth of Mother	

1900-County: Enumeration District: State: Twp/City/Street Address: Sheet #:   Super. Dist. #:

Dwelling No.	Family No.	Names of each person whose place of abode on June 1 was in this family	Relation	Color	Sex	Month of birth	Year of birth	Age	Marital Status	# of years married	Mother of # of children	# Living Children	Place of birth of this person	Place of birth of father	Place of birth of mother	Immigration year	Number of years in US	Naturalization	Occupation	Union/Confed. survivor

1910-County: Enumeration District: State: Twp/City/Street Address: Sheet #:   Super. Dist. #:

Dwelling No.	Family No.	Names of each person whose place of abode on June 1 was in this family	Relation	Color	Sex	Month of birth	Year of birth	Age	Marital Status	# of years married	Mother of # of children	# Living Children	Place of birth of this person	Place of birth of father	Place of birth of mother	Immigration year	Number of years in US	Naturalization	Occupation	Union/Confed. survivor

Family Group Sheet

Husband's Full Name

Date of:	Day Month Year	Town	County	State or Country	Additional Info.
Birth:					
Marriage:					
Death:					
Burial:					

Information Obtained From:

Places of Residence:

Occupation:	Religion:	Military Record:

Other wives:

His father:	His mother:

Wife's Full Maiden Name

Date of:	Day Month Year	Town	County	State or Country	Additional Info.
Birth:					
Marriage:					
Death:					
Burial:					

Compiler:

Places of Residence:

Occupation, if other than Housewife:	Religion:

Address:

Other husbands:

City:

Her father:	Her mother:

State:

Date:

Sex:	Children's Full Names:	Date of:	Day Month Year	Town	County	State or Country	Additional Info.
	1.	Birth:					
		Marriage:					
	Full Name of Spouse:	Death:					
		Burial:					
	2.	Birth:					
		Marriage:					
	Full Name of Spouse:	Death:					
		Burial:					
	3.	Birth:					
		Marriage:					
	Full Name of Spouse:	Death:					
		Burial:					
	4.	Birth:					
		Marriage:					
	Full Name of Spouse:	Death:					
		Burial:					
	5.	Birth:					
		Marriage:					
	Full Name of Spouse:	Death:					
		Burial:					
	6.	Birth:					
		Marriage:					
	Full Name of Spouse:	Death:					
		Burial:					
	7.	Birth:					
		Marriage:					
	Full Name of Spouse:	Death:					
		Burial:					
	8.	Birth:					
		Marriage:					
	Full Name of Spouse:	Death:					
		Burial:					

Additional Children

Sex:	Children's Full Names:	Date of:	Day Month Year	Town County State or Country	Additional Info.
	9.	Birth:			
		Marriage:			
	Full Name of Spouse:	Death:			
		Burial:			
	10.	Birth:			
		Marriage:			
	Full Name of Spouse:	Death:			
		Burial:			
	11.	Birth:			
		Marriage:			
	Full Name of Spouse:	Death:			
		Burial:			
	12.	Birth:			
		Marriage:			
	Full Name of Spouse:	Death:			
		Burial:			
	13.	Birth:			
		Marriage:			
	Full Name of Spouse:	Death:			
		Burial:			
	14.	Birth:			
		Marriage:			
	Full Name of Spouse:	Death:			
		Burial:			
	15.	Birth:			
		Marriage:			
	Full Name of Spouse:	Death:			
		Burial:			
	16.	Birth:			
		Marriage:			
	Full Name of Spouse:	Death:			
		Burial:			

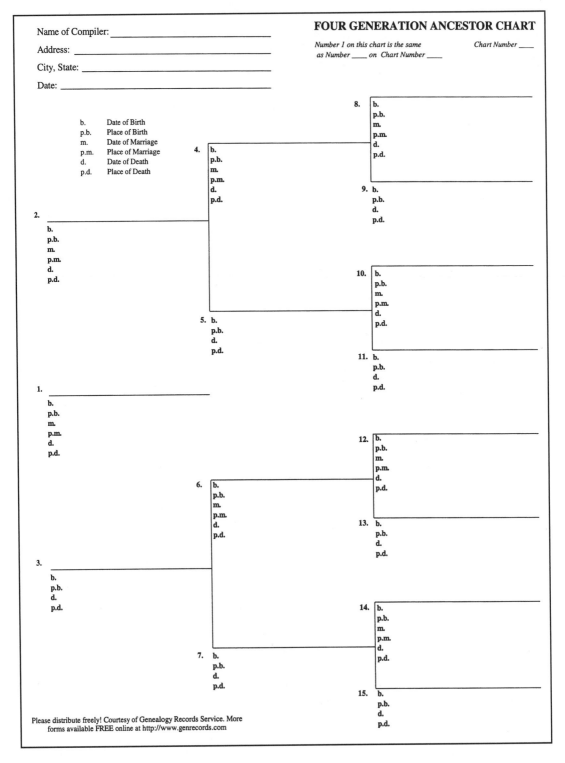

FOUR GENERATION ANCESTOR CHART

Name of Compiler: _____

Address: _____

City, State: _____

Date: _____

Number 1 on this chart is the same as Number ____ on Chart Number ____   *Chart Number ____*

b.   Date of Birth
p.b.   Place of Birth
m.   Date of Marriage
p.m.   Place of Marriage
d.   Date of Death
p.d.   Place of Death

8. _____
   b.
   p.b.
   m.
   p.m.
   d.
   p.d.

4. _____
   b.
   p.b.
   m.
   p.m.
   d.
   p.d.

9. b.
   p.b.
   d.
   p.d.

2. _____
   b.
   p.b.
   m.
   p.m.
   d.
   p.d.

10. b.
    p.b.
    m.
    p.m.
    d.
    p.d.

5. b.
   p.b.
   d.
   p.d.

11. b.
    p.b.
    d.
    p.d.

1. _____
   b.
   p.b.
   m.
   p.m.
   d.
   p.d.

12. b.
    p.b.
    m.
    p.m.
    d.
    p.d.

6. b.
   p.b.
   m.
   p.m.
   d.
   p.d.

13. b.
    p.b.
    d.
    p.d.

3. _____
   b.
   p.b.
   d.
   p.d.

14. b.
    p.b.
    m.
    p.m.
    d.
    p.d.

7. b.
   p.b.
   d.
   p.d.

15. b.
    p.b.
    d.
    p.d.

Genealogy Research Log

Ancestor's Name		Chart Number

Information Needed		Location

Date of Search	Location/ Call No.	Source	Comments	Document Number

Please distribute freely! Courtesy of Genealogy Records Service.
More forms are available FREE online at http://www.genrecords.com

369

Marriage Log

Town/County/State: _____

Courthouse Address: _____

Name of Groom	Age	Name of Bride	Age	Book	Page	Date of Wedding

Please distribute freely! Courtesy of Genealogy Record Service. More forms available online at http://www.genrecords.com

Cemetery Log

Name of Cemetery:_____

Town/County: _____   **Physical Address:**_____

Name	Age	Date of Birth	Date of Death	Inscription	Location in Cemetery

Surname Compiler for Soundex Research

ED	Sheet	County	Surname	Given Name	Race	Relationship	Age	DOB	POB

Glossary of Genealogical and Technical Terms

Abstract   An abstract is an abridged version of a document highlighting only the main points of the document.

A.G.   An A.G. is an accredited genealogist. While certified genealogists go through the Board for Certification, accredited genealogists take their test through the Family History Library in Salt Lake City, Utah.

Ancestors   The people from whom you descend—your parents, grandparents, and great-grandparents.

Ancestral File   A lineage-linked database of families submitted by fellow genealogists. This database is available on CD at your local Family History Center or online at the FamilySearch Web site.

Anthology   An anthology is a collection, such as a collection of poems, short stories, or interviews.

Banner ads   A form of advertising that appears at the top or bottom of your browser window.

Bookmark   A method of marking favorite Web pages in your Web browser software, so that you can easily and almost automatically return to that location at any time. By marking the site with a bookmark, you don't have to follow the same links you did when you originally found that site. You simply open a special section of your browser and select that site from your bookmarked URL Web site lists.

Boolean search   A search based on the mathematics of inclusion and exclusion, depending on which of the search terms (AND, OR, NOT) you use.

Bounce   A bounce is when a message does not get to its intended individual. Instead it "bounces" back or gets sent back to either the originator of the message, when sending personal e-mail, or to the list owner, in regards to a mailing list. A message can bounce because a mailbox is full or there was a typo in the e-mail address.

Browser   See **Web browser**

Bulletin boards   These areas are online message boards. The messages stay at the site where the bulletin board is located. When responding to a message, it is necessary to do so online.

Census   A recording of information taken on behalf of the government. The census results may be summarized in tabular format with very few names, or it may list the names of everyone in the household. Governments use different types of census reports: agricultural, population, and military. Each will offer you a different view of your ancestor's relevant information.

Chat rooms   A chat can be equated with the party lines that were available through the telephone company. Many people have access to the conversation. In a chat room, everyone present in the room can see the messages you post.

Civil registration   Civil registration is another name for the records of births, marriage, and death generated by civil authorities.

Computer Interest Group (CIG)   A computer interest group is usually a subset of a genealogical society that is devoted to the computer aspects of genealogy. At their meetings you will learn of new genealogy software and online sites devoted to genealogy.

Copyright   Copyright is a legal status that offers protection to authors, artists, musicians, and others to help encourage them in their creative endeavors. It does this by limiting what others may do with the works they have already completed and made available.

Cutting   The act of highlighting specific text with your mouse (or other pointing device) and then pressing the Backspace or Delete key to remove it. (Also known as deleting text.)

DAR   The abbreviation for the Daughters of the American Revolution. This is a lineage society that admits individuals only when they have proven a family connection to a qualifying ancestor.

Database   A searchable, compiled, and computerized list that contains records of information that you can sort by predefined categories. For genealogical purposes, the database could contain death records, surnames, and pedigree information.

Database program   A database program is designed to store, retrieve, and organize information. For genealogists, this could be those interred in a cemetery or those you are extracting from a census record.

Daughter-out   Refers to when you descend from a daughter. At that point the surname you are tracing, for her children, changes from her maiden name to the name of her spouse.

Descendants   Those who descend from someone. You are the descendant of your grandparents.

Digest (format of a mailing list)   Puts together anywhere from 5–30 messages into a single e-mail message before the mailing list program sends it to you.

Directories   These Web search starting points offer you a list of Web sites. Many times these lists are organized alphabetically, or under subheadings to make it easier to find a particular Web page.

Domesday Book   A general survey taken in 1086 of those who owned land in England. It has sometimes been referred to as the first English census. However, it is not a census of everyone, only those who owned land. The census got its name from its use as the document of final judgment or final proof of legal ownership of the land.

E-mail   An electronic form of writing a letter to someone, which you send directly to him at his e-mail address, and arrives within minutes to the recipient's e-mail address location. Although e-mail can occur via other methods of transmission, it is primarily considered an Internet-based method of communication. You will find yourself using it more and more, as you become more involved in using the Internet.

Emoticons   Emoticons are a way of using characters on the keyboard to denote various emotions including happiness, anger, surprise, mischief, and more.

End-of-line ancestor   An end-of-line ancestor is the last individual of any of your lines that you can currently identify.

Event fact types   Event fact types is the term used by Family Origins for the method in which Family Origins allows you to record a given event in a person's life, such as birth, marriage, graduation, death, and burial.

E-zines   These are electronic newsletters. They are published at various times on the Internet, and they vary in length and coverage of subject matter. A couple of good e-zines for genealogists are *Missing Links* at www.rootsWeb.com/~mlnews/, edited by Myra Vanderpool Gormley and Julia M. Case, and *Family Tree Finders* at www.sodamail.com, of which I am the author.

Family Group Record   A form that includes vital information on a father, mother, and children in a given family.

Family history   The recording of a family's individual members, and their collective lives and times together.

Family History Center (FHC)   A branch of the large Family History Library located in Salt Lake City, Utah. Through your local FHC, you can search the main databases on CD, and request microfilms from the main library, which currently has some 2 million rolls of microfilmed records. FHCs are found in local Latter-day Saints (LDS) (Mormon) chapels and are usually listed in the phone book.

Family traditions   Family traditions, when used in family history, are more than the activities repeated each year on given holidays. In family history, a family tradition is a story passed down through the generations, the family knowledge. It is these stories that may hold the clues you need to pursue a particular family.

Filters   Use filters as a method of automatically sorting your incoming, unread, e-mail into specific folders or files, based on specific criteria that you can preset with a selection of options that are part of your e-mail program.

Five Civilized Tribes   Those Native American Indian tribes that were moved into the half of Oklahoma originally set aside as "Indian Territory." The tribes that comprised this group included the Cherokee, Chickasaw, Choctaw, Creek, and Seminole.

Flame war   An online argument that usually escalates to involve many people in a matter of a few hours.

Frames   Frames offer a way of viewing multiple windows in a single browser window. The browser screen is divided up into two or three blocks, each displaying something different. Each frame usually has a specific function. For instance, one may list the counties of a state. When you click on one of the counties, the other frame may display the books for sale about that county.

FTP   FTP stands for File Transfer Protocol. FTP software allows your computer, where you have created your Web pages, to easily upload those pages to the Web server where they will be displayed. It offers you a little more control than trying to upload the files through your browser.

Gazetteer   A dictionary for places. Instead of giving you a definition like a regular dictionary does, it gives you details about the place, including the county in which it is located.

GEDCOM   Stands for **GEN**ealogical **D**ata **COM**munication. GEDCOM allows you to share your information with other genealogy programs without having type it all in again. You can now use the GEDCOM file to generate a Web page.

GenConnect boards   Genealogical bulletin boards with specific focuses. At present, the Internet offers GenConnect boards for separate surnames, queries, Bible records, biographies, deeds, obituaries, pensions, and wills. These boards are moderated by volunteer individuals, who keep the discussion on the topic, and ensure that the posted messages follow the threaded message system.

Genealogically-specific search engine   A genealogically-specific search engine is one that has searched out and catalogued only those sites that appear to be devoted to genealogy.

Genealogy   The recording of the descent of an individual person.

GENUKI   The premier genealogy site for the United Kingdom and Ireland. The site got its name by combining the GEN from genealogy with the abbreviation UK and the first letter from Ireland. It is a very fitting name for a site that brings you plenty of information on the United Kingdom and Ireland for genealogists.

H-GIG   This acronym stands for Horus Gets in Gear! (from the University of California, Riverside). And Horus is right there to watch you, in the shape of what appears to be a mascot frog.

Hit   A hit in search engines is a result that fits your search criteria. If the term is *genealogy,* then any Web page that has the word genealogy somewhere in the code searched by the search engine will be displayed as a hit in the results list.

Home page   This Web page is the first one of any Internet site. The home page will probably link to several other pages that make up the site, as well as links to other sites.

Homestead   A homestead in land records was generally the 160 acres an individual could acquire from the United States under the Homestead Act of 1862.

Hop   A hop represents the jumps from one computer system to another computer system that occur behind the scenes to get you from one Web page to another.

Horizontal rules   These rules are dividers within Web pages that break up your text and make it more eye-appealing. Although you can ask the Web page creation program to insert a generic horizontal rule, very often themed sets that come with Web page creating programs offer one or more horizontal rules in the color scheme of the theme you select.

HTML editor   With an HTML editor, you can work with the actual HTML codes that create Web pages. HTML code looks somewhat like programming code and will not necessarily show you what your Web page content looks like when it appears on the Web within someone's Web browser.

Independent study   Independent study courses allow you to learn at home. Many colleges offer such courses. For genealogists, Brigham Young University offers a number of specialty courses devoted to the different aspects of genealogy.

Inscriptions   In this case, an inscription refers to the information that appears on a tombstone. It can be as simple as the individual's name and the year of death, or as elaborate as a poem or other tribute by the surviving relatives.

International Genealogical Index (IGI)   The IGI was originally created as a means for LDS individuals to track religious ordinances done on behalf of their deceased families. Currently, the IGI includes over 100 million names with either birth or marriage dates, and parents' or spouses' names included.

Internet service provider (ISP)   A company or organization that offers a connection service to the Internet by modem connection for a subscription fee.

Interpretation of records   Interpretation of records refers to the inferences and assumptions we make based on the records currently available.

Land Platting   Drawing a graphical representation of the land description, as found in a land deed or patent.

Library type   Refers to the specialty for that particular library. Some library types include armed forces, college and university, government, law, public, and religious.

Lineage-linked   A database where the individuals are connected by family relationship. In the Ancestral File, this connection is displayed in the form of a pedigree or a family group view.

List (format of a mailing list)   In this context the list sends each message posted to the list as a separate e-mail message.

List owner   This person is responsible for keeping control on a mailing list. You sometimes have to subscribe or unsubscribe people. And sometimes you have to play "topic witch" to keep things on track.

Lurker   Someone who has joined an e-mail group or bulletin board, but who simply reads the messages and does not join in on the conversations.

Macro feature   In terms of photography, a macro feature lets you take extremely close-up views of any object, including documents. With the Sony Mavica digital camera that I now own, I can take close-ups of documents within half an inch, if I need, without losing the clarity.

Mailing list   A list of e-mail addresses of a group of individuals that discuss a single idea, locality, surname, or record type. The messages directed to the mailing list arrive in your e-mail box, just as your regular e-mail does.

Manuscripts   Manuscripts are generally groups of papers with a common theme or topic, and often created by or around an individual or family, for genealogical purposes. They can be a person's private papers, log books, or drafts.

Metasearch engine   A Web search site that allows you to type in your keywords, and then the search engine conducts a search throughout a number of different search engine sites.

Microsoft FrontPage extensions   These extensions refer to specific capabilities available with FrontPage, a Web page creating software developed by Microsoft. If your Web server supports these extensions, you can use FrontPage to its fullest degree. If your Web server doesn't support these extensions, you can still use FrontPage, but not all of the software package's fancy extra capabilities.

Modem   A device that allows your computer to convert its digital information to sound, which can then be sent over a normal phone line to another modem. The other modem converts it back to digital information.

Network   A system of computers connected together so that they can share files, printers, and sometimes resources. It allows you to have a file on one computer but access it with another.

Newsgroups   These areas are message areas where discussions on a given topic take place. They require a newsgroup reader to view and respond to the messages. These newsgroup readers are built into both Internet Explorer and Netscape Navigator.

NGSQ style   The NGSQ style is a numbering scheme used in published genealogies. This style assigns consecutive numbers to each individual and then adds a plus mark (+) next to those who have children.

Notary records   These records can be used to trace roots back to ancient Rome, when slaves would keep notes and correspondence for their owners. These records also now record land transactions and other property (such as a car), loans, new businesses, and the collection of state taxes.

Oath of allegiance   This oath renounced any claims by "pretenders" to the throne of England and denied the right of the Pope to outlaw Protestant monarchs. Generally, these oaths were signed by passengers as they disembarked from the ships, when they arrived in the colonies.

OCR   OCR stands for Optical Character Recognition. OCR programs take a document that has been scanned by your scanner and converts the text from that scanned image into a text document. Such PC programs have been used heavily in the digitizing of books; however, they are not 100% accurate, especially with text that is not legible.

Ortsfamilienbucher   Printed books that duplicate all the births, marriages, and deaths listed in the handwritten parish registers for a given German town. These books do not exist for every community, nor are they necessarily easily available.

Parish   A parish can refer to either an ecclesiastical (church) or civil government division.

Pedigree Chart   This chart is a road map showing your direct ancestral lineage.

PERSI   The **PER**iodical Source Index is an ongoing indexing project from the Allen County Public Library in Ft. Wayne, Indiana. The Genealogy Department of the library began to index periodicals by surname, record type, and locality.

Plug-ins   Add-on utilities for your Web browser that allow you to enter a chat room, view audio or video clips, or do other additional tasks with special features on Web pages viewable on the Internet.

Pop-up ads   Advertisements that appear as separate, self-launching windows of your browser.

Presidential libraries   These presidential libraries are established to prevent the loss of papers when a president's term is completed. The records in the currently available presidential libraries include more than 250 million pages of textual materials, 5 million photographs, 13.5 million feet of motion picture film, 68,000 hours of sound and video recordings, and 280,000 museum objects, which comprises an impressive collection.

Public domain   The public domain is where copyrighted creative works ownership revert to when the copyright laws no longer cover these works. Before you can assume something is in the public domain, you have to find out whether the material is still copyrighted.

Primary source   A source created at the time of, or close to, the event by an eyewitness.

Queries   Requests for help in regard to a particular line with which you are having problems. Before PCs, genealogists put these queries into periodicals. Now, genealogists still put them into the genealogical periodicals, but they also post them online on bulletin boards and in other message areas. They are a request for assistance to your fellow researchers.

RAM   This acronym stands for random access memory. Your PC puts information into RAM for easier and quicker access. Your PC writes and rewrites to this storage space many times during a single PC session. This type of memory is easily expandable by adding chips to your PC's motherboard. You could think of the RAM area as your PC's work space.

Real audio   A way of listening to interviews, music, and other sound from the Internet on PC.

Real estate   On the Internet, this is any space displayed in the browser window. This is where you put your graphics and text. This is where you want to connect with those surfing your site.

Register style   A numbering scheme used by published genealogists. This system assigns consecutive numbers to those individuals who had issue (had children).

Release of dower   A wife's relinquishing of her one-third right to property owned by her husband.

Remembrance   A remembrance is anything pertaining to ancestors gone by. It could be a diary, a manuscript, or a photograph. Very often these articles have found homes in private collections, museums, or historical societies.

Repository   Any building that houses records for safekeeping. It could be a state archive, a library, a museum, or a historical or genealogical society building.

Research Log   A preformatted page that allows you to track research. Most of these forms have columns for important items such as date of search, call number and repository, title of source, and results.

Research Outlines   The experts at the Family History Library have developed **research outlines**. They detail the history of the locality or record type and include information about the record availability, including addresses for repositories other than the Family History Library.

Research Planning Sheets   These sheets are designed to record pertinent information about research problems, including the ancestor's name, the source information, the search date, the goal or problem you are trying to solve, and the results of the search. You then file these planning sheets in relevant folders, along with any copies that you might have made from the source.

SASE   This acronym stands for self-addressed, stamped envelope. Whenever you are contacting anyone and requesting information from them, it is a good idea to include an SASE. You are more likely to hear back from them.

Scottish OPR Index   This index is the Scottish Old Parochial Register index—an index of entries in the old (pre-1855) church registers from the Church of Scotland. It was originally on microfiche and required that you know the shire from which the family came. The CD version combined them, making searching that much easier.

Secondary source   A source created at a later date and based upon hearsay.

Search engine   A site that is designed to help you search for specific pages on the Internet. By typing in certain keywords, the site displays a list of Web pages that it feels meets your search criteria.

Shareware   Software that you can try before paying for. You are generally left on the honor system of registering and paying for the software. Unlike demos, shareware usually doesn't stop working after a set amount of time.

Shtetl   A shtetl was an individual village in the old country.

Signature file   A closing to all your e-mail messages that is automatically inserted by your e-mail program. A signature file usually includes your name, e-mail address, and URL or Web site address.

Snail mail   The online term for mail sent through the regular postal system. While this form of mail may be faster now than in the days of the pony express, when you compare it with the speed of e-mail, it crawls.

Society of Mayflower Descendants   A lineage society that accepts membership only for those who have proven their descent from one of the passengers on that original Mayflower voyage.

Soundex   Soundex is an index based on the phonics of a surname rather than exact spelling. The soundex code is a four-digit code that takes the first letter of the surname followed by three numbers based on the next letters in the surname. The index comprises an entire state and will show you the entry information to locate your ancestor in the actual census.

Source citation   A source citation is an entry that states where you found the information of the life event. Sources can be books, land records, or vital statistics, and each type of record will have a different citation form.

Spam   Spam is the online term for unwanted e-mail. It generally refers to the advertising e-mails that you are likely to receive. One example of spam that you no doubt have seen is the e-mail telling you how to get rich quick.

Spider   A spider is an automated, computerized search tool that reads Web page information to categorize the information into a searchable database.

Spreadsheet   A spreadsheet program is often used for the recording of data in rows and columns, much like the old-styled ledger books used to track finances.

Storefront   The ability to handle purchasing and money transactions on your Web site. Such capabilities are good for societies and professional genealogists. However, your company must be set up to accept credit cards through a bank. The storefront software only handles the actual orders, not the bank processing of charges to credit cards.

Subscribe   To subscribe to a mailing list means to have your e-mail address added to the list of individuals who receive any messages sent to the mailing list's main address.

Surfing   When you go from a link on one page to a link on another page, you are surfing the Internet. From page to page, you move throughout the Internet visiting Web site after Web site, linking from one to another.

Tagline   A tagline is a one-line quote of some sort that accompanies a main title. With reference to e-mail, you can consider e-mail taglines as the "bumper stickers." The book *Everything's Relative,* compiled by Elizabeth Biggs Payne, published by the New England Historic Genealogical Society, is a collection of these taglines.

Textual holdings   Textual holdings can be letters, census pages, passenger lists, or homestead applications. This category includes anything written or typed on a piece of paper of a family orientation.

Tory   A British sympathizer. You will also find them referred to as Loyalists in many of the records. And some of the Canadian records show pensions paid by England to these Loyalists who were displaced to Canada.

Uniform resource locator (URL)   The address of a page on the Internet. Just as you and I rely on addresses to drive around town shopping and eating, we need to rely on URLs to locate pages on the Internet. Without this important string of characters, you cannot get to any Web site.

User error   Something that we hate to admit. We will always blame the PC or software program first, before we admit that perhaps we didn't enter something quite right. User error generally means we didn't type something in correctly or accurately to instruct the PC what we wanted in the first place.

USGenWeb   A huge genealogical project supported by volunteers. Some volunteers manage state sites and coordinate county volunteers who work for them. The county coordinators maintain Web sites with information of all kinds that are pertinent to the county in question.

Vital records   A term used to refer to those certificates recorded by civil authorities. Generally they include birth, marriage, and death records.

Web browser   A software application that you use to maneuver around the Internet. Through the browser software's graphical interface, you can click buttons, select links, or read text. The browser accesses the Web sites either by links within other pages or by the user typing in the URL of a Web page.

Web code   Web code is the HTML code that browser software reads to display the graphical page that we see when we view a Web page. Because this code is created by the compiler of the Web site, it falls under copyright protection.

Web page editor   With a Web page editor, you can create Web pages, usually without having to know HTML coding.

Word lists   Word lists are compiled lists of important terms of use to genealogists, as opposed to a general language dictionary, with the foreign language word and the English translation. Word lists are available for Danish, French, Latin, Spanish, and German.

Index